PUBLISHING

Executive VP Norm Deska
VP, Exhibits & Archives Edward Meyer

Publisher Anne Marshall

Editorial Director Rebecca Miles
Senior Researcher & Picture Manager James Proud
Additional Research Rosie Alexander, Charlotte Howell
Text Geoff Tibballs
Additional Text James Proud
Editors Judy Barratt, Sally McFall
Factchecker Alex Bazlinton
Indexer Hilary Bird

Art Director Sam South
Design Dynamo Design
Reprographics Juice Creative

Copyright © 2013 by Ripley Entertainment, Inc.

First published in Great Britain in 2013 by
Random House Books
Random House, 20 Vauxhall Bridge Road,
London SW1V 2SA

www.randomhouse.co.uk

Addresses for companies within The Random House
Group Limited can be found at:
www.randomhouse.co.uk/offices.htm

The Random House Group Limited Reg. No. 954009

ISBN 9781847947161
10 9 8 7 6 5 4 3 2 1

The Random House Group Limited supports
The Forest Stewardship Council (FSC®), the leading
international forest certification organisation.
Our books carrying the FSC label are printed
on FSC® certified paper. FSC is the only forest
certification scheme endorsed by the leading
environmental organisations, including
Greenpeace. Our paper procurement policy can be
found at www.randomhouse.co.uk/environment.

A CIP catalogue record for this book is
available from the British Library

Printed in China

PUBLISHER'S NOTE
While every effort has been made to verify
the accuracy of the entries in this book, the
Publishers cannot be held responsible for any
errors contained in the work. They would be
glad to receive any information from readers.

WARNING
Some of the stunts and activities in this book
are undertaken by experts and should not
be attempted by anyone without adequate
training and supervision.

Ripley's Believe It or Not!® 2014

DARE TO LOOK!

Ripley Publishing

a Jim Pattison Company

CONTENTS

Simply download our APP & try out

ODDSCAN

SEE MORE AMAZING EXTRA STUFF!

Look out for oddSCAN™ for video extras!

ROBERT RIPLEY
An American Icon!

Marco Polo, Christopher Columbus, Neil Armstrong... there are few true adventurers that can be compared to such great men—but Robert Ripley just might be one of them! In 1918, considering the limited forms of travel, Ripley's determination to visit countries barely known back home showed a pioneering spirit no less extraordinary than those intrepid explorers.

With style, in bow tie and spats, Ripley traveled to Papua New Guinea, Armenia, Tibet and beyond—his aim was to uncover the world's wonders and weird-ities, miracles and monstrosities and feature them in the Believe It or Not! cartoon he drew daily for *The New York Globe*.

Americans couldn't get enough of Ripley and he rocketed into radio and television—broadcasting from places such as a shark tank! Soon he was said to be more popular than the U.S. President!

By 1933, Ripley had opened an odditorium (museum) in Chicago to display the artifacts he'd collected.

Today, Ripley's is a global empire with 32 Odditoriums, three aquariums, a warehouse packed with artifacts, and an archive of more than 25,000 photos and 100,000 cartoons.

▲ Ripley enlisted the help of yaks to pull his car out of a snowdrift when it got stuck in a snowy mountain pass in Georgia in 1934.

In 1933–34, Ripley opened an odditorium in Chicago to house his artifacts. They were so startling, he said, that "one hundred people fainted every day and we had to have six beds!"

It's all true!

Wayne Harbour (1899–1981), a postal worker from Bedford, Iowa, devoted 29 years of his life trying to prove that Robert Ripley was wrong. He wrote 24,241 letters to people featured in the Ripley's Believe It or Not! cartoons in an attempt to find factual errors—but never received a single reply that contradicted a Ripley fact! Upon his death, his widow donated his vast collection of correspondence—80 cartons-full—to Ripley and they can now be seen in Ripley museums around the world.

❝ I have been called a liar more than anybody in the world... That short and ugly word is like music to my ears. I am complimented, because it means that my paragraph that day contained some strange fact that was unbelievable—and therefore most interesting. ❞

Robert Ripley

▲ Ripley's archive contains more than 25,000 photos, many featuring Ripley on his travels, meeting people such as this man in Korea, in 1932, who wore multiple hats.

▲ Ripley met headhunters in Port Moresby, Papua New Guinea, where he stayed at the home of the police chief and reported his experiences in his cartoons.

▼ Immaculately suited, Ripley gives a radio broadcast from Carlsbad Caverns, New Mexico, in 1939.

Facts and a figure

As Robert Ripley's full-time researcher and factchecker, Norbert Pearlroth (1893–1983) spent ten hours a day, six days a week for 52 years sitting in the same chair, at the same desk, in the reading room at New York's Public Library. In that time he pored through an estimated

> ❝ **52 years sitting in the same chair** ❞

364,000 books in search of the scarcely believable facts that made the Ripley's Believe It or Not! cartoons compulsive reading for 80 million people worldwide.

A creature of habit, Norbert left his Brooklyn home each morning, took the subway into Manhattan and worked at his office until noon, answering some of the 3,000 letters that came in on a weekly basis from Ripley readers around the world. Skipping lunch, he then headed for the library on Fifth Avenue, where he worked through the day, taking only half an hour for dinner before returning home when the library closed at 10 p.m.

Norbert retired in 1975, never having missed his weekly deadline for submitting 24 cartoon items. He died aged 89, having sourced and verified over 60,000 facts!

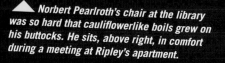

▲ Norbert Pearlroth's chair at the library was so hard that cauliflowerlike boils grew on his buttocks. He sits, above right, in comfort during a meeting at Ripley's apartment.

WE'VE BEEN OUT and about!

Here at Ripley's, we're inquisitive. Every second of every day, we've got our ears to the ground, eyes peeled and fingers flicking through files and every kind of social media—only stopping short of sniffer dogs—in the pursuit of a barely believable truth, or a person with a life more extraordinary.

We have researchers, curators, archivists and model-makers, as well as editors and correspondents who compile articles and write for the Ripley's Believe It or Not! books. Dedicated and passionate about what we do, we never tire in our mission to uncover and preserve the unbelievable side of life.

We've collected thousands of stories and hundreds of photographs for this new book. We've also traveled to find amazing people—and some of our favorites are featured here.

Each of the 4,500 shell cases that form David Palmer's portrait of President Lincoln represents 150 men who died in the Civil War.

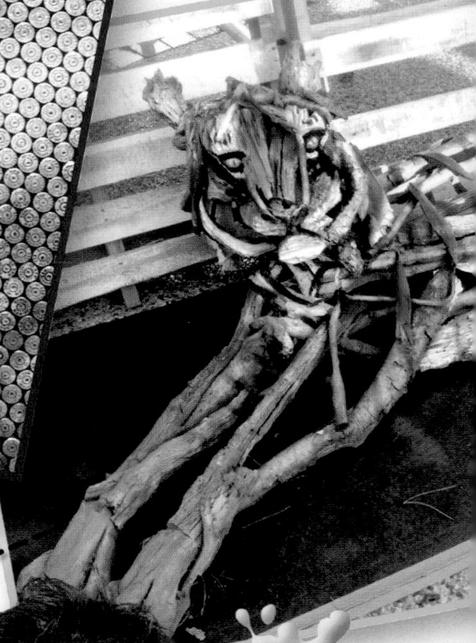

Terry Brennan's tiger was pieced together using driftwood found on Cat Island, South Carolina.

Look who we bumped into this year!

See more on page 146

See more on page 120

CRAZY CAR ART
Stacked up between countless jars of paint in Ian Cook's studio were the toy remote-controlled cars that he uses. One flick of a remote and every wheel started spinning and skidding!

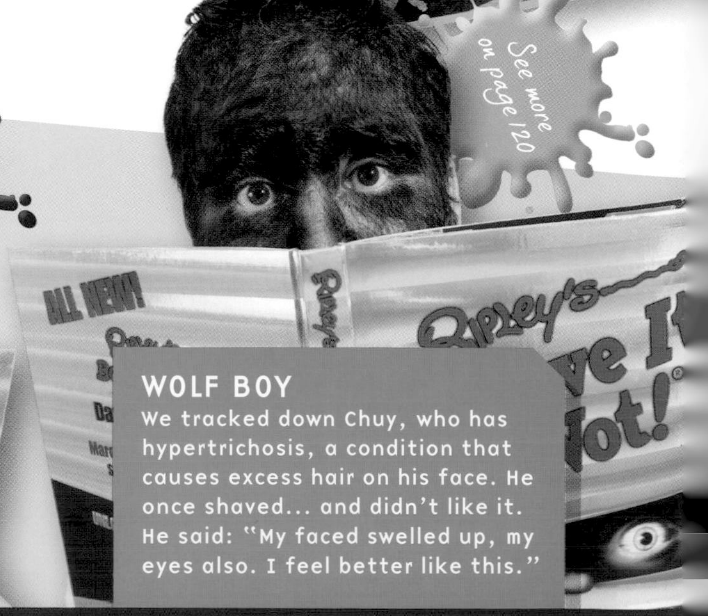

WOLF BOY
We tracked down Chuy, who has hypertrichosis, a condition that causes excess hair on his face. He once shaved... and didn't like it. He said: "My faced swelled up, my eyes also. I feel better like this."

Party Time!

Tom Sheerin's eagle contains 3,000 pieces of cutlery!

Turn to page 210 for some more crazy food, including cakes featuring brains, eyeballs and severed fingers— and just to tempt you... check out these vomit cupcakes!

Ripley's went to a cool party in London, England, to meet chefs behind some believe-it-or-not baking! Party food came in the form of an edible television, a bucket of rocks, a knife— and some vomit-covered cupcakes (left, if you can stomach them!). The TV was made from boiled sweets and trifle, the rocks were chocolate crispies and the vomit was... well, we're really not sure!

WE'VE BEEN BUYING TOO!

Ripley's Archivist, Edward Meyer, has been scouting around for new exhibits for the odditoriums and has come up with some amazing stuff.

See more on page 192.

See more on page 112.

Download our Ripley's Believe It or Not! app—see Ian Cook's car painting, hear Wolf Boy's story, experience Kelvin's pain and see exclusive pictures of King Body Art's eye tattooing!

PEG MAN
We flew Kelvin Mercado from Puerto Rico to Ripley's Florida HQ after he sent us photos of 160 pegs attached to his face! He said he could attach more and we took a picture to prove he was right!

BODY ART KING
King Body Art has tattoos that cover 90 percent of his body! Our researchers made contact, but the photo shoot had to be postponed until the swelling from his new eyeball tattoo had calmed down!

JOIN OUR WORLD!

FACEBOOK

Facebook.com/RipleysBelieveItorNot

TWITTER

Twitter@Ripleys

PINTEREST

Pinterest.com/RipleysBION

INSIDE OUR APP!

The official one-stop portal into the incredible world of Ripley's. Download the weirdest phenomena onto your mobile device. This app features Ripley's ODDSCAN, giving you the ability to scan real-world targets in Ripley's museums and books to unlock exclusive hidden content. Plus all the features below.

Ripley's Believe It or Not!®

Available on the App Store

ANDROID APP ON Google play

Visit our Odditoriums...

LIZARDMAN
AS THE LIZARDMAN
ERIK SPRAGUE
•••LY, 1972
•••+ hours and counting
•• E: 95% of body
•••••dermal Teflon ridges
pointed teeth
•••ODS: Split tongue + filed
pointed teeth
• OMG! * Can insert power drill in nose
* Has degree in philosophy * Tattoos
cost around $250,000

CARTOONS   RIPLEYZINES™

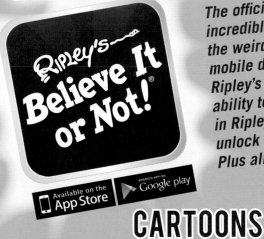

SOCIAL   ODDITORIUMS

See our amazing magazines on your handset!

...Ripleyfy™ yourself

Ever wondered what you might look like as Lizardman? Download our app and find out now! You can Ripleyfy™ yourself and send it to all your friends! At a Ripley's Odditorium? Watch out for the oddSCAN™ signs for more experiences—and collector cards with more Believe It or Not! facts.

CONTACT US

on the web...
ripleybooks.com

write to us...
BION Research
Ripley Entertainment Inc,
7576 Kingspointe Parkway,188,
Orlando, Florida 32819, U.S.A.

email us...
bionresearch@ripleys.com

SEND US STUFF

www.ripleys.com/submit

YOUR UPLOADS

Send us your Ripley birthday cakes...NOW!

▶ Havannah from Queensland, Australia, sent us this amazing birthday cake made for her by a friend —a perfect copy of our Ripley's Believe It or Not! *Incredibly Strange* book!

SEE MORE AMAZING EXTRA STUFF!!

Simply download our APP & try out **ODD SCAN**

Test it out—scan the page and see Ian Cook's art come to life!

Look out for these throughout the book!

SCAN the page

MINIMAGIC

See more on page 146

Download our Ripley's Believe It or Not! APP and activate the ODD SCAN feature to unlock amazing additional content from within the pages of this book. Every time you see the ODD SCAN icon, scan the page with your mobile device and POW! incredible extra pictures and videos will appear!

CRAZY VIDEOS

MORE PICTURES

INTERVIEWS

SILLY STORIES

WACKY WONDERS

RIPLEY'S AQUARIUM
of Canada

Over 15,000 marine and freshwater fish, including some of the most amazing underwater creatures on the planet, have taken up residence in Ripley's new aquarium right in the heart of downtown Toronto, Canada, at the base of the CN Tower.

A total of 450 species enjoy 1½ million gallons of water in 45 different habitats, ranging from the majestic kelp forests of Canada's Pacific Northwest to the spectacular color of a tropical Indo-Pacific reef. The tiniest and the mightiest are among them. Delicate sea horses cling to waving weeds, while sharks—9-ft-long (2.7-m) sand tigers among them—swim over the longest underwater tunnel in North America... right above the heads of visitors.

You can get up close and personal to beautiful turtles, giant sawfish, poisonous pufferfish, sublime stingrays and deadly piranhas, a school of which can use their razor-sharp teeth to strip an entire cow or human to the bones in just a few minutes. Luckily, the aquarium's acrylic panels are up to 1 ft (30 cm) thick.

The shark lagoon alone covers a total area of 8,000 sq ft (745 sq m)—equal to the size of a tennis court—and the water in the entire aquarium is powered by almost 100 separate pumps. The aquarium contains nearly 20 mi (32 km) of water piping and an incredible 285 mi (458 km) of electrical wiring – more than the distance from New York City to Washington, D.C.!

Ripley's already has aquariums in Myrtle Beach, South Carolina, and Gatlinburg, Tennessee. Ripley's Aquarium of Canada will conduct ongoing breeding and conservation programs for endangered species, including tagging and tracking programs for sand tiger sharks. When it comes to population numbers these sharks do not help themselves because as the unborn pups develop their embryonic teeth in the womb they eat all their brothers and sisters! All the more reason for Ripley's to look after them.

JELLYFISH
A jellyfish is 90 percent water and has no brain!

RIPLEY'S AQUARIUM OF CANADA

CLOWNFISH

By swimming among sea anemones, clownfish become immune to their deadly stings!

PUFFERFISH

There is enough poison in one pufferfish to kill 30 adult humans... and there is no known antidote!

PIRANHA

A piranha has teeth like razors and a bite force equivalent to 30 times its bodyweight!

AQUARIUM FACTS

- The aquarium holds a staggering 1.5 million gal (5.7 million l) of water

- It houses 450 different species of fish and invertebrates

- There are over 15,000 fish

- You can see 45 different tanks with live exhibits

- The largest tank is the Shark Lagoon. which is 8,000 sq ft (745 sq m) and holds 765,000 gal (2,895,840 l) of water

- The Shark Lagoon tunnel is 315 ft (86 m) long— the longest underwater tunnel in North America

- The aquarium has more than 80 sharks from 12 different species

GIANT PACIFIC OCTOPUS

A giant Pacific octopus can kill a shark by using its tentacles to break the shark's back!

STINGRAY

The barb on a stingray's tail spine measures 14 in (35 cm) and is so sharp that it can kill a human!

SAND TIGER SHARK

This shark has a full mouth of teeth that protrude in all directions, even when its mouth is shut!

BELIEVE IT! ▶

WEREWOLF SISTERS

The Sangli sisters from India, whose faces are covered in thick hair, suffer from one of the world's rarest medical conditions: hypertrichosis, or "werewolf syndrome."

The girls—from left to right, Monish, Savita and Savriti—who have three other sisters without the condition, inherited their hypertrichosis from their father. Their mother was forced to marry him as a child and first met her husband, and his hairy hypertrichosis, on their wedding day, when she had no choice but to go through with the marriage.

This genetic mutation affects just one in a billion people around the world, and results in unstoppable hair growth in abnormal areas such as the forehead and nose, and, in the case of Savita, Monish and Savitri, it has given them full beards.

There is currently no cure for the condition. Savita now uses a cream to control the spread of hair over her face, but this works only temporarily. She is sent home from her job when her facial hair starts to reappear.

People with genetic hypertrichosis, like the Sangli family, can undergo expensive chemical and laser procedures to remove hair, but it will always grow back eventually. Nevertheless, the Sangli family hope that, if they can raise the funds, laser surgery will enable the girls to find husbands, and they are actively seeking publicity to help them do this.

Ripley's RESEARCH

Hypertrichosis, which means "extra hair," is also known as "werewolf syndrome" because it leaves people looking like mythical werewolves. In the most extreme cases, the face, torso, arms and legs are all covered in hair, and the only parts of the skin to remain hairless are the palms of the hands and the soles of the feet. Very few people alive today have hypertrichosis. In fact, less than 100 cases have been recorded since the Middle Ages.

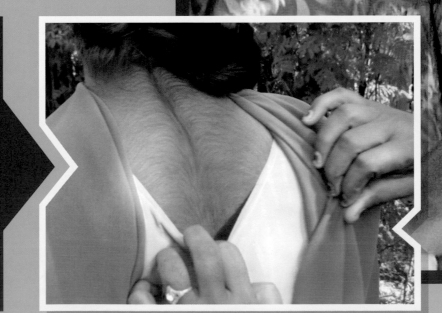

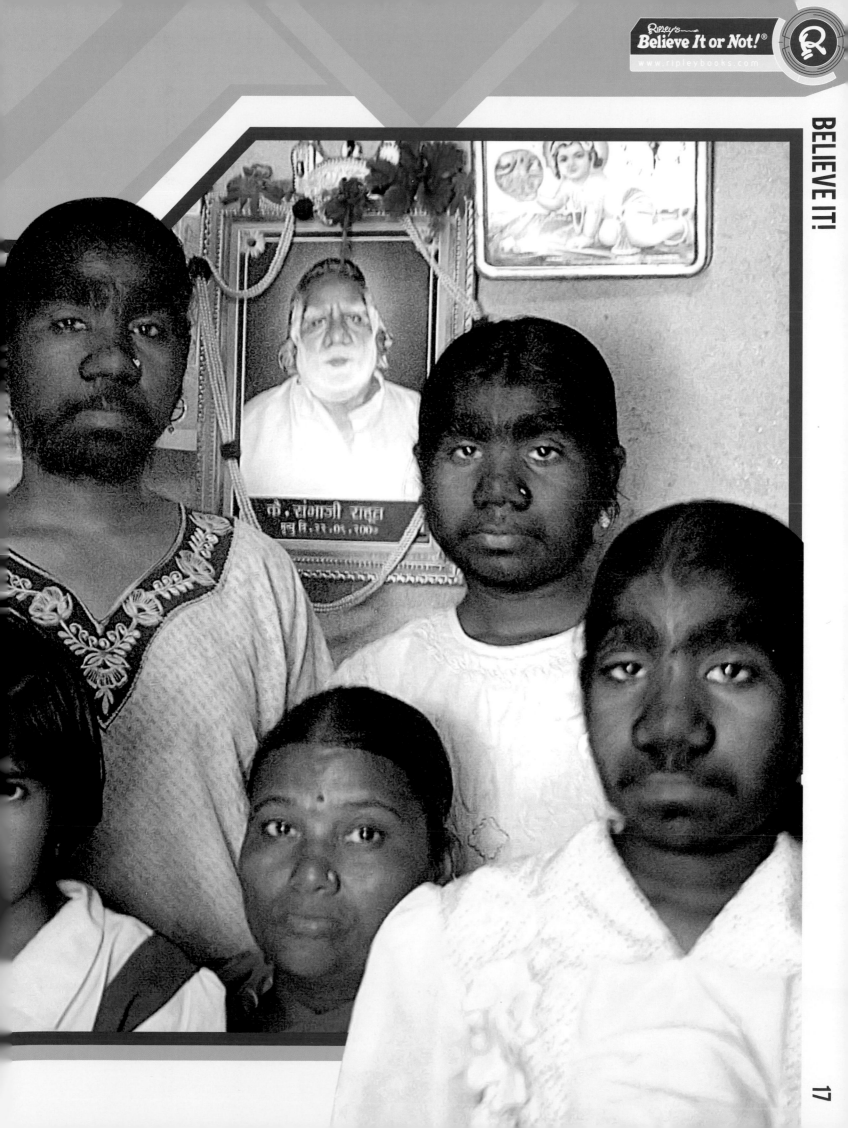

YOUR UPLOADS

BOUND TO SUCCEED ▶
Ana Lominadze, a 17-year-old Georgian schoolgirl, swam a 6,000-yd (5,500-m) stretch of the Dardanelles, a narrow strait in Turkey, in 50 minutes on August 30, 2012—with her hands and legs bound! The style of swimming, with tied hands and feet, is known as Colchian and is traditional in Georgia, where it is used for military training. Ana not only broke the world record for swimming across the Dardanelles Colchian-style, she also became the first woman to complete the crossing by that method.

CHANCE FIND ▶ Jesse Matos of Mount Shasta, California, lost his high-school class ring when he accidentally flushed it down the toilet in 1938—and it was found 73 years later in a sewer by sanitation worker Tony Congi, who graduated from the same high school in 1976 and recognized the ring immediately.

NOT ETHICAL ▶ A man was charged with stealing a book on ethics from the University of Louisville, Kentucky, and then trying to sell it to a college bookstore in the city.

FAMILY DAY ▶ Stefanie Thomas and her husband Paul of Plymouth, England, both have birthdays on September 6—and when their first child, Oliver, was born in 2011, it was also on September 6!

HUMAN DOORSTOP ▶ A would-be burglar was arrested in Brockton, Massachusetts, after his head got stuck under a garage door for nine hours. He had tried to prop open the heavy roll-up door with a piece of metal, but it slipped and the falling door pinned his head against the concrete floor until he was discovered the following morning.

HAIR RISK ▶ Hair Grooming Syncope is a pediatric disorder that results in a child suffering fainting spells whenever his or her hair is brushed or cut.

SPIDER TERROR ▶ An entire office building in Chur, Switzerland, was evacuated in July 2012 over a plastic spider. Workers panicked after seeing the lifelike creature on the boss's desk, but when police officers arrived they quickly discovered that the giant bird-eating spider was a fake.

DISTANT TWINS ▶ Reuben and Floren Blake of Gloucestershire, England, are twins, but they were born five years apart. They were conceived from the same batch of embryos during fertility treatment, but after the birth of Reuben in 2006, the remaining three embryos were frozen until his parents, Simon and Jody Blake, were ready to try for another child.

BEACH BOTTLE ▶ On the Baltic Sea coast near Kaliningrad, Daniil Korotkikh, a 13-year-old Russian boy, found a message in a bottle that had been written 24 years earlier by a then five-year-old German boy, Frank Uesbeck.

TIDY SUM ▶ Nagged for weeks by his mother to tidy up his bedroom, 19-year-old Ryan Kitching of Midlothian, Scotland, finally gave in to her wishes—and in a pile of papers in a drawer he found a £53,000 ($83,600) winning lottery ticket.

YODA COIN ▶ In 2011, the Pacific island nation of Niue released legal tender coins featuring Star Wars characters, including Luke Skywalker, Princess Leia and Yoda. Queen Elizabeth II appears on the reverse of the coins, which were issued by the New Zealand mint.

ROBOT GUARDS ▶ Scientists in South Korea have developed robot guards to patrol the country's prisons. The 5-ft-tall (1.5-m) robots run on four wheels and are fitted with sensors, which enable them to detect abnormal behavior among prisoners and then report it to the officers in charge.

SNAKE ATTACK ▶ A man who stopped to withdraw money from an ATM in Alava, Spain, got more than he bargained for when a snake slithered out of the machine and tried to attack him. The snake had somehow become trapped in the cash-point mechanism.

SLEEPY SWIMMER ▶ Alyson Bair of Burley, Idaho, twice went swimming in the nearby Snake River—while sleepwalking. On the first occasion she dreamed she was drowning, only to wake up in the river, and the second time she was found soaking wet a quarter of a mile downstream from her home.

BRAZILIAN BATMAN ▶ In 2012, city officials in Taubaté, Brazil, hired former soldier André Luiz Pinheiro to dress up as Batman and patrol the streets of the most crime-ridden neighborhoods.

SMART BED ▶ A Spanish furniture company has invented an electronic bed that makes itself. Three seconds after the last person gets out of the bed, mechanical arms automatically grab the edges of the duvet, rollers smooth down the sheets and a set of levers straighten the pillows.

PRICELESS DOORSTOP▶ A blue-and-white Ming Dynasty ceramic vase, which had been used as a doorstop by a family in Long Island, New York, was sold at an auction in 2012 for $1.3 million. The family realized the value of their doorstop only when they saw a similar piece advertised for sale in an auction house catalogue.

RADIO REVELATION▶ The elements americium and curium, discovered during the U.S.A.'s top-secret nuclear bomb project, were first announced on a 1945 edition of a children's radio quiz show, *Quiz Kids*, even before they were presented to the scientific community.

FLASH MOB▶ Jack Cushman from Boston, Massachusetts, proposed to his girlfriend Teresa Elsey by organizing a flash mob involving hundreds of complete strangers. He arranged for up to 300 people to approach her in the street as they were walking together and each hand her a single carnation. While she was surrounded, he slipped away, changed into a tuxedo and returned with a microphone to propose.

MOUNTAINTOP CEREMONY▶ Avid climbers Bob Ewing and his bride Antonie Hodge Ewing got married on the narrow summit of a 900-ft-high (274-m) mountain in West Virginia. The groom made the sheer ascent of Seneca Rocks in a tuxedo while the bride accessorized her mother's wedding gown with a helmet and hiking shoes. Her mother Evangeline, a novice climber, also made it to the top to witness the happy event.

GOOD HAIR DAY

3 ft 8 in (1.1 m) high!

▶ *Designer Kazuhiro Watanabe from Tokyo, Japan, has a spire-like Mohawk haircut that is an incredible 3 ft 8 in (1.1 m) high. He has been growing it for more than 15 years and it takes stylists two hours plus three cans of hairspray and a large bottle of gel to extend it to its maximum height.*

SALT POOL

▶ A giant, 323,000-sq-ft (30,000-sq-m) swimming pool in Sichuan Province, China, can hold up to 10,000 bathers at a time. The man-made saltwater pool, known as China's Dead Sea, was created using the area's wealth of salt resources and contains 43 different minerals and microelements. With a water salinity of more than 22 percent, swimmers float effortlessly on the pool's surface.

TELLTALE TATTOO▶ In 2011, police in Colorado captured 60-year-old Frederick Barrett 32 years after he had escaped from jail in Florida. After all that time, they were able to identify him by a tattoo of a cross and a dot on his right hand.

UNBEATABLE ROBOT▶
Scientists at the University of Tokyo, Japan, have devised a robot that is unbeatable at the game of Rock, Paper, Scissors. By using advanced motion-sensing technology, the robot needs just a millisecond to recognize the position and shape of a human hand and can therefore detect in advance what hand-shape its opponent is about to choose.

OCEAN ORDEAL▶ Nineteen-year-old Ryan Harris spent 26 hours adrift in a small plastic fishing crate in the icy waters off the coast of Alaska after being washed overboard. When his boat was sunk by huge waves, Harris, from nearby Sitka, spent the night in the crate, which measured just 4 x 4 ft (1.2 x 1.2 m), before finally being rescued by a coastguard helicopter. He kept his spirits up by singing and survived with nothing worse than a cut head and blisters from gripping the crate.

LUCKY ERROR▶ Richard Brown of Taunton, Massachusetts, was given the wrong scratch-off lottery ticket by a distracted store clerk—but he didn't complain and won $1 million.

MARRIED RESCUER▶ An avalanche survivor married the mountain rescue guide who had saved her life two years earlier—and the ceremony took place 6,000 ft (1,800 m) up on the very mountain where she was almost swept to her death. Tatjana Rasevic was buried under tons of snow on Serbia's Suva Planina mountain range until Nenad Podova dug her out.

▶*Sideshow performer James Morris could stretch his skin as much as 18 in (46 cm) from his body and could pull the skin of his neck over his head so that it looked like an elephant's trunk. He was also able to pull the skin of one leg and cover the other leg with it. Morris was born in Copenhagen, New York, in 1859 without the interior third layer of skin on his body. As a result, his skin was not bound to the flesh beneath, permitting him to stretch and pull it in any direction. A barber by trade, he used his unique talent to amuse friends and coworkers and began to perform at the dime museum of J.E. Sackett in Providence, Rhode Island. In 1882, he joined the legendary Barnum & Bailey Circus earning $150 a week, and toured the world with them to great acclaim, billed as either "The Elastic Man" or "The India Rubber Man."*

ELASTIC MAN

POTTY IDEA

▶ *You need a head for heights to use the toilet in this luxury penthouse in Guadalajara, Mexico—because it is suspended on a glass floor above a 15-story abandoned elevator shaft. When you sit on the toilet or brush your teeth, you can look straight through the floor to the bottom of the shaft.*

PHOTO SHOCK▶ Addison Logan, 13, bought an old Polaroid camera for $1 at a Wichita, Kansas, garage sale—and inside he found a photograph of a dead uncle he had never met.

SLIM CHANCE▶ George McCovery of West Palm Beach, Florida, had his jail sentence cut short by a judge in 2011 after he met a court-sanctioned weight challenge and dropped 25 lb (11 kg) in only 20 days.

LOVE LETTER▶ In July 2011, Muhammad Siddeeq of Indianapolis, Indiana, received a love letter that had been mailed to him 53 years earlier. Since then he had married twice—once to the letter writer—fathered 21 children and changed his name.

SALMON CROSSING▶ After a river flooded in Mason County, Washington, dozens of salmon were seen trying to swim across an adjacent road. Cars were not their only problem, with at least one unlucky salmon being snapped up by a passing dog.

CHRISTMAS TREES▶ Brandon Smith and Dennis Guyette decorated their home in Greenwood, Indiana, with 68 Christmas trees—and their decorations adorned every room, including the bathroom and kitchen. When they opened their festive house to the public, they had more than 600 visitors.

TOY STORY▶ After a miaowing sound was heard coming from a locked recycling container in Anglesey, Wales, fire crews and animal rescuers tried in vain to gain entry. Eventually the container was loaded onto a truck and driven 20 mi (32 km) to a specialist engineering firm, where steel saws forced it open and revealed the trapped cat in fact to be a lifelike, miaowing Disney toy of Marie the cat from *The Aristocats* movie.

MILITARY FORESIGHT▶ In the 1917 Battle of Messines of World War I, 10,000 German soldiers were instantly killed by 500 tons of explosives that had been planted underground by Allied engineers who had anticipated the battle a year earlier!

LIGHTEST MATERIAL▶ Scientific researchers in California have created the world's lightest material—one that is 99.9 percent air. Made of tiny hollow metallic tubes arranged into a micro-lattice, it is 100 times lighter than Styrofoam. In fact, it is so light that it can sit on top of dandelion fluff without damaging it.

HIGHWAY BIRTHS▶ On July 28, 2012, Siobhan Anderson from Amityville, New York, gave birth to twins on two different highways while on her way to the hospital. After going into labor a week early, she gave birth to Gavin on the Southern State Parkway in Long Island and 11 minutes later to Declan on Wantagh State Parkway.

ENGINE ATTACK▶ An 11½-ft-long (3.5-m) saltwater crocodile jumped out of the water and bit chunks out of a boat's engine during a 90-minute nighttime attack in Australia's South Alligator River. The moored boat's three occupants eventually fought off the croc by smacking it over the head with a metal pole.

ISLAND RESCUE▶ Setting off in a canoe in Wild Fowl Bay, Michigan, Nathan Bluestein carried out an elaborate, meticulously planned marriage proposal to May Gorial, but the couple then had to be rescued by sheriff's deputies after severe weather left them stranded on a nearby island.

OLDEST GROOM ▶ Hazi Abdul Noor, officially registered as 116 years old but who claimed to be 120, married 60-year-old Samoi Bibi in front of 500 guests at a ceremony in Satghari, India, in 2011. He is head of a family of 122, including two sons, four daughters and a lot of grandchildren.

MINE CLEARER ▶ Aki Ra, once a child soldier in Cambodia, digs up and defuses land mines, and he started out by using only a knife and a sharp stick. He and his team now use more sophisticated equipment and have cleared over 50,000 devices.

HAPPY ANNIVERSARY ▶ British Army Lance Corporal Scott Townson saved the life of fellow soldier Lance Corporal Craig Turley twice in a year—and both incidents occurred on September 23! First, Lance Corporal Turley was on patrol in Afghanistan when an exploding grenade nearly blew off his left hand and severed an artery, and then exactly a year later he was bitten by a venomous Egyptian cobra while training in Kenya. On both occasions Lance Corporal Townson, an army medic, was on hand to save his friend.

NUMBER SEQUENCE ▶ Laila Fitzgerald of Des Moines, Iowa, was born weighing 8 lb 9 oz on October 11, 2012, at 1.14 p.m., giving her a numerical sequence of 8-9-10-11-12-13-14.

ZOMBIFY YOURSELF ▶ People who think their wedding photos are a bit bland can now have them "zombified!" Rob Sacchetto from Sudbury, Ontario, runs zombieportraits.com, which offers people the chance to have their photos customized with hand-painted artwork that turns them into crazed zombies. He has also used ink and watercolor to zombify photos of the likes of Donald Trump, Kanye West, Alfred Hitchcock and Lindsay Lohan.

DESIGNER MONKEY

▶ Wearing a tiny shearling coat and a diaper, this seven-month-old Japanese macaque monkey was spotted wandering around the parking lot of an Ikea store in Toronto, Canada. The monkey, named Darwin, had escaped from a crate in his owner's car.

MISSING MILLIONS ▶ A bumper $96-million Lottery Euromillions jackpot went unclaimed in December 2012 because the mystery winning ticketholder from Hertfordshire, England, missed the 180-day deadline to make a claim.

DOG CALL ▶ After receiving a mysterious silent call on his cell phone from the phone in his empty house, Bruce Gardner of Orem, Utah, immediately rang the police to report that his house was being broken into—only to discover later that the "call" had come from his pet Labrador Maya. The dog had got hold of his cordless home phone and while chewing it, had happened to hit redial.

PENNY PILE ▶ Thomas Daigle of Milford, Massachusetts, paid off the final bill of his house mortgage entirely in pennies—62,000 of them! He meticulously collected pennies for 35 years until he had 400 lb (182 kg) of rolled-up coins, which he took to the loans company in two heavy steel boxes. It took the bank two days to count the coins and verify that the mortgage was paid.

PARALLEL LIVES ▶ Emilie Falk and Lin Backman, nonidentical twins born in Semarang, Indonesia, in 1983, were separately adopted by Swedish parents, but reunited 29 years later after discovering they lived only 25 mi (40 km) apart. Although raised independently, both became teachers, they got married on the same day just one year apart, and they even danced to the same wedding song, "You and Me" by Lifehouse.

CAN SCULPTURE ▶ Volunteers in Abu Dhabi, U.A.E., took six days to build an enormous aluminum can sculpture from 46,556 cans. The model of the 200-year-old Al Maqta'a Fort stood 18.6 ft (5.7 m) high and measured 13 ft (4 m) wide at the base. It was stuck together using 919 bottles of superglue and 521 cans of liquid nail glue.

DEAD BEES ▶ Matthew Brandt from Los Angeles, California, created an image of a bee, composed entirely from the crumbled parts of dead bees. He acquired his natural materials after discovering hundreds of dead honeybees scattered along the Californian shoreline.

OLD WIVES' SALES ▶ Until 1857, it was legal for British husbands to sell their wives. The going rate was £3,000 ($4,550), the equivalent in today's money of about £220,000 ($335,000).

SHARP END ▶

▶ *Shaolin monks balance their bodies on the tips of sharp spears in a demonstration of the Chinese martial art Qigong during the opening ceremony of the Fourth Southern Shaolin Martial Arts Cultural Festival in Putian. Qigong teaches the body to relax so that no pain is felt.*

HEAD IN A BOOK

▶ Artist Maskull Lasserre from Montreal, Canada, carved an intricate replica of a human skull from seven thick software manuals. Using an angle grinder and router, and working in short bursts of between 20 and 60 minutes at a time, it took him over 200 hours to complete the sculpture. He has also carved an impressive likeness of a human rib cage from a stack of old newspapers.

LEAP DAY▶ Michelle Birnbaum of Saddle River, New Jersey, was born on February 29, 1980, and in 2008, amazingly, her daughter Rose was also born on February 29—leap day.

UNDERWATER WEDDING▶ More than 200 SCUBA divers attended the July 17, 2011, underwater wedding of Alberto dal Lago and Karla Munguia, which took place 16 ft (5 m) deep in the ocean off the coast of Playa Del Carmen, Mexico. The civil judge, who wed them, and his secretary both had to learn to SCUBA dive in order to conduct the ceremony.

CLOSE SHAVE▶ A 57-year-old man who had fallen asleep in a cornfield on the outskirts of Billings, Montana, had a miraculous escape when he was run over by a large combine harvester. The man's clothing was sucked into the cutter and he was trapped in the blades, but survived with just cuts and bruises.

PIGEON MESSAGE▶ A carrier pigeon dispatched during World War II to relay a secret message, possibly about the D-Day landings, was found around 70 years later in the chimney of a house in Surrey, England—its communiqué still attached to its skeleton in a red capsule. Some 250,000 birds were used by the British military and emergency services in World War II, to form the National Pigeon Service, 32 of which received medals for distinguished service. This one never reached its destination—and its message is so secret that it is written in a code long since forgotten by British security services.

COMPLETELY NUTS!

▶ This nutty squirrel became trapped in a storm drain in the middle of a road in Isernhagen, Germany. It tried to squeeze through a small hole in the drain, but managed to fit only its head through before getting stuck. Happily the squirrel was soon freed when a local housewife came to its rescue with a bottle of olive oil that was smeared around its neck as a lubricant.

FAMILIAR FACE▶ Brazilian police charged a man in Recife with using false documents and forgery after he tried to open a bank account using an identification document bearing a photograph of Hollywood actor Jack Nicholson.

BUNGLING BANDITS▶ Two would-be robbers called a bank in Fairfield, Connecticut, on the phone and threatened to create a "blood bath" if a bag of cash was not waiting for them when they arrived. They showed up 10 minutes later and seemed surprised that police officers, alerted by the bank, were waiting to arrest them.

DISSOLVED CORPSES▶ As a green alternative to cremation, a funeral home in St. Petersburg, Florida, has installed a unit that works by dissolving the corpse in heated alkaline water. The makers say the process produces one-third less greenhouse gas than cremation and uses one-seventh of the energy.

LOST IN POST▶ Hu Seng from Chongqing, China, paid a courier to deliver him in a sealed box to his girlfriend Li Wang, but the joke backfired when the courier got lost and instead of spending 30 minutes in the box, Hu was trapped for nearly three hours. By the time the package was finally delivered to his girlfriend's office, he had passed out and had to be revived by paramedics. He said ruefully: "I tried to make a hole in the cardboard but it was too thick and I didn't want to spoil the surprise by shouting."

IDENTITY CRISIS▶ A Luciano Pavarotti impersonator for 20 years, Colin Miller from Staffordshire, England, was denied a personalized debit card because his bank refused to accept that his photo was not the real Italian opera singer.

TREE TRAUMA▶ Firefighters in Orange County, California, took 90 minutes to free a man who was stuck up to his chest inside a hollow tree trunk that extended some 5 ft (1.5 m) underground. Sheriff's deputies had located the trapped man by following the sounds of his screams down into a creek bed.

TRAPPED KITTEN▶ A team of five rescuers worked continuously for two days to save a wet and hungry kitten that had become trapped in a 6-in-wide (15-cm) concrete tube beneath a supermarket in Gothenburg, Sweden.

MOWER SNATCH▶ When keepers at the Australian Reptile Park in Gosford, New South Wales, went into the enclosure of Elvis, a 16-ft (5-m) saltwater crocodile, the aggressive reptile grabbed one of their lawn mowers, dragged it into his pond and lay at the bottom guarding it.

FLYING VISIT▶ Adventure enthusiasts Grant Engler and Amanda Volf made a spectacular entrance to their beach wedding at Newport Beach, California, by flying into the ceremony wearing water-powered jet packs, each connected by a 30-ft (9-m) hose to a boat. The bride landed on the beach aisle wearing a surfing vest, shorts and a veil, while the groom wore a white bow tie over a black wetsuit. After exchanging their vows, the couple performed the traditional first dance in midair above the ocean.

BRIDAL RACE▶ One hundred prospective brides donned wedding dresses and running shoes to take part in a 150-meter race in Belgrade, Serbia, with the winner earning a free wedding.

OSTRICH ATTACK▶ In Hastings, New Zealand, Phillip Russell was jailed for six months for assaulting his wife with an ostrich egg. He threw the huge egg at her, bruising her chest, after losing his temper because her pet pig had damaged his power saw.

SEEING DOUBLE

▶ When student Max Galuppo of Bloomsbury, New Jersey, visited the Philadelphia Museum of Art, he was stunned to see his doppelganger in Portrait of a Nobleman with Dueling Gauntlet, a 16th-century picture by an unknown artist. However, the resemblance may not be entirely coincidental as Max's grandparents come from the same area of northern Italy where the portrait is believed to have been painted.

FLOWER POWER

▸Believe it or not, these sculptures are made entirely from flowers! On the first Sunday of every September, the Bloemencorso, or flower parade, makes its way through the streets of the Dutch town of Zundert, the birthplace of artist Vincent van Gogh. Hundreds of volunteers pin specially grown dahlias to wire frames to create each float.

TESTING DAY▸ Emma French of Livingston, Scotland, took her driving test while she was in labor—and managed to pass despite having four contractions during the test. Immediately afterward, she drove herself to the hospital and gave birth just hours later.

BRIDGE STOLEN▸ A 50-ft-long (15-m) metal bridge was stolen in North Beaver Township, Pennsylvania, after thieves used a blowtorch to cut it apart.

BULLET BLOCKER▸ A storeowner in Savannah, Georgia, was shot during an armed robbery but suffered only a minor cut when the medallions hanging around his neck deflected the bullet.

MAGIC NUMBER▸ Twins Race and Brooke Belmont from Tampa, Florida, turned 11 on 11/11/11 (November 11, 2011).

FAKE FAMILY

▶ *Alice Winstone from Cardigan, Wales, has spent nearly $20,000 creating a nursery for 50 fake babies who share the house with three of her five real children. Unable to have any more children of her own, she has instead filled the house with lifelike reborn dolls, buying them racks of designer clothes, cots and strollers, and even taking her favorites out for day trips in the car. She feeds, changes, washes and sleeps with her dolls, which all proved too much for her husband who moved out over five years ago. She says: "I look after the dolls like I would my own babies—they are so lifelike and I feel such a close bond with them. It's the best of both worlds as well—I get to dress them up, do their hair and wash their clothes without the endless dirty nappies and sleepless nights!"*

Ripley's RESEARCH

Costing between $75 and $4,000 each, reborn dolls take the place of real babies for some parents who even buy fake birth or adoption certificates for them. First appearing in the U.S.A. in the early 1990s, a reborn doll is created by adding layers of paint and other features to an ordinary vinyl doll in order to make it look like a genuine baby. Veins can be painted on for an authentic newborn look, while the arms and head are often weighted with sand or rubber pellets for a more realistic feel. Buyers can request made-to-order features on the doll, such as an umbilical cord, baby fat, human hair, particular color eyes or a magnet inserted inside the mouth for attaching a pacifier. Some reborn dolls can be "fed" a fake form of milk and even be fitted with mechanisms that simulate breathing to make it appear that the doll is alive. In 2008, police in Queensland, Australia, smashed a car window to rescue what appeared to be an unconscious baby, only to find it was a reborn doll.

TREASURE TROVE ▶ After hunting in vain for buried treasure in the same area of Jersey in the Channel Islands for 30 years, amateur metal detectors Reg Mead and Richard Miles finally hit the jackpot when they unearthed three-quarters of a ton of Iron Age coins worth $15 million. Each of the 50,000 or so 2,000-year-old silver coins they dug up—the largest-ever haul of Celtic coins—has an estimated value of $300.

CROSSED WIRES ▶ A woman from Zlin, Czech Republic, had to be rescued after mistaking an electrical pylon for a bridge. She climbed the 40-ft-high (12-m) pylon in the belief that it would take her across the Morava River.

PLASTIC ARM ▶ Part of the M62 motorway in Merseyside, England, was closed by police for hours because of a plastic arm. The false limb, lying in the middle of the road, caused chaos after drivers mistook it for a genuine human arm.

FIRST GIRL ▶ In 2011, Gary and Satish Beckett of Kent, England, celebrated the birth of daughter Anaia—the first girl to be born into the family for 113 years.

UNLUCKY DAY ▶ A man got stuck in an elevator twice in one day. After being trapped for three hours on the 21st floor of Chicago's Mid-Continental Plaza on February 6, 2012, he was finally freed by fire crews. Moments later he took another elevator down, but that became stuck, too!

LOTTERY SCOOP ▶ New Taipei City, Taiwan, cleaned up its streets by offering lottery tickets to people who cleared up dog poop. More than 4,000 people collected 14,500 bags of excrement over a four-month period—and each bag was rewarded with a ticket.

KNIT WIT ▶ This plate of fish, fries, peas and two slices of lemon looks good enough to eat—but in fact the entire meal is made from wool! Artistic knitter Kate Jenkins from Brighton, England, spends hours with a crochet hook to create a whole menu of amusing, edible-looking designs—including bottles of wine, ketchup, cans of soup and fruit-topped pastries—sometimes embroidering patterns on to her tasty creations for added realism.

BUSY BIRTHDAY ▶ Sammy Kellett of Lancashire, England, has three sons, Keiran, Kaiden and Kyle, all of whom were born on September 20—in 2005, 2008 and 2011—at odds of 133,590 to one.

COVERS BLESSED ▶ Priests in Lodz, Poland, blessed all 4,000 of the town's manhole covers to try to stop scrap metal thieves stealing them.

HUNTER HUNTED ▶ A man who went duck hunting on the Great Salt Lake, Utah, was hospitalized after his dog stepped on a shotgun, shooting him in the butt.

HEAVY READING ▶ The *Earth Platinum* atlas weighed 330 lb (150 kg)—each page measuring 6 ft (1.8 m) high and 4 ft 6 in (1.4 m) wide.

TWO CRASHES ▶ On March 13, 2012, mother Annie Price and her son Antony O'Halloran survived separate head-on crashes within four minutes of each other on New Zealand's Kapiti Coast.

RING RECOVERED ▶ Sixteen years after losing her wedding ring, farmer's wife Lena Paahlsson of Mora, Sweden, found it wrapped around a carrot in her garden. She had taken off the ring while cooking in 1995 and thinks it must have fallen into the kitchen sink and become mixed up with potato peelings that were composted or fed to the farm's sheep—all her garden soil comes from either composted vegetables or sheep dung.

GOLD TRAIL ▶ When termites encounter a gold vein, they bore through it and deposit the displaced gold outside their hive. In Mali, miners use the termites' geological discoveries to plan new gold hunting expeditions.

EVIL CLOWN

▶ Swiss actor Dominic Deville hires himself out as an evil clown who stalks and terrifies children in the week leading up to their birthday. He sends them scary texts, makes prank phone calls and, finally, when they are least expecting it, he splats a cake in their face. Deville, who came up with the idea from watching horror movies, says kids love being scared senseless, but promises that if the parents become concerned, he will back off.

MINI NUN

▶ *Worshipers at a temple in Haridwar, India, bow at the feet of Anjali Barma, a nun who is just 2 ft 7 in (78.8 cm) tall. The 65-year-old, who is also known as Ganga Maa, says visitors think she is an extra-special holy woman because of her stature. However, when she was just ten years old, her lack of inches led to her being kidnapped by a circus owner who held her captive for several months and tried in vain to persuade her to perform on stage as a human oddity.*

THE HONEYMOO-MERS▷ Beef farmer Michael Hanson and his bride Hayley Morgan arrived at their bovine-themed wedding on a tractor and their wedding photos were posed in a muddy field alongside a herd of cattle in Llandefalle, Wales. They spent their honeymoon in Texas, touring cattle farms.

GOOD SAMARITAN▶ When Gerald Gronowski had a flat tire near Cleveland, Ohio, a man named Christopher Manacci stopped to help. As they talked, Gronowski realized that Manacci was the same kindly stranger who had helped him extract a fishing hook from his wounded hand eight years earlier.

FAN MAN▷ Eighty-two-year-old M. Natarajan, a Hindu devotee from Madurai, Tamil Nadu, India, has spent every day of the past 52 years fanning the visitors of local temples to keep them cool. In that time he has worn through five 6.6-lb (3-kg) peacock fans.

ILLEGIBLE NOTE▶ A bank robbery was foiled in New Castle, Delaware, when the bank teller was unable to read the illegible handwriting on the robber's note.

STRONG MATERIAL▷ Graphene, a material made from molecular sheets of carbon, is hundreds of times stronger than steel. It would take the weight of an elephant balanced on a pencil to penetrate a sheet as thin as household plastic wrap.

▶ IN 1811, NEARLY A QUARTER OF ALL THE WOMEN IN BRITAIN WERE NAMED MARY.◀

GUIDED BULLET▶ Researchers in Albuquerque, New Mexico, have invented a prototype bullet that can steer itself in mid-flight. The bullet uses tiny fins to correct the course of its flight, which enable it to hit laser-lit targets at distances of about 1¼ mi (2 km).

MOLECULAR MOTOR▷ Researchers from Tufts University of Medford, Massachusetts, created an electric motor built from a single molecule that is 300 times smaller than the width of a human hair.

SUSPICIOUS PACKAGES▶ Two men trying to board an airplane at Indira Gandhi International Airport in Delhi, India, tried to conceal live small mammals in their underpants. Suspicious customs officers discovered that the men, en route from Dubai, U.A.E., to Bangkok, Thailand, had slender lorises concealed in pouches in their briefs.

DELAYED PICTURES▷ A centenarian couple from Nanchong, China, finally posed for their wedding photos in 2012—88 years after getting married. When Wu Conghan, 101, and his wife Wu Songshi, 103, married back in 1924, they did not have the option of wedding photos.

SPACE ART

▶ Josh Taylor from Surrey, England, created a unique piece of space art at an altitude of 100,000 ft (30,500 m) using a helium weather balloon. Containing tubes of green, blue, brown and yellow paint to represent the earth, sea, desert and sun, the balloon was launched into the sky over Worcestershire and during the ascent the colors were slowly released from the tubes onto a canvas. When the balloon reached 100,810 ft (30,725 m), it burst and plummeted back down to the ground where the artwork was located by means of a tracking device.

CAT BURGLAR ▶ A trap set up to catch an office thief at an animal shelter in Swinoujscie, Poland, caught a real-life cat burglar. The secret camera captured a two-year-old Burmese cat named Clement sneaking into the office at midnight, stealing the cash and hiding it under a sofa. Her nighttime raids had netted her more than $300 in a month.

MISTAKEN IDENTITY ▶ In October 2011, a lifeboat and a helicopter from Tyneside, England, were sent on an emergency North Sea rescue mission after a member of the public mistook the planet Jupiter for a distress flare. Jupiter is particularly low in the sky at that time of year and also gives off a bright red light that can be mistaken for flares.

SQUID-BOT ▶ Scientists at Harvard University, U.S.A., have devised a rubbery, squidlike robot, which can crawl and camouflage itself, made from soft, translucent polymers. Based on the ability of certain sea creatures to control their appearance, the robot incorporates a thin sheet of special silicone containing tiny channels through which colored liquids are pumped so that its skin mimics its surroundings.

OLDEST MESSAGE ▶ Fishing off the Shetland Islands in August 2012, Scottish boat skipper Andrew Leaper discovered a message in a bottle dated June 1914, making it, at 98 years old, the oldest message in a bottle ever found. Amazingly, the previous record-holding bottle—a 93-year-old message found in 2006—was picked up in the same area by the same fishing boat, the *Copious*.

MODEL BABIES

▶ *Parents can now hold their baby before it is born—thanks to a technique that uses a 3-D printer to transform an ultrasound scan into an anatomically correct resin replica of the fetus. The models—marketed by Japanese company FASOTEC and costing over $1,000 each—come in a standard size of 3½ in (9 cm), but are also available in miniature so that proud parents can dangle their babies from a key chain.*

SPIDER NIGHTMARE

▶ Spiders from the town of Wagga Wagga, in New South Wales, Australia, spun some amazing webs while escaping floodwaters in March 2012. As the waters rushed past the town, the spiders were forced to scuttle out of the way, climbing up trees and bushes spinning their webs as they went. The results were fields that looked like they were covered in snow, bushes that looked like giant cotton candy, and dogs that could play hide-and-seek from their owners for hours!

BURIED ALIVE

▶ *Peter Skyllberg, 44, survived two months in a frozen car. He was found emaciated but alive in a car that had been buried in snow in northern Sweden for two months of a harsh winter. The car became stuck in drifts north of the town of Umea on December 19, 2011, and Peter wasn't rescued until February 17, 2012. He had survived on a few snacks and handfuls of snow, in temperatures that dropped to –22°F (–30°C). Some experts believe his body must have gone into a kind of human hibernation in order to survive the ordeal.*

BRIDGE STOLEN▶ Thieves in Slavkov, Czech Republic, escaped with a valuable haul of scrap metal after dismantling an 11-ton bridge and more than 650 ft (198 m) of railroad track.

TEDDY BEARS' PICNIC▶ A Finnish company offers people the chance to send their teddy bears on a trip to the Arctic Circle. For around $130, Teddy Tours Lapland poses the stuffed toys on horseback safari rides, taking walks in the snow and, of course, enjoying picnics.

BOTTLED MESSAGES▶ Since 1996, Harold Hackett of Prince Edward Island, Canada, has tossed more than 5,000 bottled messages into the Atlantic Ocean—and has had about 3,300 people write back from as far afield as Russia, the Netherlands, Africa and South America.

BATMAN STOPPED▶ Dressed as Batman, Lenny B. Robinson was driving his black Lamborghini "Batmobile" to surprise sick children in a hospital in Silver Spring, Maryland, when he was pulled over by police officers for having the wrong license plates on the car.

CORPSE COOKS▶ Six days after she was pronounced dead and the day before her funeral, 95-year-old Li Xiufeng of Guangxi Province, China, stunned villagers by pushing open the lid of her coffin, climbing out and cooking herself dinner.

RED FACES▶ Embarrassed parents realized that they had left their three-year-old daughter behind at a restaurant in Bel Air, Maryland, only when they saw her picture on the television news three hours later.

SILENT TREATMENT▶ A team of 120 mime artists was hired to control the traffic in Caracas, Venezuela. The initiative, dreamed up by the city's mayor, Carlos Ocariz, saw the mimes taking to the streets wearing clown costumes and wagging their fingers at any driver who violated traffic laws.

CONVERTED SHED▶ John Plumridge of Shropshire, England, spent more than four years converting his garden shed into a working pub that also displays a collection of 600 real ale and cider bottles. John's efforts resulted in first prize in a 2012 Shed of the Year competition.

LITTLE HOUDINI▶ Nicknamed "Little Houdini," Christopher Gay of Pleasant View, Tennessee, has escaped police custody 13 times—without resorting to any form of violence.

MINIATURE DIG▶ Since 2005, Joe Murray has been digging out the basement of his house in Saskatchewan, Canada, using only radio-controlled scale-model construction equipment. Working with his little tractors, excavators and a miniature rock crusher, he has been able to move an average of just 9 cubic ft (0.25 cubic m) of earth each year.

SILVER HOARD▶ In March 2012, workers in St. Petersburg, Russia, discovered more than 1,000 pieces of jewelry and silver that had been hidden behind a wall since the 1917 Bolshevik Revolution.

LATE MAIL▶ A postcard mailed in 1943 from Rockford, Illinois, to sisters Pauline and Theresa Leisenring finally arrived at their former home in Elmira, New York, in 2012—69 years after it was sent and more than 50 years after both women had died.

GETAWAY FARE▶ A would-be bank robber was arrested in Chamblee, Georgia, after returning to the scene of his crime to withdraw money for his cab fare. Fleeing empty-handed from the bank, the gunman jumped into a cab to ride to his getaway car, only to realize he had no money for the fare. So he returned to the same bank to withdraw cash legally, but was recognized by staff.

HOT LINE▶ Solenne San Jose, from Pessac, France, was horrified to receive a telephone bill for $14,766,481,895,641,556—the equivalent of nearly 6,000 times France's annual economic output. The bill should have been for around $100.

CRIME PAYS▶ An Austrian court ordered bank robber Otto Neuman to be given back $82,000 that he stole 19 years earlier because neither the bank nor its insurers wanted the money. After getting into financial difficulties, bank manager Neuman recruited two friends to help him snatch $240,000 in cash and gold bars from his branch in Vienna. By the time Neuman was apprehended and jailed, $158,000 had been spent. However, the bank was insured for the robbery and the insurance company made its money back on the rising value of the gold bars.

BARGAIN RATE▶ Isidore and Joan Schwartz stayed at the Waldorf-Astoria Hotel in New York City, on their wedding night in 1952. When they returned in 2012 for their 60th wedding anniversary, they paid the same price as their first visit—$16.80, even though rooms at the hotel now start at $319 a night.

MAGIC NUMBER▶ Kiam Moriya from Birmingham, Alabama, was born on December 12, 2000 at 12 minutes after midday, meaning that he turned 12 on 12/12/12 at 12.12 p.m.

HOT LIPS

▶ To attract pollinating butterflies and hummingbirds, the small white flowers of the shrub *Psychotria elata* are surrounded by large red leaves that look like a pair of luscious lips. No wonder the plant, which is found in Central America, is sometimes known as "Mick Jagger's lips"!

METEOR BLAST▶ A meteor measuring more than 55 ft (17 m) wide and weighing 10,000 tons entered the Earth's atmosphere at a speed of 40,000 mph (64,000 km/h) on February 15, 2013, before exploding some 15 mi (24 km) above ground with a force 33 times more powerful than the atomic bomb that destroyed Hiroshima in 1945. The largest space rock strike to hit Earth for over a century, it blew in around a million square feet (93,000 m²) of glass in the Russian city of Chelyabinsk, damaged 3,000 buildings and created a 50-ft (15-m) hole in a frozen lake. The meteor left a trail in the sky that was 300 mi (480 km) long. The shockwave from the Russian explosion was detected by sensors halfway around the world—as far afield as Africa and Greenland.

WEDDING-DAY FALL▶ Derek and Cassy McBride of Erie, Pennsylvania, were married in a hospital chapel after the groom suffered a collapsed lung and broke three ribs when he fell down a flight of stairs earlier on the day of their wedding—June 25, 2011.

SLEEPY DRIVER▶ A Swiss driver whose car veered off the road, down an embankment and plunged into a stream after he had dozed off at the wheel was still fast asleep when rescuers pulled him out. Medics thought 49-year-old Manfred Hofer, from Willisau, Switzerland, was unconscious but in fact he was just in a deep sleep.

TEENAGE TRANCE▶ Several teenage students attending an end-of-term hypnosis show at a private girls' high school in Sherbrooke, Canada, became stuck in a trance, forcing the young hypnotist to summon his mentor to snap them back into reality. The girls remained in the spell cast by 20-year-old Maxime Nadeau for several hours until his mentor, Richard Whitbread, arrived.

ROPE JUMPING

▶ In their search for new thrills, more than 3,000 young Russians have taken up the extreme sport of rope jumping, leaping from a mountain or bridge and plunging hundreds of feet through the air tied to a homemade rope. Unlike a bungee cord, the rope does not have an elastic slack, so jumpers must try to form an arc shape with it so that it cushions their fall. For an added twist, some of the youngsters have started performing the daredevil jumps on snowboards.

CHOCOLATE BABIES

▶ *Artist Annabel de Vetten from Birmingham, England, has made these disturbingly realistic, life-sized babies' heads out of solid white chocolate. The bizarre, zombie-like heads each weigh nearly 2.2 lb (1 kg), contain 5,000 calories and sell for £35 ($55). De Vetten, who calls herself "The Cake Conjurer," as she is also an amateur magician, made the heads using a latex mold after she was commissioned to create something that would shock people.*

CHILD GENIUS ▶ Heidi Hankins of Hampshire, England, has the IQ of a genius at just four years of age. The average IQ score for an adult is 100 and a "gifted" individual 130, but the youngster boasts an amazing 159—one behind eminent scientist Stephen Hawking. She could read books for seven-year-olds when she was only two and was accepted into Mensa—the high IQ society— before she had even started school.

KEEPING FIT ▶ At age 90, Edna Shepherd attends gym classes in Melbourne, Australia, several times a week, taking part in aerobics, tai chi and body pump. Her fitness regime also includes aqua classes and ballroom dancing.

LONG TRAIN ▶ To promote the 2012 Wedding Fair in Bucharest, Romania, ten seamstresses spent 100 days creating a bridal train that was 1.85 mi (3 km) long! To show off the gown, 17-year-old model Ema Dumitrescu took a ride in a hot-air balloon with the dress train flowing beneath her.

TOO LATE ▶ In May 2011, police in Walchum, Germany, arrested a 57-year-old man who tried to rob a bank that had been closed for years. He stormed the bank but was disappointed to discover that it was now a physiotherapist's office.

▶ WE SPEND AN AVERAGE OF 9 YEARS OF OUR LIFE WATCHING TV. ◀

BLIND PHOTOGRAPHER ▶ Tara Miller of Winnipeg, Canada, won a 2011 national photography competition despite being legally blind. When taking pictures outdoors she relies upon brightness and shadow in order to be able to frame a photograph, and when she shoots wildlife she relies upon her exceptional hearing to work out where the birds and other animals are so that she can snap them at the most appropriate moment.

AERIAL DANCERS ▶ Project Bandaloop, an aerial dance troupe based in California, performs many of its routines dangling from the sides of buildings and cliffs. Strapped to harnesses and ropes, the dancers have carried out breathtakingly original dance sequences hundreds of feet up in the air at Yosemite Falls, as well as performing at other U.S. and international landmarks, including the New York Stock Exchange in New York City and the Eiffel Tower in Paris, France, and in Italy's Dolomite mountains.

EXPLODING HORSES ▶ The U.S. Department of Agriculture has official, published procedures for blowing up animal carcasses with explosives. To obliterate a 1,100-lb (453-kg) horse, it recommends placing 3 lb (1.36 kg) of explosives under the carcass in four different locations as well as 1 lb (0.45 kg) of explosives in two locations on each leg. Horseshoes should be removed in advance of blowing up the horse's carcass in order to prevent flying debris.

WORLD ▶

DRESSING THE DEAD

As a way to demonstrate their love for the deceased, family members in the Toraja district of Indonesia exhume their ancestors' mummified bodies every three years and dress them in new clothes. As part of the strange ritual, called Ma'nene, the smartly attired dead are then taken for a walk around their local village.

The local people attach great importance to death and believe that family members are still with them, even if they died hundreds of years ago. Lavish funerals often take place months after death, by which time the corpses have been infused with preservatives so that they remain in good condition for centuries to come.

▲ Villagers bind cloth rolls that contain their relatives.

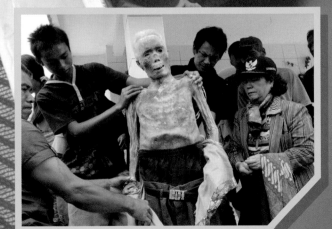

▲ The deceased relative is dressed in a new set of clothes every three years.

◀ Family members carry the coffin that contains their preserved relative dressed in new clothes.

The wealthiest people are usually buried in stone graves carved out of cliffs, while others are buried in caves. Their coffin contains possessions that the deceased will need in the afterlife. Coffins of babies or children are often hung from ropes on a cliff face or from a tree. These hanging graves last for years until the ropes rot and the coffin falls to the ground. Ma'nene takes place over a three-day period, usually in August. The coffins are lifted from their tombs and stored in a grave house at the heart of the ceremony.

▲ Family members parade their relative around the village.

YOSEMITE FIREFALL

▸ At 9 p.m. almost every summer night for 96 years, burning hot embers from wood fires were dropped 3,000 ft (900 m) from the top of Glacier Point in California's Yosemite National Park to the valley below in what looked from a distance like a glowing waterfall. The Yosemite Firefall, as it was known, was performed as a tourist attraction by several generations of the owners of the Glacier Point Hotel who would use long-handled metal implements to push the fire embers off the cliff evenly so as to simulate a steady flow. The spectacle was finally banned in 1968 and ironically the hotel burned down the following year.

CARRIAGE HOME ▸ A bungalow in Cornwall, England, is built around a 130-year-old railway carriage. The bedrooms in Jim Higgins's home are located in the restored carriage dating from 1882.

FISH RICH ▸ Lake Malawi, Africa's third largest lake, has an estimated 1,000 species of fish—more than every lake in North America combined.

STORMY DAY ▸ In a single day—June 28, 2012—the U.K. was hit by a record 110,000 lightning bolts, with more than 200 strikes recorded every minute at the height of the storms. This was 40 times higher than an average lightning storm and represented the equivalent of four months' worth of strikes in one day.

ICE SHOCK ▸ A huge block of ice fell from the sky and crashed through the roof of Brentwood Cathedral in Essex, England, during Sunday service, leaving members of the congregation trembling with shock. The ice is believed to have fallen from an airplane.

WOMEN DIVERS ▸ The fishing divers of Jeju Island, South Korea, are all women, a tradition that dates back hundreds of years. The average age of the 5,000 or so divers is 50, but some are over 80 years old. The practice began when a loophole in the law allowed women to sell their catch tax-free, while men were heavily penalized.

HOT RAIN ▸ The hottest rain ever recorded—115°F (46°C)—fell during a desert thunderstorm at Needles, California, on August 13, 2012. Owing to the low humidity, most of the rain evaporated before it hit the ground.

RED CITY ▸ Streets, sidewalks and open spaces in the Chinese city of Foshan were covered in red clay in July 2012 after a typhoon washed the clay down from nearby mountains. Even when the floodwaters subsided, a red clay residue coated the ground and lower levels of buildings.

NEAR MISS ▸ On February 29, 2012, a tornado came within 40 ft (12 m) of the Ripley's Believe It or Not! Odditorium in Branson, Missouri—a building deliberately designed to look like it has been hit by an earthquake! The 1,200-ft-wide (366-m) tornado tore the roof from the motel next door but, believe it or not, spared the Odditorium, whose distinctive crumbling façade has made it one of the most photographed buildings in the world. It was erected in 1999 to commemorate the massive 1812 Missouri earthquake that made the Mississippi River run backward for three days and made church bells ring in Philadelphia, nearly 1,000 mi (1,600 km) away.

STONE FOREST

TOP TANKS▸ Water tanks on the roofs of residential buildings in Guiyang, China, are decorated as giant soccer balls. Local authorities thought that regular tanks would look too ugly, so they made them into a quirky feature of the neighborhood.

UNDERSEA ERUPTION▸ An underwater volcano erupted off the coast of New Zealand to create a mass of white, floating pumice that covered 10,000 sq mi (26,000 sq km) of the ocean—equivalent to the size of Belgium. The small, buoyant volcanic rocks were the size of golf balls and were formed when lava from the volcano came into contact with seawater.

▸ A stone forest consisting of hundreds of razor-sharp vertical rocks—many up to 330 ft (100 m) high—covers a remote 230-sq-mi (595-sq-km) area of Madagascar. Known as the Tsingy, which translates as "where one cannot walk barefoot," the spectacular structure was formed by tropical rainfall eroding the limestone rock into spiked towers. Although it looks inhospitable, the landscape is home to a wide variety of animals, including 11 species of lemur.

FIREBALL FIGHT▸ To commemorate the mighty volcanic eruption of 1658 that forced the entire town to be evacuated, residents of Nejapa, El Salvador, have gathered every August 31 since 1922 to hurl fiery, gasoline-soaked rags at each other. Although there are no rules for the fireball fight, amazingly there have been few serious injuries.

EXTRA TIME▸ An extra second—known as a leap second—was added to time at midnight on June 30, 2012, because the Earth's rotation is slowing down.

UGLY CONTEST

▶ *Contestants in the Concurso de Feos in Bilbao, Spain, twist and distort their eyes and mouths into hideous poses in a bid to scare—and impress—the judges as to who can make the ugliest face. The ugly competition is part of the nine-day Aste Nagusia festivity, which also includes music, circuses, bullfights and fireworks.*

FLOUR BOMBS▶ At the Els Enfarinats festival in Ibi, Spain, an event that dates back more than 200 years, revelers dressed in mock military uniforms pelt each other with flour and eggs.

FALLING FRUIT▶ An avalanche of more than 100 apples rained down like giant hailstones on a busy road in Coventry, England, on December 12, 2011, forcing stunned drivers to swerve and brake sharply. The fall of fruit is thought to have been caused by a freak mini tornado that lifted the green apples from a garden or orchard before dropping them in the city.

MINE HOST▶ Sweden's Sala silver mine has a hotel room located 508 ft (155 m) below ground. Access is by a mine lift shaft, and it took nearly ten years to carve out the room, which, because it is set in a warm air pocket, has a pleasant temperature of 64°F (18°C), compared to the chilly 36°F (2°C) elsewhere at the bottom of the mine.

ELECTION DAY▶ National elections in the U.S.A. always take place on a Tuesday owing to a law dating back to 1845 that gave people time to reach a voting station when traveling by horse. Tuesday was chosen because it did not clash with Sunday worship or market day, which was Wednesday in many towns.

DULL AND BORING▶ In 2012, the town of Boring, Oregon, voted in favor of becoming a "sister community" to the Scottish village of Dull. Boring was named after William Boring, an early resident of the area, and Dull is thought to have taken its name from the Pictish word for field.

INVISIBLE BRIDGE▶ Visitors can reach the historic Fort de Roovere in the Netherlands via a sunken bridge, which runs beneath the water level of the surrounding moat. As the water on either side comes right up to the edges of the bridge, the walkway is virtually invisible to the naked eye when viewed from a distance.

STRANDED GOATS

▶ Two young goats spent two days stuck on the narrow, 6-in-wide (15-cm) ledge of a railway bridge 60 ft (18 m) above a highway near Roundup, Montana, before being rescued with a crane.

GLACIER THEFT▶ In January 2012, police in Chile arrested a man on suspicion of stealing five tons of ice from the Jorge Montt glacier near the Patagonian border to sell as designer ice cubes in bars and restaurants. Officers intercepted a refrigerated truck containing more than $5,000 worth of illicit ice.

SAFE HOUSE▶ In 2011, a home created from a nuclear missile silo in Saranac, New York State, went on sale for $1.76 million. It came complete with its own private airstrip and 15,000 sq ft (1,400 sq m) of underground space that was built to withstand tornadoes, hurricanes and nuclear attacks.

CRASH LANDINGS▶ Thousands of migrating birds were killed or injured in Utah in December 2011 when stormy weather conditions caused them to mistake wet parking lots for ponds.

PIED PIPER▶ The German town of Hamelin was in need of a new Pied Piper in 2012 following a fresh invasion of rats. The rodents, attracted by people feeding birds, chewed through electrical cables, putting a local fountain out of order.

MEN AT RISK▶ More than 80 percent of lightning strike victims are male. This is not because men are usually taller than women (lightning often strikes the tallest object), but because they tend to spend a greater amount of time outdoors.

DRIVE-IN CHURCH▶ Reverend David Ray, a Presbyterian Church pastor in Texas, holds some of his church services in the style of drive-in movie theaters, with parishioners seated in their cars in a parking lot.

PRESS GANG▶ Under the "Barney Fife" ordinance, police officers in Johnson City, Tennessee, can draft citizens into law enforcement duties during illegal assemblies or riots—with refusal to serve being a crime.

DO NOT DISTURB▶ The Mashco-Piro tribe, an isolated Amazon tribe in southeastern Peru, seeks to avoid contact with the outside world by firing tipless arrows as warning shots for tourists and park rangers to keep away.

INLAND BEACH

▶ Although it is 330 ft (100 m) from the sea in the middle of a green meadow, Playa de Gulpiyuri, near Llanes, Spain, is a flooded sinkhole that has its own beach and even its own waves. About 130 ft (40 m) long, it is affected by tides because the salt water of the Cantabrian Sea has carved a network of underground tunnels that constantly feed water to the beach from the Bay of Biscay. The gentle waves and crystal-clear water make the inland beach a popular tourist spot, but the water is colder than normal, having traveled underground.

WITCH WORSHIP▶ The U.S. military has built an $80,000 Stonehenge-like stone circle at its Air Force Academy in Colorado so that cadets, including druids, pagans, Wiccans and witches, who practice "Earth-based" religions have somewhere to worship.

MIDDLE AMERICA▶ The town of Kinsley, Kansas, has a road sign pointing to San Francisco, California, on the west coast and New York City on the east, with a distance of 1,561 mi (2,512 km) to each one.

DEADLY SEA▶ Although the Dead Sea's high salt content allows a person to float effortlessly on the surface, drownings there are common. It is Israel's second most dangerous swimming area.

FAMILY HOME▶ Berkeley Castle in Gloucestershire, England, has been home to the Berkeley family for 900 continuous years. The current heir, Charles Berkeley, will be the 27th generation of the family to live there.

▶ *KETTLE DRUMS WERE ONCE USED AS CURRENCY ON ALOR ISLAND, INDONESIA.* ◀

TIME FLIES!▶ At the end of 2011, Samoa changed its time zone to the west side of the International Date Line, making it possible to celebrate a single holiday two days in a row by flying 30 minutes east to American Samoa, which opted to stay east of the Date Line.

DRIFTING DOCK▶ A 66-ft-long (20-m) concrete and metal dock that was carried away from Japan by the 2011 tsunami washed ashore on a beach near Newport, Oregon, in June 2012. It was identified via a commemorative plaque and by the discovery of a starfish native to Japan that was still clinging to the structure 15 months after it went adrift. In total, more than 1.5 million tons of tsunami debris drifted across the Pacific toward the west coast of North America.

STREET EELS▶ Dozens of slimy eels were found in puddles and gutters in the flooded streets of Masterton, New Zealand, in March 2012 following heavy rain and storms. The eels came from nearby sewerage ponds that had overflowed with the torrential rain.

WOMAN'S WORLD▶ In the Indian state of Meghalaya, people live in a matrilineal culture—where property and wealth pass to daughters rather than to sons, and children take the mother's surname.

CLIFF CORRIDOR

▶ Until 40 years ago, the only way to reach Guoliang village in Henan Province, China, was via 720 steep steps—but then 14 villagers joined forces to build a precarious 4,100-ft-long (1,250-m) road tunnel perched 360 ft (110 m) up on a cliff face. With no electricity or heavy machinery, they used their hands to chisel and hammer the 16-ft-high (5-m), 13-ft-wide (4-m) cliff corridor out of the mountainside over a five-year period, during which they went through 10 tons of drill rods and 4,000 hammers.

CHURCH PERCH▶ The 130-ft-tall (40-m) Katskhi Pillar near Chiatura, Georgia, has an orthodox monastery perched on top that dates back more than 1,200 years. Its inaccessibility meant that the monastery stood deserted for 700 years, but visitors can now reach it by climbing an iron ladder that extends all the way from the ground to the summit.

HIGH SCHOOL▶ To reach their school in Pili in China's mountainous Xinjiang Uygur region, some 40 pupils, guided by parents and teachers, must carefully pick their way along a narrow rocky pass located 1,500 ft (457 m) above a sheer drop.

SINKING CITY▶ The Italian city of Venice has been sinking into the water and tilting east into the Adriatic Sea by 0.08 in (2 mm) per year over the last decade—five times quicker than previously thought.

SHOW AND SMELL▶ Sweden's Lund University displays a collection of more than 100 plaster casts of noses belonging to notable Scandinavians, including a cast of the false silver-and-gold nose of Danish astronomer Tycho Brahe (1546–1601), who lost his original nose in a sword duel.

NOSE PLUGS

▶ *Tailyang Yaming, a member of the Apatani tribe from the Ziro valley in India's Arunachal Pradesh state, shows off her facial tattoos and bamboo nose plugs, the result of a painful and bloody teenage tradition. Coveted for their beauty, young Apatani women were often kidnapped by neighboring tribes, so to combat this they were deliberately defaced. Soot-covered thorns were jabbed under their skin to create tattoos and nose plugs were inserted into holes cut in their upper nostrils. Although the gruesome ritual has largely died out, a few women still practice it today.*

TSUNAMI BIKE ▶ A Harley-Davidson motorbike was washed up on the coast of British Columbia, Canada, in April 2012, having been swept into the sea by the Japanese tsunami 13 months earlier. The rusty bike with a Japanese license plate was found on Graham Island and was traced to an owner in Miyagi Prefecture, a region of Japan badly damaged by the tsunami.

NO-FLY ZONE ▶ In 2012, environmental authorities in Beijing, China, introduced new regulations stipulating that none of the city's public lavatories should contain more than two flies.

WORM-EATING PLANT ▶ Brazil's *Philcoxia minensis* plant grows leaves underground that are used to trap and eat tiny worms. The carnivorous plant's subterranean leaves, each about the size of a pinhead, secrete a sticky gum that traps roundworms and slowly digests them.

TOM'S DAY ▶ Thomas C. Eakin, a humanitarian from Aurora, Ohio, has had over 300 counties and cities proclaim a Thomas C. Eakin Day in his honor.

SHINING LIGHT ▶ A 55-watt lightbulb hanging in the porch of Roger Dyball's home in Lowestoft, Suffolk, England, has been burning brightly for more than a century. The bulb was manufactured in July 1912, three months after the *Titanic* sank.

GREEDY TREE

▶ This tree on Vashon Island, Washington, has eaten a bicycle! The story behind the bizarre phenomenon has been the stuff of legend for years—even spawning a children's book—but recent new evidence suggests that the red bicycle was abandoned next to the tree by local boy Don Puz in 1954 and that the trunk subsequently grew around it. Even so that does not explain why the bicycle is more than 6 ft (1.8 m) above the ground. Maybe there is still a final part of the mystery waiting to be solved.

HYPNOTIC ROBBER ▶ A woman was arrested in Volgograd, Russia, in 2009, on suspicion of hypnotizing bank tellers into handing over tens of thousands of dollars in more than 30 separate robberies. The tellers often did not realize they had been robbed until a couple of hours later.

UNKNOWN LANGUAGE ▶ A British archeologist excavating a 2,700-year-old palace in Tushan, Turkey, has discovered evidence of a previously undocumented language. The mystery language—which was probably spoken by a formerly unknown people from Iran's remote Zagros Mountains—was found by Cambridge University's Dr. John MacGinnis as he deciphered an ancient clay writing tablet.

HUMAN HAMSTERS ▶ A Ferris wheel in New Delhi, India, has no motors and is powered instead entirely by human muscle. The men hang from the inner bars of the wheel and use their weight to propel it around like human hamsters.

AEROBIC TREMOR ▶ A 10-minute tremor that caused hundreds of people to flee screaming from a high-rise building in Seoul, South Korea, on July 5, 2011, was caused by 17 middle-aged fitness fanatics enjoying a vigorous gym exercise workout on the 12th floor.

HARMS' WAY ▶ Virgil Harms has served as mayor of Paoli, Colorado, for more than 50 years, having never faced an opponent during an election.

DEATH RITUAL ▶ When a person dies among the Jarawa people of the Andaman Islands, relatives place the body beneath a tree where it sits until it is reduced to a skeleton. Then the members of the tribe tie the bones to their own bodies to bring luck while hunting pigs and fishing for turtles.

LUCKY VILLAGE ▶ Every French soldier to serve from the small village of Thierville in Normandy has come back alive in the country's last five wars—including World War I and World War II.

METEORITE TOWN ▶ The town of Manson, Iowa, sits on top of a 74-million-year-old meteorite crash site that disrupted the underlying rock so badly that it is nearly impossible to drill water wells in the area.

STATE LINE

▶ Ripley's were sent this picture by Dick Larson of West Palm Beach, Florida, showing that the Virginia–North Carolina state line on the Blue Ridge Parkway is an actual line painted on the road!

YOUR UPLOADS

GHOST SKULLS

Thirteen golden human skulls form a macabre religious shrine in Bangkok, Thailand, guarding the newly dead and preventing their souls from turning into malevolent ghosts.

The shrine was built more than 60 years ago by a volunteer ambulance company—and the skulls belonged to nameless ambulance patients who died while being transported to the hospital and whose bodies were never claimed. After having the corpses cremated, the company kept the skulls, cleaned them, covered them in gold paint and gold leaf and later inserted small gold lamé cushions into the eye sockets. When the ambulance company eventually moved from its warehouse headquarters, it left the shrine behind, the skulls' spirits acting to safeguard the building.

▶ *As they originally belonged to dead paupers or unidentified "John Does," the skulls are seen as kindly benefactors, protecting the bodies of the deceased and comforting their spirits during the period between death and disposal of the body.*

◀ *Local superstition states that the souls of the poor and the anonymous are particularly susceptible to ghostly interference and that unless a fresh corpse is cared for, the spirits of these downtrodden folk will linger and become infested with evil.*

NOCTURNAL ORCHID ▶ On New Britain Island, near Papua New Guinea, botanists have discovered the world's first night-flowering orchid. Of the 25,000 species of orchid, *Bulbophyllum nocturnum* is the only one with flowers that consistently open after dark and then close up in the morning.

LOST BALL ▶ A soccer ball that was swept out to sea by the Japanese tsunami in March 2011 was found more than a year later on a beach on Alaska's Middleton Island over 3,000 mi (4,800 km) away and returned to its owner, 16-year-old Misaki Murakami.

CLAN CAMPBELL ▶ When the town of Phil Campbell, Alabama, was hit by a tornado on April 27, 2011, men and women named Phil and Phyllis Campbell from all over the world raised nearly $35,000 for relief efforts.

SKY-HIGH ▶ Opened on May 22, 2012, the Tokyo Sky Tree is the world's tallest free-standing tower. The steel structure weighs over 45,000 tons and houses a staircase of 2,523 steps. At 2,080 ft (634 m) tall, the Japanese landmark is nearly twice the height of the Eiffel Tower.

UNIQUE LAVA ▶ Carbonatite lava, which is only about half the temperature of typical lava, flows freely with a viscosity similar to motor oil and can be found in only one place on Earth— Ol Doinyo Lengai, a volcano in Tanzania.

SIX STRIKES ▶ Carl Mize, a University of Oklahoma utility employee, has miraculously survived six different lightning strikes. The odds of being struck by lightning just once in a lifetime are 5,000 to 1, which makes Mize a guy in several million.

MANHATTAN SOLSTICE ▶ On two days of the year—the first occurring around the end of May and the second in the middle of July—the sun sets precisely in line with the street grid of Manhattan, New York City. The extraordinary phenomenon is known as "Manhattanhenge" (named after the solstice site of Stonehenge in the U.K.) or "the Manhattan Solstice."

DRY SNOW ▶ A snowball cannot be made at the snow-covered South Pole. The snow there is too dry and powdery to clump together.

LAVA LAKE ▶ The Democratic Republic of Congo's Mount Nyiragongo has one of the world's largest permanent lava lakes, with a huge 1,800°F (982°C) pool of molten rock often measuring 1,300 ft (396 m) deep and holding an estimated 282 million cubic ft (8 million cubic m) of lava.

WEIRD LAKE ▶ Lake Untersee, which lies under a thick layer of ice in Antarctica, has water as alkaline as bleach and sediments that produce more methane than any other lake on Earth.

RED RIVER ▶ On December 12, 2011, an industrial accident involving chemical dye caused the Jian River in Henan, China, to turn blood red.

ALGAE BLOOM ▶ In July 2010, the Baltic Sea experienced a blue-green algae bloom covering an area of 145,500 sq mi (377,000 sq km)— larger than the size of Germany. It was triggered by a lack of wind, prolonged high temperatures and fertilizers being washed into the sea from surrounding farmland.

LIVING DEAD ▶ The seedpod of the ice plant, *Delosperma nakurense*, can open and close itself even after it has fallen from the plant and died.

TOXIC DUMP ▶ The city of Orlando, Florida, pumped tens of thousands of gallons of molasses into the ground to clean up a toxic dump. The molasses was injected into the ground to break up the chemical that had contaminated the land.

MOSSY ISLAND ▶ Buckeye Lake, Ohio, is home to an 11-acre (4.5-ha) floating island made of sphagnum moss covered in countless rare species, cranberry plants and trees. The bog is a relic of the Ice Age.

LIPSTICK DAMAGE ▶ The tomb of Irish writer Oscar Wilde in Paris, France, needed restoration in 2011 due to it being eaten away by lipstick from tourists kissing the monument.

PRESERVED FOREST ▶ Scientists have discovered a huge 298-million-year-old forest buried intact beneath a coal mine near Wuda, Inner Mongolia, China. As the forest had been covered and preserved for all those centuries by volcanic ash, entire trees and plants were found exactly as they were at the time of the eruption.

GEL STORM ▶ During a freak 20-second hail storm over Bournemouth, England, on January 26, 2012, when the sky turned a peculiar dark yellow, about 20 blue jellylike spheres, each the size of a marble, fell to the ground. Tests later showed them to be floristry hydrating gels, but nobody knows how they came to fall from the sky.

QUAKE SCALE ▶ An 8.7 earthquake is about 23,000 times more powerful than a 5.8 earthquake. The release of energy in an earthquake multiplies by nearly 32 times with every whole number increase on the Richter scale.

VOLCANIC ERUPTIONS ▶ At any one moment there are about 20 volcanoes actively erupting around the world. Of the 600 or so volcanoes that have erupted in history, about 10 percent erupt each year.

MANY TONGUES ▶ There are more than 800 languages spoken on the island of New Guinea—about a third of the world's indigenous tongues—making it the most linguistically diverse place on Earth.

EXPLOSIVE HEAT ▶ Scientists have created the hottest temperature ever seen on Earth— an incredible 10 trillion degrees Fahrenheit (5.5 trillion degrees Celcius), 250,000 times hotter than the Sun. The ultra-hot explosions, each of which lasted for less than one-billionth of a second, were created on a giant atom smasher at the Large Hadron Collider outside Geneva, Switzerland.

BACK TO LIFE ▶ Russian scientists have successfully grown plants of *Silene stenophylla* from tissue material that had remained intact, frozen in the ground in Siberia for 30,000 years.

TOWERING INFERNO

▶ In September 2012, filmmaker Chris Tangey was scouting movie locations in Alice Springs, Australia, when he captured a fire tornado on camera. This rarely witnessed natural phenomenon occurs when flames on the ground are whipped into a whirlwind that can spiral as high as 1,000 ft (300 m) and last for more than an hour. Chris described the fire as sounding like a "fighter jet."

CORPSE BRIDE

For more than 80 years, visitors from all over the world have been lured to a wedding gown shop in Chihuahua, Mexico, to study the spookily lifelike bridal mannequin in the window. According to legend, the mannequin is not really a model at all, but the perfectly preserved corpse of the previous owner's daughter.

Most are so captivated by the mesmerizing gaze of La Pascualita, as she is known, that they leave convinced that she is a mummy rather than a dummy. She was first installed in the window in 1930, but people soon realized that she bore an uncanny likeness to the store's owner at the time, Pascuala Esparza. They concluded that the apparent mannequin was really the embalmed body of Esparza's daughter who had died recently on her wedding day after being bitten by a black widow spider. Esparza denied the story, but the rumors persisted, and La Pascualita began to take on a life of her own. It is said that a love-struck French magician would arrive at night and bring her to life, taking her out on the town. Others say her eyes follow them around the store and that she changes positions during the night. One shop worker, Sonia Burciaga, who has to change the dummy's outfits twice a week, says: "Every time I go near Pascualita my hands break out in a sweat. Her hands are very realistic and she even has varicose veins on her legs. I believe she's a real person."

CHILLY CHURCH ▶ Residents of the German village of Mitterfirmiansreut built a church from snow and ice in December 2011, complete with a 62-ft-tall (19-m) tower. It held 200 people and was built to commemorate a similar snow church constructed there exactly 100 years earlier.

EGG ROULETTE ▶ At the Russian Egg Roulette World Championships, held in Lincolnshire, England, each competitor picks an egg from a box of six, five of which have been hard-boiled and one left raw. The eggs are then smashed against the competitors' heads, the losers being the ones left —literally—with egg on their face.

MR. CLEAN ▶ Don Aslett of Pocatello, Idaho, has opened the Museum of Clean, which features 6,000 vacuums, dust busters, rug beaters and other items relating to the history of cleanliness. Among the artifacts are a horse-drawn vacuum dating back to 1902, an antique Amish footbath and a 1,600-year-old bronze toothpick. The seats in the museum continue the theme, being fashioned out of garbage bins, a claw-foot bathtub and a 1945 washing machine.

FLOUR BOMBS ▶ Every February in Galaxidi, Greece, dozens of people put on goggles, face masks, plastic suits and cow bells to fight each other by hurling hundreds of small bags filled with a combined total of more than two tons of colored sticky baking flour. Lasting for several hours, the Flour War creates such a mess that houses and boats in the coastal town have to be covered in plastic.

RED LAKE

▶ A lake in the Camargue area of southern France turned blood red in August 2012 as a result of its high salt concentration linked to the tiny brine shrimp that live in the lake. When the salt concentration in the lake is very high, the shrimp die and saline algae spreads rapidly to give the water its unusual color.

LARGE PRINT

▶ The parking garage at Kansas City Public Library, Missouri, is covered by a "shelf" of huge wooden book spines, each measuring 25 x 9 ft (7.6 x 2.7 m). Known as the "Community Bookshelf," the 22 titles, which include *The Lord of the Rings*, *Romeo and Juliet* and *To Kill a Mockingbird*, were suggested by library users.

BOTTLE HOMES ▶ Twenty-five homes in Yelwa, Nigeria, are being built entirely from sand-filled, discarded plastic water bottles, placed on their side, one on top of the other, and bound together with mud. The recycled bottles serve as good insulation, and are both inexpensive and bullet-resistant. Each house uses around 7,800 bottles.

POWER OUTAGE ▶ Following the collapse of three electrical grids, a massive two-day power outage in India on July 30–31, 2012, affected more than 600 million people—about half the country's population.

KNIT WIT ▶ The Hotel Pelirocco in Brighton, England, has a room where everything is made from wool—including a vase of flowers, curtains, a toothbrush, a tube of toothpaste and even the breakfast. Using 11 lb (5 kg) of wool, designer Kate Jenkins also knitted a bedspread from 100 different colors and crocheted covers for the phone, lampshade, teapot and cup.

HIVE OF ACTIVITY

▶ Collecting the precious honeycomb can take several hours. The harvesters use simple bamboo sticks.

▶ The honeycomb is lowered to the ground in a handmade basket.

Continuing a tradition that dates back hundreds of years and has claimed many lives, the Rai people of Nepal make ladders out of braided bamboo to climb 250 ft (76 m) up a steep mountain cliff and harvest the prized honey of the world's largest bee, the Himalayan honey bee.

The harvesters light a fire at the base of the cliff to smoke the bees from their honeycombs and then, often under attack from up to 100,000 swarming bees, they retrieve the 5-ft-wide (1.5-m) honeycombs with long sticks in a delicate four-hour mission before lowering the booty to the ground.

The climbers wear no facial protection to guard against stings—their only safety precaution is to tie their feet to the homemade ladders to reduce the risk of a fall. Ironically, the red honey, which sells for five times the price of regular honey, is poisonous owing to a toxin in the pollen and nectar of the rhododendron plants used to make it. When consumed straight out of the honeycomb, it can result in stomach cramps and vomiting, so it is often used as a substitute for sugar and as an ingredient in pancakes. Despite its toxic properties, the honey remains sought-after, as it is believed to possess healing and relaxing powers.

◀ A Rai honey harvester carrying a huge honeycomb.

RING ROAD

▶ When an elderly couple in Wenling, China, refused to let their five-story house be demolished to make way for a new road, planners simply built the road around it. Luo Baogen and his wife lived in the last house standing, being circled by cars and trucks.

SILVER BULLION▶ In 2012, a record haul of around 48 tons of silver bullion, worth around $44 million, was recovered from a World-War-II wreck 15,000 ft (4,570 m) deep in the Atlantic off the coast of Ireland. The 1,203 bars of silver were retrieved from the S.S. *Gairsoppa*, a British cargo ship that was sunk by a German torpedo in 1941.

FLYING ANGEL▶ Italy's annual 12-day Venice Carnival begins with the "Flight of the Angel," where a young woman is suspended on a wire from a bell tower 330 ft (100 m) above St. Mark's Square and is gradually lowered to the ground.

ABOVE GROUND▶ More than half of the London Underground's 250-mile (400-km) subway network is actually overground.

SCARY POOL▶ The glass-bottomed swimming pool at the Holiday Inn hotel in Shanghai, China, partly hangs over a 24-story drop, giving swimmers a scary bird's-eye view of the street below. The 100 x 20 ft (30 x 6 m) cantilever pool is designed to make guests feel as if they are swimming in the sky.

IDENTICAL SHRUBS▶ Every King's Lomatia, a shrub from Tasmania, is genetically identical. The plants never produce fruit or seeds and can only reproduce when a branch falls off and grows a root of its own.

DISAPPEARING SEA▶ The Aral Sea—on the border of Kazakhstan and Uzbekistan—was once the fourth-largest inland lake in the world, covering 26,300 sq mi (68,000 sq km) with more than 1,500 islands dotted in its waters. However, after 50 years of water diversion, it is now mostly desert split into four lakes and has shrunk to one-tenth of its original size. In the 1950s, Muynak was located on the edge of the water; today it is a desert town more than 62 mi (100 km) from the sea. The disappearance of the Aral Sea has been blamed for local climate change, with summers becoming hotter and drier, and winters colder and longer.

HEAVY CLOUDS▶ The water droplets in a medium-sized cumulus cloud weigh as much as 80 elephants. Large cumulonimbus clouds can be twice the height of Mount Everest.

BALL STORM▶ Hundreds of tiny, yellow plastic balls fell from the sky over Dylis and Tony Scott's garden in Leicester, England, during a thunderstorm on August 19, 2012. Mysteriously, the lightweight balls, which may have been picked up many miles away by the wind and transported in the storm, were soon washed away by the rain.

CLOUD RIDERS▶ A mysterious and rare meteorological phenomenon known as the morning glory cloud appears every fall above the small town of Burketown, Queensland, Australia. Each year, glider pilots convene to ride the tubular clouds, which can stretch for 620 mi (1,000 km), be as low as 330 ft (100 m) above ground and move at speeds of 37 mph (60 km/h).

ECCENTRIC OLYMPICS▶ As an alternative to the 2012 Olympics, London also staged the Chap Olympiad, a celebration of English eccentricity featuring events such as bicycle jousting, butler baiting, throwing a bowler hat into a fishing net, and ironing board surfing, where competitors are carried atop an ironing board while holding a cocktail that they must not spill.

SNAIL HOUSE▶ A five-story family house in Sofia, Bulgaria, has been designed in the shape of a giant snail. The brightly colored snail house has horns on its head and butterflies on its back and took nearly ten years to build without a single straight wall or corner. The interior is equally quirky, with heating radiators in the form of a frog, a ladybug and a pumpkin.

▶ THERE ARE OVER 10 MILLION BRICKS IN THE EMPIRE STATE BUILDING. ◀

DRIP... DRIP▶ Ohio State University in Columbus, Ohio, has an international hall of fame dedicated to water drainage.

RECKLESS DRIVER▶ A driver from Zurich, Switzerland, committed 15 traffic violations in just over ten minutes—including speeding, driving on the hard shoulder, running a set of red lights and failing to stop for police.

BUBBLE HOTEL▶ At the Bubble Hotel, set in the countryside outside Paris, France, guests sleep in inflatable rooms that have a transparent dome so that they can admire the wonders of nature.

ANCIENT LOVE▶ Archeologists in Modena, Italy, have unearthed the skeletal remains of a Roman-era couple who have been holding hands for the past 1,500 years. The man and woman died around the late 5th century and were buried apparently looking longingly into each other's eyes.

FOAM VILLAGE ▶ Houses and vehicles in the fishing village of Footdee, near Aberdeen, Scotland, were covered in a blanket of white foam in September 2012. The freak foam—a mix of water and sand—was whipped up by heavy rain and strong winds battering the coast.

REMOTE ACCESS

▶ The 200 villagers of Yushan in Hubei Province, China, are completely cut off from the outside world except for a 3,300-ft-long (1,000-m) aerial ropeway stretched between two sheer cliffs. To go shopping, they must ride in a diesel-powered steel cage suspended precariously from cables 1,300 ft (400 m) above the valley floor. Before the cable link was built, the villagers had to walk for several days to reach the nearest village.

JELLYFISH LAKE

Jellyfish Lake on Eil Malk, an island in Palau, is home to over 20 million jellyfish—yet people can swim safely among them because, over time, the strength of their sting has been greatly reduced. Isolated for thousands of years from the Pacific Ocean that surrounds the island, the jellyfish thrive in the landlocked, algae-rich lake with no predators. As a result, they don't need a powerful sting, and their lake has become a huge hit with divers.

DON'T LOOK DOWN

▶ A house appears to have dropped onto the top of the University of California, San Diego, and stuck seven stories up, but it's actually a project by artist Do Ho Suh from South Korea. The project was seven years in the making and cost more than $1 million. The house is fully furnished and there is even a small garden, and visitors can go inside. However, the view from the windows is not for the faint of heart.

PEDAL POWER ▶ Guests at the Cottage Lodge bed-and-breakfast hotel in Brockenhurst, England, can keep fit and help the environment by watching a bicycle-powered LCD TV in their room. To generate electricity for the set to operate, guests hop on the bike and pedal the power into the TV's battery pack.

POLAR RUN ▶ Amundsen-Scott South Pole Station is home to the "300 Club," where participants warm up in a 200°F (93°C) sauna, then go out into –100°F (–73°C) or colder weather and run around the ceremonial South Pole—naked except for a pair of boots!

10,000-YEAR CLOCK ▶ Amazon.com founder Jeff Bezos is funding the $42-million construction of "The Clock of the Long Now," which is being built 500 ft (152 m) deep inside a Texas mountain, and is designed to keep time for 10,000 years. The clock will be 200 ft (60 m) tall, have a 5-ton pendulum and will chime a different melody every day.

TOWERING CITY ▶ Hong Kong is the skyscraper capital of the world. Its soaring skyline boasts more than 2,300 buildings at least 330 ft (100 m) tall—three times more than New York City.

RUSSIAN PRESENCE ▶ The Norwegian island of Svalbard, which lies halfway between Norway and the North Pole, is home to only 2,000 people—yet it has its own Russian consulate.

WRONG PLACE ▶ Chris and Frances Huntingford have been ordered to demolish their $375,000 four-bedroom dream home in Suffolk, England, because they built it 15 ft (4.5 m) to the right of where it should be.

WALL COLLAPSE ▶ A 100-ft-long (30-m) section of the Great Wall of China in Zhangjiakou collapsed in 2012 after weeks of torrential rain—coupled with building work directly in front of the wall's foundations—that caused tons of bricks and rubble to crumble.

HIDDEN VOLCANOES ▶ British surveyors have discovered a chain of 12 previously unknown undersea volcanoes off the coast of Antarctica, with a few coming within just 225 ft (70 m) of the surface.

TIMBERRR!

▶ This incredible photograph shows lumberjacks working in the redwood forests of Humboldt, California, in the early 19th-century. Before the days of chainsaws and heavy machinery, giant trees were felled with axes and handsaws, and it could take a team of men a whole week to bring down one redwood, the largest trees in the world. The work was as risky as it looks, and even today, logging is one of the most dangerous occupations in the world.

▶ Skarphedinn Thrainsson and Örvar Atli Porgeirsson explored the strange blue world under Europe's largest glacier, Vatnajökull, in Iceland, to capture on film the bizarre yet beautiful ice caves that lie hidden beneath. Air is squeezed out of the ancient ice in the glacier as it travels, making it a bright, clear, blue color. Venturing into these caves is a risky business, not just because of temperatures dropping to 10°F (−12°C) but because of the shifting ice, which has previously claimed the life of a photographer.

UNDERWORLD

ANIMALS ▶

CATCOPTER

▶ After his pet tabby cat was killed by a car, Dutch artist Bart Jansen turned the animal's body into a radio-controlled flying model helicopter. Bart kept Orville (named after aviation pioneer Orville Wright) in a freezer for six months before having him stuffed. He then attached propellers to each of the cat's paws and an engine inside his stomach to create the "Orvillecopter," a "half cat, half machine" that can fly at a considerable speed. A fin attached to Orville's tail aids steering. He has also been fitted with a plastic undercarriage to allow dignified landings.

CAT FLAP

▶ Having driven around for hours mystified as to why his car was struggling for power, a motorist in Rio Verde, Brazil, checked under the hood—and found a kitten stuck inside the engine. It was trapped inside the metal air intake pipe, with just its head and a paw sticking out. Firefighters used a hacksaw to cut the kitten free and, incredibly, it survived. It had climbed into the engine to keep warm but had then been suddenly sucked in when the driver started up the car.

MISSING PET ▶ Monika Moser of Munich, Germany, was reunited with her pet cat Poldi more than 16 years after he went missing. He walked out of the family home in 1996 and was not seen again until he was found 20 mi (32 km) away living in a forest and was identified by a mark on his ear.

MASTER MIMIC ▶ Chook, a superb lyrebird at Australia's Adelaide Zoo, learned to mimic perfectly the sounds of construction, including drills, handsaws, trucks and radio conversations, while workers were near his enclosure.

TV STAR ▶ Seeking a warm refuge from an unseasonal blizzard, Laura the cow escaped from her field in Serfaus, Austria, and walked into a sportswear store at a nearby shopping mall, chewing her way through two bras and a T-shirt. The sports company, Intersport, was so impressed by Laura's taste that it signed her up as the star of its new TV advertising campaign.

HAMSTER RAMPAGE ▶ Houdini the hamster left his owners with a £1,000 ($1,500) repair bill after escaping from his cardboard box, climbing into the car engine and chewing through the electrics while being driven to his new home in Derbyshire, England. He was rescued from the engine after a two-hour search.

LOYAL FRIEND ▶ After 68-year-old Lao Pan, a resident of Panjiatun, China, died in November 2011, his dog took up residence by his grave site, refusing to leave even to look for food. Villagers were so touched by the dog's devotion that they brought him food and built him a graveside kennel.

BEAR BASH ▶ When a black bear tried to snatch her pet dachshund Fudge, Brooke Collins, a hairdresser from Juneau, Alaska, scared the predator off by punching it on the nose. The bear immediately let go of the dog, who escaped with minor claw and bite marks.

HUNTING LESSONS ▶ Fishermen in Honduras have been training sharks to hunt poisonous lionfish, which have invaded a reef near the island of Roatan and whose voracious appetite is reducing local fish stocks and threatening the fishermen's livelihood. Sharks had always avoided lionfish because of their spikes, but when fishermen started spearing the lionfish and leaving them alive and struggling in the sea, they found that the sharks soon became attracted to them and learned to recognize them as natural prey.

TRAIN JOURNEY ▶ A lucky black cat survived a 120-mi (193-km) rail journey from Southampton, England, to Cardiff, Wales, in June 2012 by clinging on to the underside of the train.

FUGITIVE PENGUIN ▶ A Humboldt penguin that jumped over a wall and slipped through a fence at the Tokyo Sea Life Park remained on the loose for 82 days in the Japanese capital before finally being caught. While on the run, the penguin was frequently spotted swimming in rivers but always managed to elude keepers.

KITTEN RESCUE ▶ A mother cat and her three kittens were rescued from beneath the concrete floor of a garage in a house in West Jordan, Utah. They had crept into the space beneath the floor shortly before the concrete was poured, but when construction workers heard meowing, they cut a hole in the newly laid floor so that the animals could be saved.

RAISED ALARM ▶ When disabled Victoria Shaw of Wrexham, North Wales, collapsed in the shower, Louis, her Yorkshire terrier, summoned help by pressing the panic alarm in her home. She had trained him to hit the button in case of an emergency, and was delighted when he remembered what to do.

EASY RIDER

▶ Tom Bennett and his dog Brody, a five-year-old golden doodle, ride on a jet ski on Pigeon Lake near Bobcaygeon in Ontario, Canada. Brody, who has only ever fallen off once, wears goggles to keep dragonflies from hitting him in the eyes.

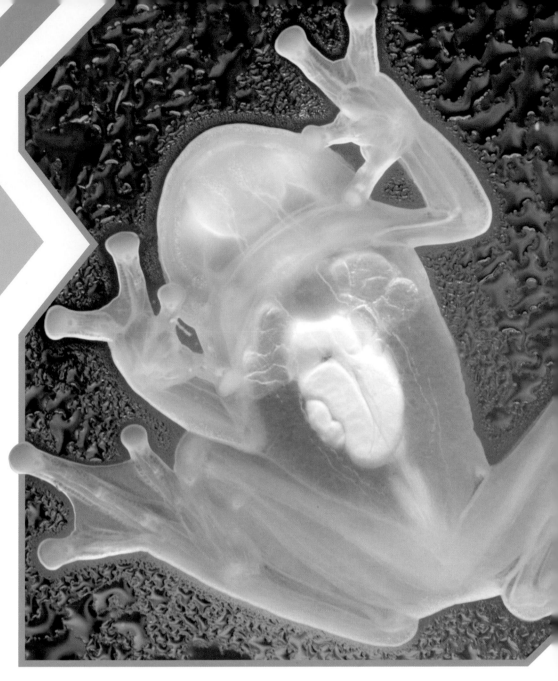

MIGHTY MICE ▶ Birds nesting on Gough Island in the South Atlantic Ocean risk being eaten by packs of the 700,000 oversized mice that populate the island. The mice have evolved into super-rodents that are three times the size of the normal house mouse. Instead of being vegetarian, these monster mice have turned into carnivores that eat chicks from their nests.

BAT INVASION ▶ The town of Katherine in Australia's Northern Territory was invaded by more than 250,000 fruit bats in February 2012. The risk of catching rabies from a bat bite or scratch was sufficient for authorities to close down the town's main sports ground until the bats left.

THICK COAT ▶ The sea otter has the thickest coat of any mammal, with a million hairs covering an area the size of a postage stamp.

QUICK CHANGE ▶ As the species consists largely of males, the two-banded anemonefish, a native of the Red Sea, has males that can turn into female fish at will, in order to mate.

SEE-THROUGH FROG

▶ *Glass frogs from the forests of Central and South America have a transparent skin through which you can see their beating heart, and their stomach, liver, intestines, lung and gall bladder. Their green translucent bodies enable them to blend in with their leafy background, thereby protecting them from predators.*

BLOOD SUCKER ▶ The Cooper's nutmeg snail searches the sea floor in the Eastern Pacific Ocean for electric rays—it then climbs on top of them and drinks their blood.

GEOMETRIC WEB

▶ An orb-weaver spider in a Hong Kong park spun this incredible web in an intricate geometric shape. These amazing patterns are believed to attract insect prey by reflecting ultraviolet light. They may also help camouflage the spider from predators.

LUNCH LAUNCH ▶ To catch seals off the coast of Cape Town, South Africa, 2,000-lb (900-kg) sharks swim up rapidly from beneath, sometimes launching both themselves and their prey as high as 10 ft (3 m) out of the water.

ETERNAL YOUTH ▶ Honey bees can reverse the brain decline brought on through old age by tackling duties usually done by much younger bees. Scientists at Arizona State University found that when older, foraging bees were tricked into doing social tasks inside the nest, the molecular structure of their brains changed, significantly improving their ability to learn new things.

CANNIBAL TOADS ▶ As much as 66 percent of a young Australian cane toad's diet is made up of other, smaller cane toads.

STOWAWAY LIZARD ▶ A stowaway 6-in-long (15-cm) brown *Chioninia* lizard not only survived a 3,000-mi (4,800-km) flight in passenger Sue Banwell-Moore's luggage as she returned from vacation in the Cape Verde Islands to the U.K., it also coped with her inadvertently putting it into the washing machine along with her dirty laundry. She spotted the lizard as she was hanging out the washing after 30 minutes on the delicates cycle. Nicknamed Larry, the lizard recovered from its ordeal and now lives at a nearby wildlife park.

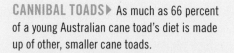

ANT RAFTS ▶ Fire ants can survive flood conditions for weeks at a time by linking together to form living rafts with their bodies. Their hairy bodies allow the ants to trap air bubbles, which, with all the insects jammed together, fuse to form a protective air layer that stops the colony from drowning. A single raft can contain more than 10,000 ants.

MIRROR TRICK ▶ To encourage its lonely flamingos to breed, China's Shenzhen Zoo surrounded their enclosure with 45 ft (14 m) of mirrors, each over 3 ft (90 cm) high, to make them feel as if they were in a large colony. When the birds first arrived at the zoo from Japan, they failed to breed because their flock was too small for them to feel confident enough to have chicks.

CORPSE CARRIER
▶ To deter predators such as spiders, the assassin bug of Malaysia makes itself look bigger by carrying at least 20 dead ants on its back at a time. The assassin bug kills the ants by injecting them with a deadly saliva containing an enzyme that quickly turns their insides to liquid. The liquid lunch is then sucked up by the bug and the dry carcasses are heaped on its back.

GIANT WASP ▶ A newly discovered giant wasp on the island of Sulawesi, Indonesia, is 2½ in (6.4 cm) long and has jaws longer than its front legs.

WING SONG ▶ The club-winged manakin, which lives in the forests of Colombia and Ecuador, is the only bird known to sing with its wings. Whereas most birds have lightweight, hollow wing bones, the club-winged manakin has dense, solid wing bones that help it to emit a violin-like sound. To attract a mate, instead of singing through its beak, it rubs its wings together.

DESIGNER SHEEP ▶ The latest collectible for wealthy Chinese people is a $2-million Dolan sheep bred in the ancient city of Kashgar. With their distinctive curved nose, twin tail and floppy ears, there are only 1,000 Dolan sheep in the world.

TAKE ME HOME ▶ A lost budgerigar was taken back to its home after reciting its entire address to a police officer. The talkative bird had escaped from a house in Yokohama, Japan, and flown to a city center hotel where it was caught and handed over to the police.

SELF-SUFFICIENT ▶ Yeti crabs grow their own food. The crabs, which are found near deep hydrothermal vents, get most of their food from bacteria that they cultivate on their hairy arms.

WRONG TURN ▶ In June 2011, a young emperor penguin took a wrong turn and washed ashore on a beach in New Zealand, more than 2,000 mi (3,200 km) from its Antarctic home. It was the first confirmed sighting of an emperor penguin in New Zealand for 44 years.

ALBINO TURLE

▶ *A rare albino baby green sea turtle swims at a conservation center on Khram Island, Thailand, where 15,000 turtles are hatched each year under the protection of the Thai Navy before being released into the sea.*

POPULATION PLUNGE▶ White-rumped vultures of southern Asia once numbered in the tens of millions, but during the past ten years, the population has dropped by about 99.9 percent.

WONDER WHISKERS▶ Dormice can climb trees by using their whiskers. The tiny animals, which spend winter on the ground but live in trees in summer, vibrate their whiskers up to 25 times a second to help them navigate their way safely along uneven branches and through tight gaps.

HIGH SPOT▶ A cat climbed to the top of a 30-ft (9-m) saguaro cactus in the Arizona desert and stayed there for more than three days. After being filmed by a TV crew from a helicopter, the daredevil cat calmly climbed down from its lofty perch and wandered off.

HOMESICK HOUND▶ Buck, a three-year-old Labrador, traveled 500 mi (800 km) to be reunited with his owner. No longer able to keep a dog in his Myrtle Beach, South Carolina, home, Mark Wessells had left Buck with his father in Winchester, Virginia, but the dog had other ideas and several months later turned up near his old home.

SNAKE BITE▶ A 13-month-old toddler from Shefa'Amr, Israel, chewed the head off a snake. Little Imad Aleeyan used his six teeth to bite into the head of the 12-in-long (30-cm) nonvenomous snake.

DOG WIGS▶ Ruth Regina from Bay Harbor Islands, Florida, makes custom wigs for dogs. Her enterprise started when her niece asked her to make a wig for her basset hound and now she sells doggie hairpieces in a wide range of styles, including the Sarah Palin, the Elvis and the Beatle.

SECRET EATER▶ Although giant pandas were thought to be strictly vegetarian, with 99 percent of their diet being bamboo, a camera at the Wanglong Nature Reserve in Sichuan, China, recorded on video one animal eating a dead antelope in December 2011. However, it is not thought that the panda killed the antelope, but that it stumbled across the corpse in the forest.

IMMORTAL WORMS▶ Flatworms can regenerate time and time again, giving them the ability to live forever unless they succumb to disease or a predator. If a flatworm is cut in half, the head portion grows a tail and the tail portion grows a head—a feat that allowed scientists at Nottingham University in England to create a colony of 20,000 identical flatworms, all from one original specimen.

HIGH TEA▶ Sure-footed Tamri goats of Morocco love the tasty berries of the argan tree so much that as many as 16 goats have been seen perched on the narrow branches of a single tree, some as high as 30 ft (9 m) above the ground. Amazingly, the goats' cloven hooves help them to climb and balance while their soft soles enable them to grip the bark of the tree.

DOUBLE TROUBLE
▶ This two-headed California Kingsnake at San Diego Zoo presents a headache for keepers at feeding time. They have to feed each head separately (covering one with a hood) in case one head tries to snatch the other's food and causes injury. The snake started out as twins, but the embryo failed to split properly, causing the rare two-headed reptile.

FOUR BEARS▶ A bear and three cubs broke into a cabin in northern Norway and finished off all the food and drink—including marshmallows, chocolate spread, honey and over 100 cans of beer.

KNOTTED BOAS▶ Some captive boa constrictors and pythons suffer from a fatal disease called Inclusion Body Disease, which can cause them to tie their bodies in knots from which they are unable to escape. The disease is thought to be caused by a previously unknown strain of arenavirus—a type of virus that normally attacks rodents.

BLOOD LUST▶ Some species of mosquito fly up to 40 mi (64 km) to find a meal of blood, and people can attract mosquitoes from that far away simply by breathing. When a person exhales, their carbon dioxide and other odors waft through the air, letting mosquitoes know that a tasty meal is within their flight range.

FALSE LEGS▶ Lemon Pie, a dog from Mexico City who lost both his front legs, has learned to walk again thanks to a pair of $6,000 state-of-the-art prosthetic limbs.

GLASS WINGS

▶ The glasswing butterfly, *Greta oto*, of Central America has translucent wings that appear to be made of glass. The tissue between the veins of its wings lacks the colored scales present in other butterflies, resulting in its unique appearance and Spanish name *espejitos*, meaning "little mirrors." Although fragile-looking, the wings are just as strong as those of other butterflies and if it were not for the wings' dark orange borders, the glasswing would be virtually invisible to the human eye.

◀NO NOSE

▶ *Kabang, a German shepherd cross, lost her snout while saving the lives of two young girls in a motorcycle crash in the Philippines. Her owner's daughter and niece were about to be run over by the bike until Kabang heroically stepped into its path, but in doing so the dog got her head caught in the bike's front wheel and her snout and upper jaw were ripped off. However, an Internet campaign spearheaded by Karen Kenngott, a nurse from Buffalo, New York, raised $20,000 for Kabang to be taken to the U.S. for remedial surgery.*

INSECT LIGHTS▶ The Jamaican click beetle, the world's brightest glowing insect, was once used by tribesmen around the Caribbean to light their huts at night. Unlike other bioluminescent creatures, different Jamaican click beetles can emit different colors, ranging from green to orange.

BOOM TIME▶ Around 100 male crocodiles at a breeding farm in the Golan Heights in the Middle East began their mating calls prematurely after the animals mistook the sonic booms made by Israeli warplanes flying overhead for the calls of rival males.

LONG TONGUE▶ First discovered in Ecuador in 2005, the tube-lipped nectar bat—*Anoura fistulata*—has a tongue that is one-and-a-half times longer than its body. The bat is about 2 in (5 cm) long, but its tongue is nearly 3½ in (9 cm) long, giving it the longest tongue, relative to body length, of any known mammal. When not collecting nectar from flowers, the bat's tongue is retracted and stored in the animal's rib cage.

OLD TOWN▶ The world's oldest horse and the world's oldest dog both live in the same town in Essex, England. Shayne the horse is 51 years old and has lived in a Brentwood horse sanctuary since 2007 while Pip, a 24-year-old terrier-whippet cross, lives nearby with her owner Tiffany Dyer and is still active enough to perform with the Essex Dog Display Team. In human years, Pip would now be 170 years old.

ACIDIC VENOM ▶ The venom of the Texas coral snake contains compounds that produce an intense pain by making nerves react as if they are being attacked with acid.

DONKEY DREADS ▶ In June 2012, a pack of long-haired Baudet du Poitou donkeys at a farm in Hampshire, England, had their locks cut for the first time in 17 years to help them cope with the hot weather. The rare French donkeys are not usually groomed—their fur is usually left to grow into dreadlocks that stretch all the way down to the ground.

ROAR ENERGY ▶ On a still night, a lion's roar can be heard 5 mi (8 km) away. Both males and females roar, the sound starting as a low moan and progressing in stages to higher and louder tones. The roar can reach 114 decibels— louder than a jackhammer.

LARGEST EGGS ▶ Whale sharks are born from the world's largest eggs—12 in (30 cm) long— that remain in the mother's body until after the eggs hatch.

FLYING PLANKTON ▶ Tiny shrimplike plankton called copepods escape predatory fish by bursting through the surface of the ocean and flying through the air. The creatures, which live close to the surface, are so adept at this evasive action they actually travel further in the air than in water.

DOG IN DISGUISE
▶ When they saw this strange creature roaming the streets, residents of Xinxiang, China, thought a genetically modified pig was on the run from nearby medical laboratories. In fact the animal was not a pig at all but a rare pedigree Chinese crested hairless dog whose bizarre tufty head and bare, pink, spotted body make it look much more like a pig than a dog.

INSTANT ANTLERS ▶ The blackbuck antelope, which is native to India, grows a full set of 30-in (75-cm) antlers in just 12 weeks—this is the fastest-growing body part in the animal world.

LIVING POOP ▶ After being eaten, some marine snails survive inside ducks' guts for up to five hours, even traveling many miles in flight before popping out alive and completely unscathed in the bird's feces.

WOOFSTOCK FESTIVAL ▶ More than 300,000 dog lovers and their pets attend the annual Woofstock Festival in Toronto, Canada. First held in 2003, the event includes a fashion show and a talent contest for dogs, with an award for the best-dressed dog. Yorkshire terrier Remy, dressed as a biker in a black leather jacket, helmet and sunglasses, was the star of the 2012 show. Previous winners include a dog dressed as Bob Marley and another wearing a costume inspired by the *Men in Black* movie trilogy.

MINI LIZARD ▶ *Brookesia micra*, a newly discovered chameleon from Madagascar, reaches a maximum length of just 1.1 in (29 mm). It is the tiniest chameleon ever found and is so small it can stand on the head of a match.

VANISHING ACT ▶ The 8½-in-long (22-cm) smalleye pygmy shark of the Western Pacific Ocean has bioluminescent cells in its belly, which causes its silhouette to vanish when seen by predators from below.

BUSY BURROWERS ▶ Naked mole rats are only a few inches long, but a colony of several dozen can create an underground burrow that spans up to 20 football fields in area.

HARD TO SWALLOW
▶ This 2-ft-long (60-cm) night adder looked to have bitten off more than it could chew as it attempted to devour a toad head-first in a garden in Natal, South Africa. In a bid to swallow the toad, the snake stretched its mouth to an angle of almost 180 degrees.

ANT BRIDGE

▶ *Faced with a gap between two leaves that was several times wider than their body length, these weaver ants in Jakarta, Indonesia, showed incredible ingenuity by linking their bodies together to form a bridge that other ants in the army could then walk across.*

KILLER CROC▶ A 14½-ft-long (4.4-m) saltwater crocodile in the north of Australia ate up to nine pet dogs in a savage killing spree. The croc, which had also snatched wallabies, was eventually caught near the settlement of Daly River, 140 mi (225 km) south of Darwin.

DELAYED BIRTHS▶ An eastern diamond-back rattlesnake recently gave birth to 19 healthy offspring—10 females and nine males—five whole years after mating. The normal gestation period for rattlesnakes is six to seven months. The snake had mated in the wild as a sexually immature juvenile and had somehow managed to store the sperm in its body for five years.

LAST TORTOISE▶ For more than 40 years— up until his death in 2012—Lonesome George was the world's only remaining Pinta Island giant tortoise. Researchers had tried in vain to get him to mate, offering $10,000 to anyone who discovered a female Pinta Island giant tortoise.

RAT TRAP▶ Along with humans, the African crested rat is the only mammal that uses poison that it didn't produce itself. The rat chews the poisonous roots and bark of the acokanthera tree—the same deadly venom used to tip poison arrows—then smears the toxic slobber on its specially adapted fur to deter predators.

REVENGE MISSION▶ After being bitten by a common cobra while working in a paddy field near Kathmandu, Nepal, Mohamed Salmo Miya was so angry that he chased the snake, caught it and bit it until he killed it.

BACK FROM THE DEAD▶ Rhino the hamster came back from the dead after clawing his way out of a 2-ft-deep (60-cm) grave. After finding the pet "cold and lifeless" in his cage, Dave Eyley of Oxfordshire, England, buried him in the garden, but the next day Rhino was seen scampering around, having dug a 2-in-wide (5-cm) hole and climbed to the surface.

▶▶ THE GIANT PANDA HAS A MORE POWERFUL BITE THAN ITS MUCH LARGER COUSIN, THE POLAR BEAR. ◀

ARTIFICIAL JELLYFISH▶ Biophysicists at Harvard University, Cambridge, Massachusetts, have built an artificial jellyfish using muscle cells from the heart of a rat and silicone. When placed in an electric field, the synthetic creature looks, moves and swims like a real jellyfish—but genetically it is still a rat.

KOALA CALL▶ Although koala bears weigh only about 15 lb (6.8 kg), their bellow is as loud as a cow weighing more than a ton. The marsupials are able to make such loud noises to attract partners during the mating season because they have human-type voice boxes where the larynx sits deeper in the throat than it does in other species.

TINY FROG▶ A tiny frog, *Paedophryne amauensis*, has been discovered in Papua New Guinea that measures just 0.3 in (7.7 mm) in length as an adult and is so small it fits easily on a U.S. dime.

FAT CAT▶ After being kidnapped from the garden of a house in Landskron, Austria, Cupid, a 28-lb (13-kg) pedigree Maine Coon cat worth $4,500, was returned two weeks later because the thieves could not cope with the animal's enormous appetite of more than three cans of cat food at a single sitting.

SAFETY IN NUMBERS▶ Periodical cicadas are incapable of defending themselves, so the insects all emerge from the ground as adults at the same time—in their thousands—making it impossible for all of them to be eaten by predators.

LONG NERVE▶ Giraffes have a nerve that travels all the way down their neck to their chest and back up to connect the brain to their larynx— an organ that lies only inches away.

LOVE SONGS▶ Staff at Drusillas Zoo Park, Sussex, England, tried to get their Chilean flamingos in the mood for love by piping Barry White songs into their enclosure at night—and it resulted in the hatching of the zoo's first chick in three years.

WING SCENE▶ *Macrocilix maia*, a Malaysian moth, mimics an entire scene on its wings—a pair of flies approaching bird droppings. The moth also emits a foul odor, and so tries to fool predators by both sight and smell.

ROUNDUP RABBIT▶ Champis, a five-year-old pet dwarf rabbit owned by Nils-Erik and Greta Vigren of Käl, Sweden, rounds up and herds the farm's sheep as if he were a sheepdog. The rabbit has never been trained for the job but seems to have picked up the necessary skills from watching the actual sheepdogs on the farm.

MIGHTY BITE▶ Scientists from Florida have found that extinct crocodiles generated bite forces in excess of 23,000 lb (10,500 kg)—that's twice as powerful as the bite of a Tyrannosaurus rex.

RELATED COWS▶ By extracting DNA from ancient cow bones found at an Iranian archeological site, scientists have found that all the domesticated cows in the world today—that's about 1.3 billion of them—come from a herd of just 80 that existed 10,500 years ago.

ARTISTIC ELEPHANT▶ By holding a paintbrush with her trunk, Shanti, an Indian elephant at Prague Zoo, Czech Republic, creates paintings that sell for more than $2,000 each. The proceeds from her artwork bought a new enclosure for Shanti and her herd.

CARING CAT▶ A cat in Qingdao, China, lives in a birdcage with five chicks she has adopted. The unusual relationship began when owner Li Tongfa left the door of the birdcage open and the cat climbed in, but instead of eating the birds, she played with them.

BIRDS OF A FEATHER

▶ The normal-looking budgerigar on the left seems puzzled as to why her six-month-old offspring resembles a feather duster. The bizarre budgie from Zhengzhou, China, has long curly feathers all over its body, probably as a result of a rare mutation that causes unrestricted feather growth and leads to a decidedly disheveled appearance.

WORKING TOGETHER▶ Elephants possess human-like powers of empathy that enable them to work together. In the wild, elephants have been seen stopping and teaming up to rescue another elephant that had fallen into a pit.

COLOR SENSITIVE▶ Gunnison's prairie dogs, squirrel-like rodents native to the U.S., can distinguish between the different colors of clothing people wear. The rodents make different alarm calls depending on whether they see a blue, a yellow or a green shirt.

SIZZLING PORK▶ Fifty-three pigs were electrocuted by a single lightning bolt that struck their sty in Guangming Xinqulou, China, on July 5, 2012. Farmer Mrs. Chen found them all lying on their backs, motionless, apart from one pig in the sty, which survived with a broken leg.

PIG HANGED▶ In 1386, a pig went on trial in the French town of Falaise accused of causing the death of a child. Dressed in human clothes for the proceedings, the pig was found guilty, mutilated and publicly hanged.

GREEN BOTTLE
BUBBLES

▶ *Martin Amm from Kronach, Germany, captured this amazing image of a green bottle fly in a meadow on a foggy morning. The bizarre-looking bubbles are actually morning dew. Martin told Ripley's that he can sometimes search for hours before he finds an insect to photograph, and that this type of super-close-up image, which requires a special lens, is easier to take on a cold morning because the cold-blooded insects can't fly away!*

LATE DEVELOPERS ▶ Female loggerhead sea turtles take as long as 45 years to mature and begin laying eggs—yet in the wild they rarely live much beyond the age of 50.

COMPLEX DNA ▶ The marbled lungfish, *Protopterus aethiopicus*, has a DNA genome that is 133 base pairs long—that's 44 times longer than a human's.

DIVE BOMBING ▶ Peregrine falcons can dive at over 200 mph (320 km/h), knocking smaller birds to the ground for an easy meal.

LARVAL SPRAY ▶ Sweden's elk botflies spray their young into the noses of elk, where they feed on blood and mucus. Occasionally the botflies mistakenly spray a human's eyes instead. Human victims have had more than 30 eggs shot into their eye at a time. The larvae cause a burning sensation and, if not removed, attach themselves to the cornea and eyelid where they may cause extensive damage.

FEARSOME FLEAS ▶ 165 million years ago, dinosaurs were plagued by giant flea-like insects—ten times the size of a modern flea—which fed on their blood with a bite thought to be as painful as being injected with a hypodermic needle.

TREE LOBSTER ▶ The Lord Howe Island stick insect, aka the Tree Lobster, was rediscovered in the 21st century after being thought extinct since 1920. The size of a human hand, the insect feeds on only one species of shrub. It is thought that there are just 30 specimens in the wild—on a rat-free volcanic outcrop off the coast of Australia.

SWALLOWED SPOON ▶ Fruit-loving Max, a ten-year-old Rottweiler owned by Annette Robertshaw of West Yorkshire, England, needed surgery after gulping down a strawberry... along with the teaspoon on which it was served. The spoon lodged in Max's stomach, and although it was successfully removed, the experience seems to have put him off eating strawberries for life.

GRIZZLY CUSTOMER ▶ A 250-lb (113-kg), 18-month-old grizzly bear named Billy has become a regular at a pub in Vancouver, British Columbia, where he enjoys a game of pool. After going to the pub with his owners, animal handler Mark Dumas and his wife Dawn, Billy goes back to their home to watch TV, or splash and play ball with them in their swimming pool.

CYCLOPS GOAT ▽

▶ *No kidding! Kyndra Batia of Garden City, Texas, sent Ripley's this amazing picture of a baby goat born on April 26, 2012, with just one eye in the middle of its face.*

YOUR UPLOADS

OLDEST INSECTS▶ Scientists working in Italy's Dolomite mountains have discovered a fly and two mites that have been perfectly preserved in amber for 230 million years, making them the oldest insects found in amber by 100 million years. The tiny bugs, which are invisible to the human eye, were found in millimeter-sized droplets of amber, a fossilized resin produced by extinct coniferous trees.

DEVIL WORM▶ A new species of "devil worm"—*Halicephalobus mephisto*—has been discovered living 2.2 mi (3.5 km) below the Earth's surface—the deepest-living animal ever found.

CANNIBAL SHARKS▶ A species of carpet shark known as the wobbegong eats other sharks. Remains of sharks have previously been found in wobbegongs' stomachs, and in 2012 Australian divers and photographers observed at first hand a tasseled wobbegong devouring whole a brownbanded bamboo shark along the Great Barrier Reef.

SAVIOR SEAL▶ After being attacked by a 15-ft-long (4.6-m) great white shark off Cape Town, South Africa, British expat Michael Cohen was saved by a seal, which fended off the shark as it prepared to make a second and probably fatal attack. Cohen still lost more than 15 pt (7 l) of blood after having his right leg ripped off.

FISH MIMIC▶ Scientists in Indonesia have recorded a tiny jawfish mimicking a mimic octopus, which in turn mimics other fish! The usually reclusive yellow-and-black-striped jawfish will swim alongside the similarly colored octopus, wiggling its body like a tentacle and taking advantage of the camouflage either to seek food or a new burrow.

SHARK WHISPERER

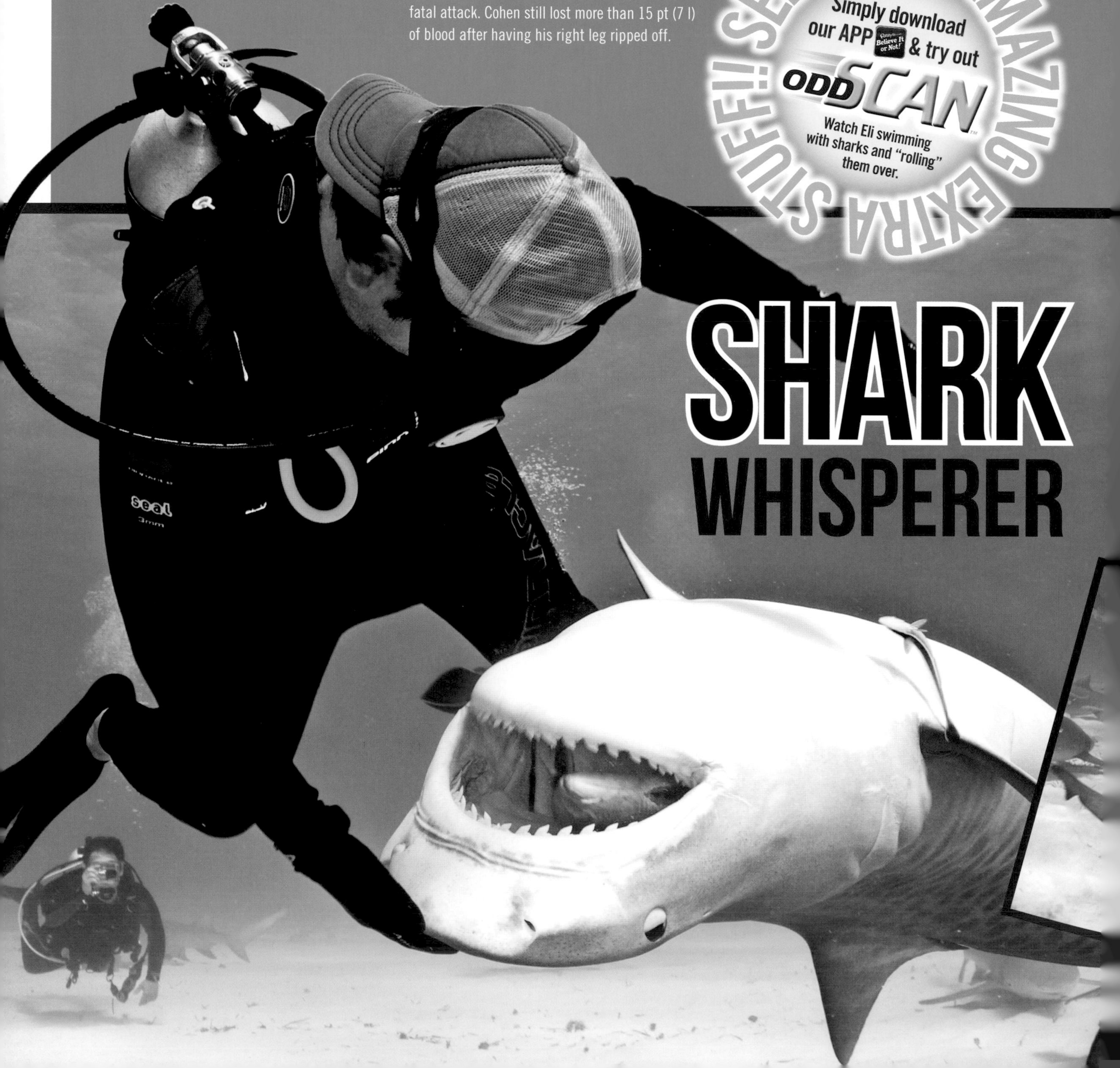

CONTACT LENS ▶ Win Thida, a 45-year-old Asian elephant at Artis Zoo in Amsterdam in the Netherlands, was fitted with a contact lens after her eye became scratched in a fight with another elephant. Since elephants are unable to lie down for long before their weight impairs their breathing, the operation was performed with Win Thida anesthetized standing up, the veterinarian using a ladder to climb up and insert the lens.

60 EYES ▶ A new species of flatworm that has a staggering 60 eyes in its body—but that's just 0.5 in (12 mm) long—has been found by scientists near Cambridge, England.

PET TIGER ▶ Michael Jamison and Jackie Smit share their home in Brakpan, South Africa, with 14 dogs and a 378-lb (172-kg) Bengal tiger called Enzo, which they bought as a cub. He used to ride in their yellow Lamborghini until his daily diet of 11 lb (5 kg) of meat meant he got too big.

BRAIN OVERSPILL ▶ Some tiny spiders measuring less than 0.04 in (1 mm) across have such huge brains for their body sizes—taking up nearly 80 percent of their total body space—that their brains actually spill over into their legs.

FEEDING FRENZY

▶ *Although they weigh up to 79,000 lb (36,000 kg) and measure as much as 52 ft (16 m) long, humpback whales regularly lift 90 percent of their bodies out of the water before twisting and landing on their backs—an action known as breaching. Attracted by a mass of sardines, this hungry humpback surfaced in shallow waters near San Luis Obispo, California, to the amazement of kayakers and sailors who were able to get within a few feet of the ocean giant. The picture was taken by Bill Bouton, who had been trying unsuccessfully to photograph birds until his luck changed with a picture that got 200,000 views within 16 hours of being posted on Flickr.*

▲ Photographers arrive to take shots of Eli as the local tiger sharks come to play with him.

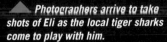
▲ A tiger shark comes in for a "high-five" with Eli.

▶ Diver Eli Martinez has trained deadly, 16-ft-long (5-m) tiger sharks—second only to great whites in terms of attacking humans—to roll around like playful puppies just by tickling them. The shark whisperer, from Alamo, Texas, has been visiting Tiger Beach off the Bahamas for ten years and has struck up such a bond with the local sharks that he can get them to "high-five" him with their fins and even roll 360 degrees around his hand. He is still very cautious, though, and aware that "they are so wild you can never get 100 percent comfortable."

Animal Whisperers

▶ **HORSE** American horse trainer Monty Roberts believes that horses use a nonverbal language, which he calls Equus. He uses this language—a series of silent gestures—to communicate with them.

▶ **LION** Using endless patience, Kevin Richardson, a ranger at the Lion Park near Johannesburg, South Africa, has developed such a rapport with lions that he has slept next to them, eaten with them and lived with them.

▶ **SNAKE** Paul Kenyon uses his experience at recognizing what mood a snake is in to catch and handle the world's most venomous snakes around his base in Western Australia.

▶ **GATOR** Jeanette Rivera from the Florida's Everglades Alligator Farm, plays with and wrestles monster gators that weigh 56 lb (25 kg) more than her. She shows her confidence by placing her chin on their snouts.

ALWAYS GROWING ▶ Bowhead whales can live for more than 200 years, and because their spine does not fuse, they never stop growing.

READING SKILLS ▶ Baboons can learn reading skills. In 300,000 tests conducted by French scientists, six baboons were able to distinguish between real and fake words flashed up on a computer screen 75 percent of the time. The star of the group, four-year-old Dan, achieved an 80-percent success rate and learned to recognize 308 four-letter words.

CRUSH-TACEANS ▶ Florida stone crabs have crushing claws that can exert a force of up to 19,000 lb per square inch (1,336 kg/cm²)—several times stronger than an industrial car crusher.

URINE WASH ▶ Male capuchin monkeys make themselves more attractive to females by urinating onto their hands and then rubbing the urine into their fur like a human would rub cologne onto the skin. When a fertile female capuchin is on the hunt for a male partner, the smell of the male's urine indicates to her that he is sexually mature and available.

ELEPHANT DETERRENT ▶ Farmers in Tanzania have devised a new way to keep elephants off their land—by smearing fences with a mixture of chili peppers and engine oil. The elephants never forget the intense burning smell of the chilis, which makes them sneeze, while the engine oil helps the spicy concoction stick to the fences, even in heavy rain.

MILK MACHINE ▶ Smurf, a 15-year-old Holstein cow from Embrun, Canada, has produced over 57,000 gal (216,000 l) of milk in her lifetime—three times more than the average dairy cow and equal to more than one million glasses of milk.

CHIMP HANDSHAKES ▶ Chimpanzees pass down a secret handshake through the generations—and the form of the handshake differs from group to group. Researchers in Zambia found that some chimps prefer to clasp hands while others like to clutch the wrists.

BEAR RIDE ▶ In December 2011, a black bear made its way into downtown Vancouver, Canada, by hitching a ride in a garbage truck. The bear had been hunting for food in a dumpster when the dumpster's contents, including the bear, were tipped into the truck.

HIGH LIFE ▶ When Richard Haughton goes to work repairing the thatched roofs of cottages in Norfolk, England, his dog Axel joins him up on the roof. Axel, a Labrador, Newfoundland and rottweiler cross, catches a lift on his owner's shoulder to get up and down the ladder and shows no fear of heights.

BEES' NEST ▶ Tommy Hill of Brighton, Tennessee, found that overnight 25,000 bees had made their home in the engine of his car. He tried to lose them by driving down the highway at 60 mph (96 km/h), but not one bee left the nest until eventually they were all lured out with a box of honey.

WAXY MORSEL ▶ In addition to feeding on the ticks and parasites of Africa's large mammals, red-billed oxpecker birds dine on the mammals' tears, saliva, mucus, blood and earwax!

FAT CAT ▶ Believed to be the world's fattest cat, Sponge Bob weighed 33 lb (15 kg)—the same as a four-year-old child—when he first arrived at an animal shelter in Manhattan, New York City.

FLYING CAT ▶ Sugar the cat fell 19 stories from a high-rise window in Boston, Massachusetts, and walked away without any broken bones or cuts.

TRAPPED BULL ▶ A bull fell through an open manhole in Santiago, Chile, and spent two days trapped in the drainage ditch before the animal was finally rescued.

PARROT DIALECTS ▶ Since many of a parrot's calls are learned rather than instinctive, parrot populations often develop local dialects in their songs, depending on what birds they grew up with.

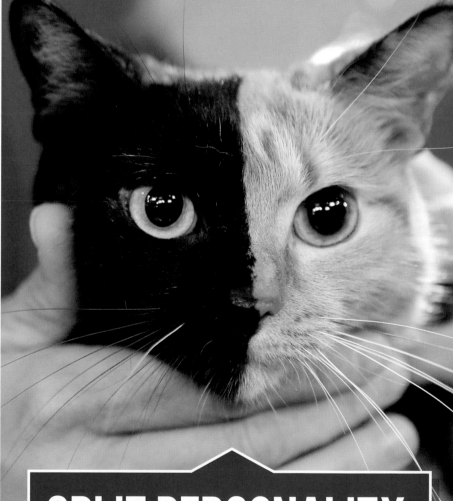

SPLIT PERSONALITY

▶ *Venus, a chimera cat from North Carolina, has become a celebrity on Facebook because her face appears to be perfectly divided into two halves. Her face is half black and half calico, and the condition heterochromia has given her one blue eye and one green.*

PYTHON PASSENGER

▶ A 16-ft-long (5-m) python made its home under the hood of Marlene Swart and Leon Swanepoel's car while they were on holiday in South Africa's Kruger National Park. When the reptile refused to budge, they had to drive the stowaway snake 3 mi (4.8 km) to the nearest lookout point, where they were finally able to remove it.

TIGHTROPE WALKER▶ An Alaskan malamute dog in Chongqing, China, has learned to walk a tightrope and can walk along two parallel 33-ft-long (10-m) wires in just a minute. Wang Xianting and his colleagues have been training dogs so that they can access difficult areas and help firefighters deal with disasters.

GLOWING DONKEYS▶ 500 donkeys in Botswana were fitted with glow-in-the-dark ear tags in an attempt to reduce the number of accidents on country roads at night. The animals' impoverished owners often leave them to roam freely in search of food, and in northern Botswana one in ten road crashes involves a donkey.

MONSTER SNAKE▶ A female Burmese python caught in the Florida Everglades in 2012 measured 17.6 ft (5.3 m) long, weighed almost 165 lb (75 kg) and was carrying an incredible 87 eggs.

BRAVERY AWARD▶ Yogi the golden retriever won a heroic dog award for rescuing his owner in true Lassie style. When Paul Horton of Austin, Texas, was knocked unconscious after falling off his bicycle, Yogi ran to get help, finding Horton's neighbors and barking at them until they followed him back to the injured cyclist.

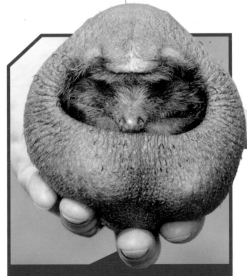

BALD HEDGEHOG
▶ Betty the hedgehog suffers from a mystery skin condition that has left her without any spines. Abandoned by her mother, Betty was taken to an animal rescue center in Norfolk, England, where she has to stay out of the sun because her skin is so dry and sensitive. The youngster is scared of other hedgehogs, which may make it impossible for her to find a mate.

LOT OF BULL▶ Jocko, a 27-year-old bull from France, died in March 2012 after fathering 400,000 offspring during his lifetime. By donating 1.7 million sperm straws, Jocko helped keep alive the Prim'Holstein cattle strain, and in France alone, his daughters are present in over 23,000 farms.

CAT COMMUTER▶ Graeme, a cat belonging to Nicole Weinrich of Melbourne, Australia, follows his owner to the train every day when she leaves for work—then returns to the station to wait for her at the end of the day. Occasionally, he even jumps on to the train and rides for a couple of stations before getting off again.

MUSICAL ELEPHANT▶ Shanthi, a 36-year-old Asian elephant at the Smithsonian National Zoo in Washington, D.C., has started playing the harmonica. She uses her trunk to play the instrument, which is attached to the side of her enclosure.

RAY ATTACK▶ Jenny Hausch was boating off the coast of Islamorada, Florida, when a 300-lb (136-kg) spotted eagle ray leapt from the water into her boat, pinning her to the deck.

HAPPY SNAP

▶ Photographer Marina Scarr captured this image of a hapless gar fish jumping straight into the jaws of a hungry alligator in Florida's Myakka River. The water level was low at the time and the fish did not stand much chance as there were at least 70 other alligators in the river.

SHARK FALL▶ A live, 2-ft-long (60-cm) leopard shark fell from the sky and landed near the 12th tee on San Juan Hills Golf Club in California. The shark had puncture wounds where it appeared that a bird had grabbed it from the Pacific Ocean some 5 mi (8 km) away. Club officials rushed the injured shark back to the ocean and it swam off.

TALKING ELEPHANT▶ A 22-year-old male Asian elephant called Koshik can mimic human speech and say five words in Korean—hello, no, sit down, lie down, and good. A resident of Everland Zoo in South Korea, Koshik puts the tip of his trunk into his mouth to transform his natural low rumble into a convincing impression of the human voice.

WRESTLED GATOR▶ Sixty-six-year-old grandfather Steve Gustafson from Lake County, Florida, wrestled a 7-ft-long (2.1-m), 130-lb (60-kg) alligator to pry his West Highland terrier Bounce from the reptile's jaws. Seeing the alligator heading into the water with the little dog in its mouth, Gustafson made a flying leap onto the creature's back and fought it underwater until he was able to free Bounce. When the gator snapped at his hand, he grabbed its jaw and pinned it shut. After swimming off, the alligator was killed by a trapper a few days later and bought by Gustafson to be stuffed as a permanent reminder of his crazy wrestling match.

CLEVER BOY!▶ A pet cockatoo named Figaro from Vienna, Austria, has learned to use his beak to make tools from sticks so that he can get at food that would otherwise be out of his reach. He is able to cut twigs to the right size to grab nuts placed outside his cage. Wild cockatoos are not known for making tools, and scientists believe Figaro is the first cockatoo to do so.

▶ A PLATYPUS CAN STORE 600 EARTHWORMS IN ITS CHEEK POUCHES FOR FOOD. ◀

DOLPHIN ALERT▶ Dolphins can stay awake for at least 15 days by sleeping with only one half of their brain at a time. This allows them to remain alert and active so that they can regularly come to the surface to breathe and keep a constant lookout for predatory sharks.

SECURITY CAT▶ A major toy warehouse in Southampton, Hampshire, England, employed a cat as a security guard to protect its Christmas stock. Millie the Bengal cat secured the post through her excellent climbing abilities and loud purr. She was paid with cat food and fish.

CROC ESCAPE▶ Baggage handlers at Melbourne Airport, Australia, had a shock when they began unloading passengers' luggage from the hold of a Qantas airplane—and found a crocodile running loose. The reptile was being transferred from Brisbane but had escaped from its container during the two-hour flight.

DEADLY BITE▶ A single bite from the inland taipan or fierce snake of Australia contains enough venom to kill 100 adult men or 250,000 mice within 45 minutes. Yet because it rarely comes into contact with people, there are very few recorded human deaths from its bite.

TRUNK AND DISORDERLY▶ Fifty elephants went on a drunken rampage in Dumurkota, India, after drinking 18 containers of mahua, a strong alcoholic brew. The herd demolished dozens of houses, ransacked a shop and ruined crops in their search for more liquor.

NEW TEETH▶ An Australian saltwater crocodile's teeth are constantly replaced. The toothy animals go through 3,000 teeth in a lifetime.

LOW TRICK▶ Zookeepers in Linyi, China, trained a giraffe to duck so that the animal could pass under more than 20 low bridges, electricity pylons and highway signs on the journey to her new home. They spent months teaching 15-year-old Mengmeng to dip her head whenever she saw a low obstacle, but it still took seven hours to move her just a few miles.

PARALYSIS CURE ▶ Paralyzed in an accident, Jasper the dachshund lost the use of his hind legs until scientists at Cambridge University, England, injected cells from the dog's nose into the injured part of his spine so that he could walk again.

SAVED LIFE ▶ When Aysha Perry from Nottinghamshire, England, started choking on a piece of chicken, her Japanese Akita dog Sheba saved her life by bounding into the room and hitting her on the back with one of her huge paws, dislodging the piece of meat. Afterward, Sheba licked her owner's face to make sure she was okay.

DOGGY DRIVER

▶ A dog in New Zealand has been taught to drive a car. Having first put the car into gear, with his left front paw on the steering wheel and his right back foot on the accelerator (modified so that he could reach it), Porter steered a Mini Cooper along an off-road track in Auckland. Porter's two months of daily instruction by trainer Mark Vette began with mock car controls, then moved on to a real car with an instructor, until finally Porter performed his solo test. The Auckland Society for the Prevention of Cruelty to Animals wanted to showcase how clever dogs are.

SPIDER RIDER

▶ *This close-up of a female wolf spider shows it carrying hundreds of young spiderlings on its back. The wolf spider is the only spider that carries her eggs in a round silken globe attached to her abdomen—much like a human would carry a growing baby. When the eggs hatch, they move on to the mother's back until they are old enough to hunt on their own.*

ROLY POLY A hedgehog at an animal rescue center in Somerset, England, was so fat that he was unable to roll into a ball. Roly Poly weighed 4 lb 7 oz (2 kg), more than three times the weight of an average hedgehog.

JOINED RACE A stray dog ran for 1,138 mi (1,830 km) and 24 days to keep pace with a bicycle race across China. Xiao Sa's amazing journey began when one of the cyclists fed her, and she then joined the long-distance race from Wuhan to Llasa, in the process climbing ten mountains higher than 13,000 ft (4,000 m).

FOSTER MOM After being rejected by her natural mother, a baby chimpanzee at a Russian zoo was adopted by the keeper's 100-lb (45-kg) pet mastiff dog. Within hours, the chimp had settled in and started eating and sleeping with the family's dogs.

FRISBEE CATCH Sixty dogs from six countries demonstrated their Frisbee-catching skills at the 2012 Extreme Distance Frisbee European Championships for Dogs in Budapest, Hungary. Categories include toss and fetch and freestyle, where the dogs perform a routine to music.

SURFING GOAT Wearing her yellow life jacket, "Goatee" the goat regularly surprises beachcombers on California's Pismo Beach by balancing her hooves on the surfboard of her owner Dana McGregor and riding the waves.

EMERGENCY CALL George, a two-year-old basset hound, saved his own life in March 2012 by dialing emergency services after becoming strangled by the cord of an old-fashioned phone. George had knocked over the heavy phone in owner Steve Brown's home in West Yorkshire, England, but despite choking with the cord wrapped around his neck, managed to dial 999 with his paw. The emergency operator heard heavy breathing and gasping on the other end of the line and alerted medics and a neighbor.

DOGGIE WHEELS Eighteen months after breaking her back, Carnage, a shih tzu-Maltese cross, can run around again thanks to a set of $300 wheels. Owner Jude McMinn from Queensland, Australia, bought the wheels, which take the place of the dog's back legs, after being told Carnage would have to be put down.

RARE KITTEN At the Audubon Center for Research of Endangered Species in New Orleans, an ordinary domestic cat has been used as a surrogate mother to create a rare African black-footed kitten. In a world first, nine-year-old frozen sperm from African black-footed cats, of which there are fewer than 10,000 left in the wild, was used to form embryos that were transplanted by IVF into the house cat.

SURF'S PUP

▶ A world record 17 dogs squeezed onto a single surfboard during the 2012 Loews Coronado Bay Resort Surf Dog Competition in California. A total of 20 dogs started out but three jumped off as soon as the board began to move.

DUCK DRIVE

▶ *A farmer holds up traffic while driving a huge herd of 5,000 ducks along a road on their way to a pond in Taizhou, China. Farmer Hong has been herding his ducks through the city for several months and claims never to have lost a single one.*

FRIEND OF THE STARS▶ In his lifetime, Lucky, a little white Maltese dog owned by U.S. TV personality and animal campaigner Wendy Diamond, was photographed with more than 300 famous people, including ex-President Bill Clinton, TV personality Kim Kardashian, movie star Kristen Stewart and musician Kanye West. Sadly, Lucky died in June 2012 at age 15 from spleen cancer.

PERMA-KITTEN▶ Lil Bub, a dwarf cat from Bloomington, Indiana, is a perma-kitten, meaning that she will be the size of a kitten and have kittenlike features for her entire life. She was born with several genetic mutations, making her legs disproportionately small compared with the rest of her body. She has no teeth but has an extra toe on each foot, giving her a total of 22 claws—four more than is usual.

MONKEY BUSINESS▶ A white-capped capuchin monkey has become such a talented artist that 40 of his paintings were exhibited in Toronto, Canada, in 2011. Pockets Warhol, a resident of Story Book Farm, a primate sanctuary in Sunderland, Ontario, paints with his tail, hands, feet and sometimes a brush. His colorful artworks have been sold for up to $400 apiece to buyers from as far afield as Europe and Israel.

POOP SNIFFER▶ A black Labrador mix named Tucker has been trained to become the only working dog able to sniff out and track the scent of killer whale feces in the ocean as far as a mile away. By detecting the orca scat around the San Juan Islands, Washington State, the one-time Seattle stray helps marine biologists monitor the health of the whales.

DOUBLE TROUBLE
▶ A pig in Zhangjia, China, was born with two mouths—and it eats and drinks through both of them. The strange little piggy also has two snouts. These deformities prevented it from suckling, so farmer Bai Xuejin fed it by hand until it was old enough to take solid food.

77

ILLUMINATED CREATURES

▶ Adult **female glowworms** use the eerie green light at the base of their abdomens to attract mates. Once a female has mated, she turns out her light, lays her eggs and dies.

▶ Living in the depths of the Atlantic where there is no light, the female **anglerfish** entices prey with a fishing-rod-like projection from its mouth, the end of the rod being illuminated by bacteria.

▶ The **hatchetfish** emits greenish-white lights as a defensive camouflage. When sunlight on the water casts a shadow of the fish, it turns on its lights to disguise the shadow and hide from predators below.

▶ The **cookiecutter shark** glows luminescent green for camouflage, but a small patch on its underbelly remains dark so that it resembles a small fish to hungry tuna and mackerel, which are then eaten by the shark when they attack.

▶ A species of **giant South American cockroach** has three glowing spots on its back to mimic the appearance of the toxic click beetle, thereby deterring predators.

▶ **Headlight beetles** of the West Indies emit so much light that islanders used to tie a few to their toes so they could see where they were going at night.

Female glowworm

▶ Nineteenth-century English nurse **Florence Nightingale** rescued a baby owl when she visited Athens, smuggled it home and often kept it in her pocket.

▶ As a boy, Aerosmith front man **Steven Tyler** had a **raccoon** that he used to take on fishing trips.

▶ French poet **Gérard de Nerval** used to walk his **lobster** on a length of ribbon through Parisian gardens.

▶ Spanish painter **Salvador Dalí** owned an **ocelot**, Babou, which traveled everywhere with him, even on luxury cruise liners.

▶ Sixteenth-century Danish astronomer **Tycho Brahe** had a **moose** that used to roam free during parties and drink large amounts of alcohol.

▶ English poet **Lord Byron** kept a **bear** at Cambridge University—because dogs were not allowed.

▶ **Michael Jackson's chimpanzee** Bubbles slept in a crib in the singer's room and even used his toilet.

▶ U.S. President **John Quincy Adams** had an **alligator**—a gift from the Marquis de Lafayette—which he used to keep in a bathroom in the White House.

▶ **Napoleon Bonaparte's wife Josephine** had an **orangutan** that was allowed to join her at the table for meals.

Tamarin monkeys

ANIMAL CANNIBALS

▶ The female Australian **redback spider** often devours the smaller male during mating.

▶ While still in the womb, **baby sand tiger sharks** develop teeth, which they use to eat their younger siblings. The mother has two uteruses and only one pup survives in each of them.

▶ A **Papuan python** was once found with a carpet python in its stomach.

▶ **Mormon crickets** walk up to 50 mi (80 km) in a migratory season in search of food—and if one cricket stops marching, the others will eat it.

▶ Less than 1 percent of **freshwater crocodile** eggs grow into adults—with cannibalism one of the major causes of mortality in young crocs.

▶ **Spotted hyena cubs** practice their hunting skills on their brothers and sisters, mauling them to death even as the adults try to separate them.

▶ **Female green anacondas** that can grow 16 ft (5 m) long and weigh 215 lb (97.5 kg) sometimes eat their smaller male partners in order to survive their seven months of pregnancy.

▶ A hungry **female praying mantis** often bites off the male's head while mating, but his sex drive is so strong that he can continue to mate even while being slowly eaten.

▶ Although they are usually devoted mothers, **tamarin monkeys** have also been seen biting through their babies' skulls and eating out the brain.

ANIMALS
THAT SAVED HUMANS

▶ When a rattlesnake attacked 11-year-old Sean Callahan in Texas, Leo, a poodle, leaped between the snake and the boy. Despite receiving six potentially deadly bites to the head, Leo survived, and saved Sean from the attack.

▶ Seeing surfer Adam Maguire attacked by a shark near Sydney, Australia, a school of dolphins thrashed around in the water, circled the shark repeatedly and chased it to stop it moving in for the kill.

▶ Schnautzie the kitten alerted Trudy Guy to a potentially fatal gas leak at her Montana home by repeatedly tapping her on the nose and sniffing the air.

▶ Priscilla, a pig owned by Victoria Herberta of Houston, Texas, rescued 11-year-old Anthony Melton from drowning in Somerville Lake by swimming to his aid, using her snout to keep his head above water until he could hold on to her collar, and then dragging him to the shore.

▶ After Noel Osborne shattered his hip in a fall at his farm in Benalla, Australia, his goat Mandy huddled by his side for five cold days and nights, not only keeping him warm but also allowing him to milk her for sustenance.

▶ As a cougar prepared to pounce on 11-year-old Austin Forman in British Columbia, Canada, the boy's golden retriever Angel jumped directly into the big cat's path and bore the brunt of the attack instead.

▶ When a three-year-old boy fell into the gorilla enclosure at Brookfield Zoo, Illinois, Binti Jua, a female gorilla, guarded the boy from the other gorillas, then cradled him in her arms while her own baby was on her back and carried him to an entrance where keepers were able to retrieve him.

Fangtooth fish

FREAKY FISH

▶ The **globefish can inflate itself** to three times its normal size by filling an air bladder inside its body.

▶ The **climbing perch** uses its spiny gills and its fins to help it **climb trees.**

▶ Some species of **shark never stop swimming** even when they are asleep—if they did, they would drown.

▶ The **archerfish** squirts water up a tube between its tongue and palate to fire at insects sitting on leaves up to 3 ft (1 m) above the surface. The shot **knocks the insect off the leaf** and into the water where the fish is waiting to eat it.

▶ The **copperband butterflyfish** has a **false eye** near its tail so that enemies will think its tail is its head and therefore snap at the wrong end of the fish.

▶ The **swordfish** has a **special heater in its brain and eye muscles**, which keeps its vision sharp enough to catch food in dark depths of 2,000 ft (600 m).

▶ The **fangtooth** has the **largest teeth of any ocean fish,** proportionate to body size—about one-tenth of its total body length, the equivalent of adult humans having 10-in-long (25-cm) teeth.

PORCUPINE ATTACK

▶ When bulldog Bella Mae got into a fight with a porcupine near her home in Norman, Oklahoma, she ended up with 500 quills stuck in her face, neck, legs, chest and paws—though miraculously they all missed her eyes. Porcupines hit victims with their tail, leaving some of their 30,000 barbed quills embedded in the skin. Veterinarians eventually managed to dig out the quills and set Bella Mae on the road to recovery.

BLIND FISH▶ Mexico's blind cave fish are actually born with eyes, but skin soon grows over them and they are rendered sightless. They find their way around by bouncing sound waves off nearby objects.

LONG JOURNEY▶ A calico cat named Willow that belonged to the Squires family of Boulder, Colorado, and went missing in 2006, was found five years later roaming the streets of Manhattan, more than 1,800 mi (2,900 km) away.

GUARDIAN ANGEL▶ One night, Patricia Peter from Camrose, Canada, was woken by her cat Monty repeatedly biting the fingers of her left hand—the hand she used to monitor her blood-sugar levels for her recently diagnosed diabetes. When she woke, Patricia felt sick, whereupon Monty ran and sat beside her diabetic testing kit. Taking her cue from the cat, Patricia discovered that, sure enough, her blood-sugar levels were dangerously low. Monty persisted in keeping Patricia awake until they returned to normal.

SPOT THE DIFFERENCE▶ Zoe, a Dalmatian dog at a farm in South Australia's Barossa Valley, adopted a look-alike lamb, which had a black-and-white spotty coat. The lamb was so confused by the resemblance that he even tried to suckle from the dog, who responded by allowing him to sleep inside her kennel.

DOG DOCTOR▶ Sharon Rawlinson from Nottinghamshire, England, discovered she had a cancerous tumor in her breast only because Penny, her Cavalier King Charles Spaniel, kept sniffing and pawing at it. The dog's bizarre behavior continued for several months until finally Penny stepped on her owner's chest, causing sufficient pain to trigger Sharon into investigating futher. Closer inspection revealed the lump.

ROUND TRIP▶ The northern wheatear, a tiny 1-oz (28-g) songbird, makes an epic, annual 18,600-mi (29,930-km) round-trip migratory journey between sub-Saharan Africa and the bird's Arctic breeding grounds.

WEALTHY KITTY▶ In 2011, Tommaso, a lucky black cat who was rescued from the streets of Rome, Italy, and given a home by an elderly widowed heiress, inherited nearly $13 million from her in the form of cash, shares and a property empire including homes in Rome and Milan and land in Calabria. Maria Assunta had become so enamored with her adopted pet that, two years before her death, she wrote out a will bequeathing her entire estate to Tommaso.

FIVE LEGS▶ Benny, a five-year-old dog owned by Leah Garcia of Texas, has five legs, with an extra limb located under his right front paw. He has three elbows and five paws but walks on only three legs, as his two right front legs are nonfunctional. Leah adopted Benny after he was abandoned at her workplace as a puppy.

YOUR UPLOADS

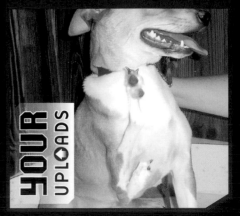

GROUNDHOG DAY▶ In the period around Independence Day 2012, groundhogs removed more than 75 flags from Civil War graves in Cedar Park Cemetery, Hudson, New York. Police identified the culprits after special cameras revealed a number of flags hidden down the animals' underground holes.

LAST STRAW▶ Crunchie, a male strawberry roan Welsh mountain pony, has to sleep on a bed of shredded waste paper at his stable in Cheshire, England, because he suffers from hay fever! He was diagnosed as being allergic to the dust in traditional straw beds after suffering a near-fatal asthma attack in 2009.

STOWAWAY CAT▶ A stowaway black-and-white cat survived with just minor burns after riding 200 mi (320 km) through Ohio, from Xenia to Cleveland, under the hood of a car.

TWO HEADS▶ A two-headed California kingsnake was born at a zoo in Yalta, Ukraine. The snake's two heads eat separately and react differently, so one head has to be isolated with a special spatula to prevent the second head from blocking its swallowing.

FREQUENT FLYER

▶ Oscar the dog has visited more than 30 countries in three years, flying twice the circumference of the Earth and taking in such landmarks as the Great Wall of China, the Eiffel Tower in France and the Golden Gate Bridge in California. As well as traveling by airplane, he has also been up in a hot-air balloon and taken a helicopter ride over the Grand Canyon. He travels with owner Joanne Lefson, who rescued him from a South African kennel in 2004—just a day before he was due to be put down.

On board an airplane

In India

At the Eiffel Tower

At the Golden Gate Bridge

Looking down on the Grand Canyon

KITTEN COMFORT ▶ A male long-tailed macaque monkey in Bali's Ubud Monkey Forest adopted a stray ginger kitten, nuzzling and grooming it and caring for it as a pet.

SHRINKING HORSES ▶ Early horses shrunk in size as the climate became warmer. When horses evolved around 56 million years ago, they were about the size of a small dog, but then became even smaller during a period of global warming. Then when the Earth's temperature subsequently cooled, horses dramatically increased in size.

RECORD TONGUE

▶ Although he is only a fraction of the size of a Saint Bernard or a Great Dane, Puggy the Pekingese has got the opposition licked. For he is the dog with the world's longest tongue—a whopping 4½ in (11.43 cm). It is so long that it almost reaches the ground. He lives in Fort Worth, Texas, with owner Becky Stanford after having been abandoned as a puppy—perhaps because his oversize tongue made him look expensive to feed!

BEAR NECESSITY ▶ Two-year-old Lieke Stenbreker helped save the life of a baby sloth at a zoo in Arnhem, the Netherlands, by giving it her favorite teddy bear. The sloth's mother was not producing enough milk, so zookeepers tried feeding the baby by hand. However, attempts failed because baby sloths need to cuddle while they feed. Once Lieke had donated her teddy, the tiny sloth was able to cuddle the toy while taking milk from a syringe.

MUD RESCUE ▶ Up to her waist in quicksand-like mud, Nicole Graham stayed by the side of her horse Astro for three hours, desperately keeping his head above water after the 1,100-lb (500-kg) animal had been swallowed up by the coastal mud near Geelong, Victoria, Australia. Astro was eventually pulled free by a farmer's tractor just minutes before the tide came in.

NUTS ABOUT MUSIC ▶ Sammy, a gray squirrel adopted by piano teacher Shirley Higton of Yorkshire, England, has started playing his own miniature toy piano. After developing an interest during the Higton children's piano lessons, Sammy has learned to press the keys with his paws.

TWO-HEADED BIRD ▶ Hearing a commotion in the backyard of her home in Northampton, Massachusetts, April Britt went out to investigate and found a baby Cardinal chick with two heads and three beaks.

TWO-LEGGED KITTEN ▶ A video showing a two-legged kitten playing with a ball and a feather went viral on YouTube. Found and adopted by artist Carrie Hawks from Pensacola, Florida, little Anakin was born without a pelvis and his two back legs. He manages to get around by pushing his front feet back, so that they are almost in the middle of his body, and using his tail for balance.

SEE MORE AMAZING EXTRA STUFF!

Simply download our APP & try out
ODD SCAN
Watch and listen to Puggy slurping ice cream!

ILLUMINATED WEBS ▶ Orb weaver spiders spin webs that reflect ultraviolet light, making them visible to birds that would otherwise fly through the webs and ruin them.

LIVING PROOF ▶ Until January 2012, when pictures were taken in remote mountain rain forests on the Burma–China border, the rare Myanmar snub-nosed monkey—*Rhinopithecus strykeri*—had never been photographed alive. Before that, the species had been described only from a dead specimen collected by a local hunter.

HEAVY PATIENT ▶ When a 1,050-lb (477-kg) polar bear at the Highland Wildlife Park in Inverness-shire, Scotland, developed a toothache, it needed 12 dentists, veterinarians and dental nurses to carry out a three-hour root canal operation. The dentist's chair for five-year-old Arktos consisted of a specially reinforced table made from scaffolding poles and planks.

GOAT TOWER ▶ The Fairview Farm in Paarl, South Africa, has a two-story tower built for the exclusive use of the farm's 750 goats. The tower was built with spiral staircases as goats can climb more efficiently when the object they are climbing is positioned at an angle.

ELEPHANT MAN ▶ Known locally as "the Elephant Man," Andy Swan of Sacramento, California, has collected more than 10,000 elephant-related items, including miniature models, plush toys, jewelry, album covers and clothing.

PIG RECRUIT▶ A 200-lb (91-kg) pig called Dominic has joined Avon Fire and Rescue Service in England to help firefighters learn how to handle escaped animals.

DOLPHIN CALLS▶ Although each dolphin has its own individual whistle, dolphins often communicate by mimicking the sounds of their closest companions. Research shows that the mammals' signature whistles copy only those dolphins they share strong social bonds with and want to be reunited with.

INK CLOUDS▶ Caribbean reef squid hide from predators by squirting out clouds of ink and then disguising themselves to look like the billows of ink that they just created.

SPEED KINGS▶ Houston Zoo, Texas, has borrowed a racetrack so that its pair of five-year-old cheetah brothers, Kito and Kiburi, can stretch their legs. Adult cheetahs need a 200-yd (182-m) straight run for healthy exercise, and with space limited at the zoo, they were able to approach their top speed of 65 mph (104 km/h) at the nearby Sam Houston Race Park.

SLAM DUNK▶ Eddie, a 16-year-old sea otter at The Oregon Zoo in Portland, Oregon, has started playing basketball in his pool to help ease his arthritis. To the delight of visitors, he picks up a plastic ball, swims with it toward a specially built, low-level hoop and then slam dunks it in the basket.

PURPLE COW▶ In January 2012, a black-and-white cow in Cacak, Serbia, gave birth to a calf with purple-tinted fur. The coloring is thought by doctors to be some kind of genetic mutation.

BEAVER COLLECTION▶ Since starting her collection in the 1970s, Betty Davis of Redlands, California, has acquired more than 600 different items of beaver-related memorabilia.

SEE MORE AMAZING EXTRA STUFF!!

Simply download our APP & try out ODDSCAN

Cool stuff... Ratatouille, the snowboarding opossum in action!

SNOWBOARDING OPOSSUM

▶ Ratatouille, a snowboarding opossum, has become such a celebrity at the Liberty Mountain Resort in Pennsylvania that he even has his own lift pass. Wearing his favorite green sweater, he regularly takes to the slopes atop a special mini snowboard that he steers with the help of his tail.

04

SPORTS ▶

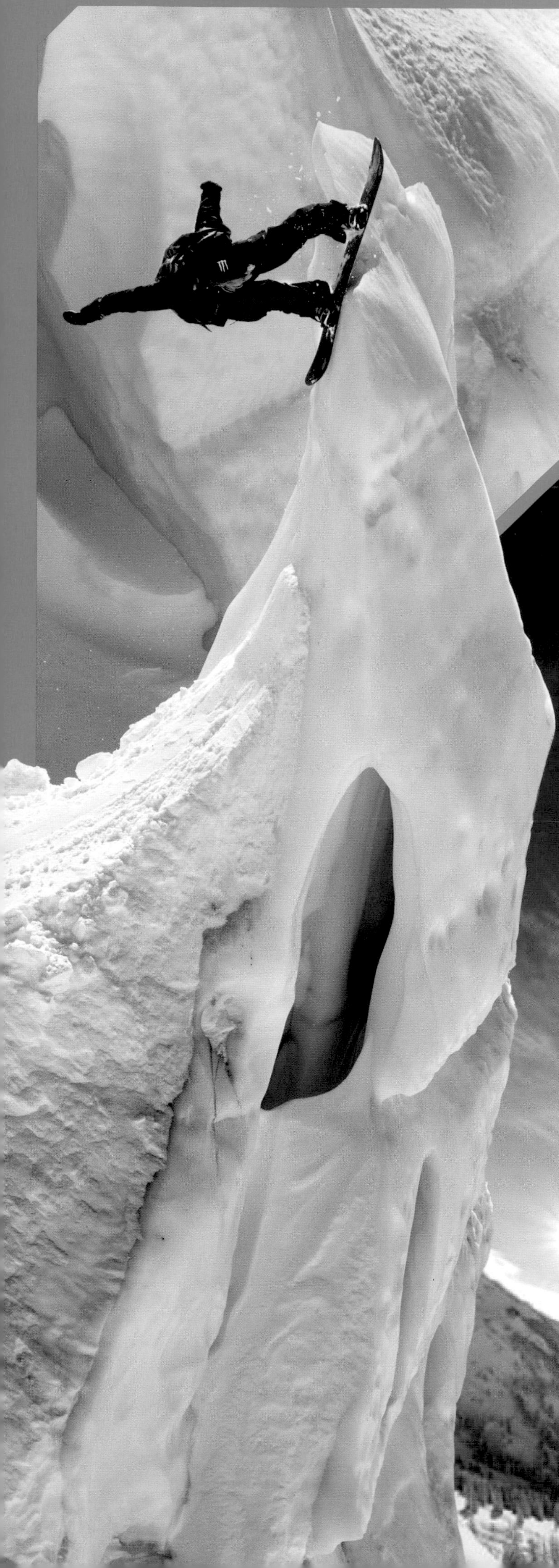

While snowboarding on an icy glacier in Methven, New Zealand, Canada's Mark Sollors teetered on top of a natural quarter-pipe with a massive 40-ft (12-m) drop just inches ahead of him. Glacier snowboarders must also keep watch for dangerous holes in the ice that blend into the scenery. This spot was so inaccessible that Sollors had to be dropped there by helicopter.

Jumping from heights of up to 600 ft (183 m) without parachutes, extreme skiers plummet through the air at around 125 mph (200 km/h), yet they usually escape serious injury because they land in thick, soft snow. The snow cushions their fall, and that is why free skiers make their jumps in locations that always have plenty of fresh powder—such as Utah's Alta Ski Resort, which has an incredible 500 in (1,270 cm) of snowfall a year.

Julian Carr launches into a trademark flip off a 60-ft-high (18-m) cliff at Utah's Alta Ski Resort.

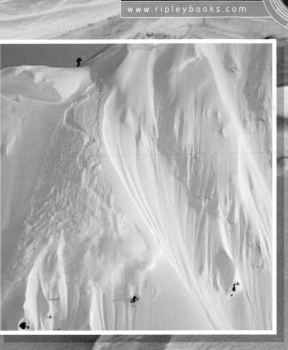

EXTREME SKIING

After months of planning, photographer Patrik Lindqvist captures Tomas Bergemalm's stunning leap from a 600-ft-high (183-m) French mountain cliff.

Extreme skiing takes this winter sport to the max, with competitors defying the ever-present threat of deadly avalanches to ski or leap hundreds of feet down vertical mountain cliffs. Not content with simply jumping into the snowy abyss below, many extreme skiers perform daring twists and flips in midair during their fall.

When the late Jamie Pierre made a 255-ft (78-m) free-fall cliff drop— known as a huck— in Wyoming in 2006, without a helmet or parachute, he landed headfirst, creating a 10-ft (3-m) crater in the deep snow. Amazingly, his only injury was a cut lip—from the shovel his friends were using to dig him out of the hole!

That record height was more than doubled in 2011 by Swedish free skier Tomas Bergemalm, who jumped off a 600-ft-high (183-m) mountain cliff face near Chamonix, France, and landed safely—an incredible leap of faith that required five months of training. Thirty-five-year-old Tomas, who once skied across Greenland in just 47 days and has competed in ski competitions all over the world from Slovenia to Canada, wanted to make one last spectacular jump before retiring from the sport to spend more time with his family.

To record the jump—twice the height of the Statue of Liberty from ground to torch—Tomas teamed up with professional sports photographer Patrik Lindqvist. The thrill was as great for the photographer as the skier. Patrik loves his job so much, he says: "If I have to climb mountains and sleep overnight in a tent at minus 20 degrees, then so be it."

Another extreme skier who risks life and limb in pursuit of the ultimate adrenalin rush is Julian Carr from Salt Lake City, Utah. He regularly launches himself off cliffs, and in 2006 set a new world record by performing a front flip off a 210-ft-high (64-m) cliff in Switzerland.

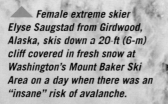

▲ Female extreme skier Elyse Saugstad from Girdwood, Alaska, skis down a 20-ft (6-m) cliff covered in fresh snow at Washington's Mount Baker Ski Area on a day when there was an "insane" risk of avalanche.

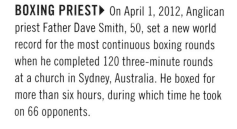

BELLY FLOP

▶ The 16th annual Colorado College Belly Flop Contest landed with a splash at Water World, outside Denver, in July 2012, with fearless floppers hurling themselves with little grace into the water from a height of 12 ft (3.7 m) in order to make the biggest wave. The pain is not without gain, however—as well as belly-flop glory, winners took home prizes and scholarships worth $5,000, with Paul Salcido taking the overall honors.

BACKWARD RUNNER ▶ Garret Doherty from Dublin, Ireland, can run a mile backward in fewer than seven minutes. The 33-year-old successfully defended his title at the 2012 U.K. Backwards Running Championships, finishing in 6 minutes 57 seconds—more than a minute ahead of his nearest rival.

CLEAR WATER ▶ Hong Kong held a swimming race across its Victoria Harbor in 2011—the first swimming race there for 33 years owing to long-standing concerns about pollution.

BOXING PRIEST ▶ On April 1, 2012, Anglican priest Father Dave Smith, 50, set a new world record for the most continuous boxing rounds when he completed 120 three-minute rounds at a church in Sydney, Australia. He boxed for more than six hours, during which time he took on 66 opponents.

NEW NAME ▶ In September 2011, Ron Artest, a professional basketball player with the Los Angeles Lakers, legally changed his name to Metta World Peace.

RARE CARDS ▶ Baseball fan Karl Kissner picked up a dirty old cardboard box in the attic of his late grandfather's house in Defiance, Ohio, and found it contained a collection of rare, 100-year-old baseball cards worth around $3 million. He discovered some 700 cards—all in excellent condition—and featuring greats such as Ty Cobb, Christy Mathewson and Connie Mack.

LONG SHOT ▶ In 2010, 14-year-old archer Zak Crawford, a Robin Hood fan from Northamptonshire, England, fired an arrow nearly 1,640 ft (500 m)—the length of five soccer pitches. His feat beat the previous world record by an incredible 492 ft (150 m).

HAND CLIMB ▶ In June 2012, Spencer West of Toronto, Canada, climbed the 19,308-ft-high (5,885-m) Mount Kilimanjaro in Kenya at the age of 31—on his hands. Both of his legs were amputated when he was five, but Spencer still managed to climb Africa's highest peak by propelling his torso forward, one hand after another, up the mountain for seven days.

LOSING RUN ▶ Toronto Blue Jays' pitcher Joseph "Jo-Jo" Reyes started 28 consecutive games without a single win—from June 13, 2008 until May 30, 2011.

SMURF SUPPORT

▶ Fans of England's Hartlepool United soccer team found a bizarre way to show their dedication to the cause when they traveled to the last game of the 2011–2012 season dressed as Smurfs. Surreal photographs of hundreds of blue-faced supporters making the 230-mi (370-km) trip to London for the game against Charlton Athletic spread worldwide. Dressing up for the last day of the season is a 25-year tradition at the club—unfortunately the Smurf invasion of London was not enough to secure a win for the team.

SAME NAME▶ A soccer match took place in the town of Bungay in Suffolk, England, in May 2012 where all 22 players, the referee, the linesmen and the reserves had the surname Bungay. In addition to players who had come from the U.K., the U.S.A. and Australia, the mascot was eight-year-old Carla Bungay and the doctor on hand to treat injuries was Dr. Elizabeth Bungay.

DOUBLE HIT▶ During a baseball game between the New York Yankees and the Colorado Rockies on June 25, 2011, Rockies' shortstop Troy Tulowitzki managed to hit a ball twice with a single swing of his bat.

MARATHON DRIBBLE▶ Mark Ott of Jackson, Michigan, ran the 26-mile 2010 Martian Marathon in Dearborn in 3 hours 23 minutes 42 seconds while dribbling a basketball.

ETHNIC GAMES▶ A demonstration of traditional ethnic Yao games at Nanning, China, included tossing a ball of fire into an opponent's basket, running across burning logs to hurl fruit at a 16-ft (5-m) target, and climbing a mountain of knives, where barefoot competitors scale a 23-ft-high (7-m) pole embedded with 36 razor-sharp blades.

HORSEY HEROINE▶ Australian racehorse Black Caviar is so popular that a major Aussie Rules football match was rescheduled to avoid clashing with one of her races. When she first raced abroad, at Royal Ascot, England, in June 2012, thousands of people watched her record her 22nd straight win on a giant TV screen in Melbourne's Federation Square, even though it was nearly one o'clock in the morning.

▶ IN 1946, AL COUTURE BEAT RALPH WALTON IN A BOXING MATCH IN 10.5 SECONDS— INCLUDING THE COUNT! ◀

LONGEST GAME▶ At O'Fallon, Missouri, in July 2012, 50 baseball players took part in a game that lasted 60 hours 11 minutes 32 seconds—the world's longest. In all, 169 innings were played and 451 runs scored over three afternoons with temperatures topping 100°F (38°C).

FASTEST SKATEBOARDER▶ On June 18, 2012, Mischo Erban from Vernon, Canada, set a new world record for the fastest skateboard speed from a standing position. He clocked 80.74 mph (129.9 km/h) on a downhill run in Quebec.

CRACK CLIMBERS

▶ A pair of determined daredevils from the U.K. traveled to Utah to become the first climbers ever to complete an infamous sheer-rock ascent. Tom Randall and Pete Whittaker squeezed themselves up Century Crack, a terrifying 120-ft (37-m) rock fissure in the Canyonlands National Park, by sliding their hands, feet and limbs into narrow crevices only inches wide and hauling their bodies upward. The climb is so challenging that nobody had ever completed it before. The width of the crack means that regular climbing techniques are of little use, and the men had to complete most of the ascent by hanging upside down with their feet jammed above their heads. Randall and Whittaker did not take the Century Crack lightly, undergoing two years of intensive training that involved spending hours hanging from a replica of the crack in the cellar of Randall's house!

ANT ALERT ▶ A September 2011 high school football game between Hunter-Kinard-Tyler and Calhoun County at Neeses, South Carolina, was postponed because of fire ants. The referee found up to 20 large and active fire ant mounds on the field and despite attempts to dig them up and pour salt on them, the game had to be called off.

TRIPLE TIE ▶ Three greyhounds in a race in Essex, England, on January 19, 2011, made history by crossing the finish line in a triple dead heat, beating odds of many millions to one. Even the track's photo-finish technology was unable to separate them, and what made the three-way tie all the more remarkable was that the dogs were running over the maximum distance of 1,011 yd (925 m).

SURE SHOT ▶ Shooter Kimberley Rhode won the women's skeet gold medal at the London 2012 Summer Olympics to become the first U.S. competitor to win an individual shooting medal in five consecutive Olympics. She finished with 99 points, missing only one of the 100 clay targets she shot at all day.

POLE POSITION ▶ In the crazy Japanese sport of Bo-Taoshi, two teams of 75 players compete—one team defending a tall wooden pole while the other team tries to knock it down. By pulling, punching, grabbing and kicking their opponents, the attackers have about 2½ minutes to lower the defending team's upright pole to an angle of 30 degrees or less. If they fail to do so, the defending team wins.

NO FEET ▶ Eleven-year-old Brazilian schoolboy Gabriel Muniz was invited to train with Spanish soccer giants Barcelona—even though he has no feet. Despite being born without feet, he is one of the best players at his school and impressed Barcelona chiefs when they saw his incredible ball skills on TV.

BROKEN LEG ▶ U.S. 4 x 400 meters relay runner Manteo Mitchell ran half of his race at the 2012 London Summer Olympics with a broken leg! He felt a bone snap partway through running the first leg of the relay, but he kept sprinting through the last 200 meters because he didn't want to let his team-mates down. Despite his injury, he still ran the 400 meters in 46.1 seconds and helped the U.S.A. to finish as joint-fastest qualifiers.

COW RACE

▶ At the annual Pacu Jawi Cow Race in West Sumatra, Indonesia, jockeys ride pairs of cows along a muddy course while desperately hanging on to their mounts by their tails. To make the cows go faster, the jockeys bite their tails. The event, which dates back hundreds of years, was originally contested by farmers for relaxation at the start of the rice-harvesting season.

GENTLE OGRE

DRAG RACER ▶ Belle Wheeler from Northamptonshire, England, passed her drag-racing driving test becoming the world's youngest drag car racer—just one day after her eighth birthday. She has gone on to compete against drivers more than twice her age in her specially modified dragster, which can rocket from 0 to 50 mph (80 km/h) in just 12 seconds.

SUPER GIRL ▶ When she won the women's 400 meters individual medley at the 2012 Olympics, 16-year-old Chinese swimmer Ye Shiwen swam the last 50 meters faster than American Ryan Lochte covered the same distance in the corresponding men's race—the first time a woman had ever beaten a man's time at that stage of the race. Her total time of 4 minutes 28.23 seconds was so fast it would have won the men's gold medal at the Olympics in 1964, 1968 and 1972.

▲ Maurice "The Angel" Tillet—seen here waving his official papers—became a citizen of the United States in 1947.

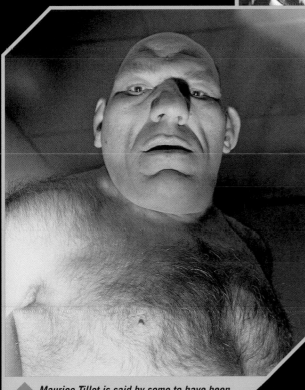

▲ Maurice Tillet is said by some to have been the inspiration behind the movie character Shrek.

▶ Maurice Tillet, a Russian-born French professional wrestler of the 1940s, was such a beautiful child that he was nicknamed "The Angel"—but when he was 17 he noticed a mysterious swelling in his feet, hands and head and was diagnosed with acromegaly, a pituitary disorder that results in the abnormal growth of these areas.

Maurice could speak several languages and had wanted to become a lawyer, but his disfigurement prevented him doing so and instead he took up wrestling in the U.S.A. Known as "The French Angel," he was also dubbed "the freak ogre of the ring." His proportions—he weighed 280 lb (127 kg) and had huge hands and an oversized head but was a modest 5 ft 8½ in (1.74 m) tall—made him difficult to wrestle against and for many years he was billed as "unstoppable." A huge box office draw, Maurice was twice recognized as world heavyweight champion by the American Wrestling Association. He died in 1954, aged 50, a year after his last professional fight.

OLYMPIC YARN

▶ An anonymous "yarnbomber" wrapped the town pier at Saltburn in North Yorkshire, England, with a 150-ft-long (46-m) scarf depicting woolen athletes competing in a variety of Olympic events, including synchronized swimming, rowing, weightlifting and cycling.

FALL GUYS

▶ *Daredevil kayakers Steve Fisher and Dale Jardine from South Africa and Sam Drevo of the U.S.A. paddled up to the very lip of the world's largest waterfall, the Victoria Falls, knowing that one slip would send them plunging more than 350 ft (106 m) to their death—no person has ever survived a fall into the raging torrents below. Also braving the crocodiles and hippos that lurk in the calmer waters at the top of the mile-wide falls between Zambia and Zimbabwe, they stood on one of the small rocky outcrops that appear at the edge of the falls in the dry season and peered over for the view of a lifetime.*

SOCCER BARBIE

▶ For her diploma in visual arts at Strasbourg, France, student Chloë Ruchon designed "Barbie Foot," a Barbie-themed table soccer game, where, instead of soccer players, two teams of fashion-conscious Barbie dolls spin their legs at the ball. The limited edition game went on sale in Paris for $12,000.

VERTICAL SPRINT▶

Attached to a safety rope, Belgian athlete Mark Sluszny completed a vertical run down the side of a 334-ft-high (102-m) building in Brussels in just 15.5 seconds.

MOTH MENACE▶ St. Louis Cardinals baseball player Matt Holliday exited a game against the L.A. Dodgers on August 22, 2011, in the eighth inning because he had a moth in his ear. Trainers had to pull the moth out using tweezers.

ACCIDENT PRONE▶ Since 1995, British racehorse jockey Robert "Choc" Thornton has suffered more than 360 falls and 40 serious injuries, including breaking all 24 ribs in his body, his right collarbone six times and his left collarbone three times. He has also broken and lost several teeth.

SEVEN UP▶ A bet placed on 2012 Wimbledon men's singles tennis champion Roger Federer nine years earlier earned £100,000 ($160,000) for the charity Oxfam. In 2003, Nick Newlife from Oxfordshire, England, wagered £1,520 at odds of 66 to 1 that the Swiss player would win seven Wimbledon titles by 2019, a feat he achieved by defeating Scotland's Andy Murray seven years ahead of the expiry date. Mr. Newlife had died in 2009 but had left the betting slip to Oxfam in his will.

PILLOW FIGHT

▶ Hundreds of combatants attacked each other with pillows during a half-hour battle in Trafalgar Square, London, England, on April 7, 2012. As part of the Seventh Annual Pillow Fight Day, similar mass scuffles took place in more than 100 cities across the world, including Los Angeles, Sydney, Madrid, Sao Paulo and Shanghai.

CHESS PIECE ▶ The Chess Club and Scholastic Center of St. Louis, Missouri, unveiled a king chess piece that was 14½ ft (4.4 m) tall and 6 ft (1.8 m) wide at the base—45 times larger than a standard chess piece.

BALLOON RUN ▶ Rob Ginnivan ran a half marathon while in a hot-air balloon high in the sky above Canberra, Australia. He ran the 13 mi (21 km) on a treadmill powered by a small generator inside the basket and finished in 2 hours 18 minutes.

QUICK KICKER ▶ Kickboxer Raul Meza, 33, of Sioux Falls, South Dakota, completed 335 martial arts kicks in a minute with one leg in November 2011. He once performed more than 18,000 kicks in a single eight-week period.

BABE AUCTION ▶ A New York Yankees jersey worn by Babe Ruth around 1920 sold for $4.42 million at an auction in California in 2012. At the same auction, his 1934 cap sold for $537,278 and one of his 1920s bats went for $591,007.

MUD RUN ▶

▶ *Covered from head to toe in thick muck, a bearded athlete battles his way through the 2012 Bluegrass Mud Run, staged over a grueling 3-mi (5-km) course in Lexington, Kentucky. The mud is more than waist-deep in places and to make it even tougher, the competitors also have to crawl through the swamp beneath low obstacles.*

SEE MORE AMAZING EXTRA STUFF!

HOT WHEELS▶ In an incredible life-sized Hot Wheels stunt, Team Hot Wheels drivers Greg Tracy and Tanner Foust raced two vehicles through a six-story double vertical loop at the 2012 X Games in Los Angeles, California, in June 2012. At speeds of more than 50 mph (80 km/h), they defied gravity and felt about 7Gs of g-force—the same as jet pilots experience in flight. During the stunt Foust had to make grunting noises to stop himself from blacking out.

WRONG COUNTRY▶ More than 400 Spanish soccer fans heading to the 2012 Europa League final landed in the wrong country after mixing up the names of two cities. The confused Athletic Bilbao supporters ended up in Budapest, Hungary—hundreds of miles away from the match in Bucharest, Romania.

BALL CATCHER▶ Zack Hample of New York City has caught more than 6,000 home-run and foul baseballs from Major League baseball games in over 50 different stadiums. In July 2012, he even caught a baseball dropped from a helicopter hovering 762 ft (232 m) above LeLacheur Park in Lowell, Massachusetts.

SKI CRAZY▶ Rainer Hertrich, a German-born snowcat operator at Copper Mountain, Colorado, skied every single day for 2,993 straight days—that's more than eight years. In that time he covered 98 million vertical ft (30 million m). He finally stopped on January 10, 2012, after he was diagnosed with a dangerously irregular heartbeat.

SOLITARY SQUID▶ A total of 74 competitors took part in the 2012 All England Squid Championship in Brighton, England, but at the end of five hours they had managed to catch only one squid between them—and that was just 0.4 in (1 cm) long. Nevertheless, it was enough for Davide Thambithurai to win the title for the second year running.

KENYAN MONOPOLY▶ Since 1968, a Kenyan athlete has won the men's 3,000-meter steeplechase every time the country has competed in the Olympics. At the London 2012 summer Olympics, Kenya won gold for the eighth time in a row and has now won 10 of the last 12 steeplechases, missing out only in 1976 and 1980 when the nation boycotted the Games.

▶ THERE CAN BE UP TO 500 DIMPLES ON A REGULATION GOLF BALL. ◀

PIGEON TRIANGLE▶ A small area of England has been dubbed the Bermuda Triangle of pigeon racing after hundreds of birds mysteriously vanished during races in 2012. In one event, only 13 out of 232 birds released in Thirsk, North Yorkshire, made it back to their homes in Scotland.

LONG STRIDES▶ It took Jamaica's Usain Bolt just 41 strides to break the Olympic men's 100-meters record with a time of just 9.63 seconds at the 2012 Olympic Games. Bolt's fellow countryman and Olympic silver medalist Yohan Blake took 46 strides to run the same distance.

YOUNGEST RACER▶ Stock car driver Braden DuBois from Indian River, Michigan, raced his Chevrolet four-cylinder car at Onaway Speedway for a full season at age nine, making him the world's youngest ever stock car racer.

TRICK SHOT▶ New York City chef Antony Riniti successfully performed a trick shot with 75 pool balls racked in triangles 25 stories high, making a tower more than 5 ft (1.5 m) tall. He carried out the trick by hitting the cue ball to pocket one of the balls at the base of the tower without the structure falling down.

TWIN RUNNERS▶ Identical twins Kevin and Jonathan Borlee of Belgium both reached the men's 400-meter final at the 2012 Olympics. Although split by the width of the track, they finished fifth and sixth respectively, separated by just 0.02 seconds.

NO REST▶ Seventeen-year-old U.S. swimmer Missy Franklin won gold in the women's 100-meters backstroke at the 2012 London Olympics less than 20 minutes after swimming in the 200-meters freestyle semi-final and qualifying for the final.

BULGING BICEPS

▶ New York City bodybuilder Gregg Valentino has biceps that measure a gigantic 28 in (71 cm) in circumference, making his arms larger than some people's waists. A bodybuilder since the age of 14, Gregg uses his mighty muscles to bicep-curl 300 lb (136 kg) and bench-press 550 lb (250 kg).

FIELD GOALS▶ On October 9, 2011, Craig Pinto of Mineola, New York State, kicked a record 1,000 regulation 40-yard (36.5-m) American Football field goals in 24 hours.

SAMOAN JOY▶ American Samoa were the joint-lowest-ranked national soccer team in the world when they won their first-ever international match, beating Tonga 2–1 in a World Cup qualifier in November 2011. With a population of just 55,000, the U.S. protectorate had lost every competitive game they had played in more than 17 years, including a 31–0 mauling by Australia in 2001.

HOCKEY MARATHON▶ In May 2012, a hockey game at Chestermere, Alberta, Canada, lasted an epic 246 hours—that's more than ten days—making it the longest hockey game ever.

MEN BANNED▶ When fans of teams from the Turkish Soccer Association get excessively rowdy, adult men are temporarily banned and only women and children are permitted to attend the games.

KITEBOARDING RECORD▶ Setting off from Whale Harbor, Islamorada, Florida, in February 2012, Lithuanian-born Rimas Kinka kiteboarded an astonishing distance of 401 mi (645 km) in just 24 hours.

MAKESHIFT SHOES▶ When he was younger, Kenyan athlete David Rudisha, who won gold at the 2012 Olympics when he ran the fastest-ever 800 meters, would cut up used car tires to serve as makeshift running shoes.

KING KAYAK

▶ At a little over 407 ft (124 m) long, this enormous kayak can seat 100 people! Built to mark the centenary of outdoor retailer L.L. Bean, the king-sized craft—made up of 100 standard kayaks—took its maiden voyage at Freeport, Maine, in June 2012.

PLAYING IN THE LAKE▶ In the drought-hit area around Imotski, Croatia, in November 2011, two local soccer teams were able to play on the dry bed of a lake that normally contains millions of gallons of reservoir water. The makeshift soccer field was carved out of the dust at Modro Jezero (The Blue Lake), which is usually as much as 500 ft (150 m) underwater.

FIRST 1080▶ At Tehachapi, California, on March 30, 2012, 12-year-old Tom Schaar from Malibu nailed the first-ever 1,080-degree skateboard turn by making three complete revolutions in midair before landing. Tom, who has been skateboarding since the age of four, achieved the historic feat on the 70-ft-tall (21.3-m) MegaRamp, which launches skaters up to 15 ft (4.5 m) in the air.

LUCKY SOCKS▶ At the London 2012 Olympics, veteran Great Britain rower Greg Searle wore the same pair of lucky socks that he had worn when winning gold at the 1992 Barcelona Olympics, making the socks older than four of his 2012 team-mates!

FAMILY PUNISHMENT▶ For touching a gate in the qualifying round of the men's kayak competition at the 2012 London Olympics, New Zealand's Mike Dawson was handed a two-second penalty by his mother, Kay, who was a judge at the Games.

BLIND ARCHER▶ South Korean archer Im Dong-hyun is a world record holder in his sport despite being legally blind, with only ten percent vision in his left eye and 20 percent in his right eye. When he looks at the targets, he sees colors with blurred lines between them.

FOOD BALL▶ Yubi lapki, an ancient seven-a-side rugby-like game played in Manipur, India, uses a coconut as a ball. Before the start of the game, the players rub their bodies with mustard oil and water so that they are difficult to tackle.

SENIOR TRIATHLETE▶ In June 2012, Arthur Gilbert of Somerset, England, completed his 41st triathlon—at age 91. The grandfather did a 550-yd (500-m) swim, followed by a 12½-mi (20-km) bicycle ride and a 3-mi (5-km) run, finishing in 2 hours 47 minutes 22 seconds. His rigorous training regime includes going to the gym twice a week, cycling 25 mi (40 km) every Sunday and swimming 50 lengths of his local pool every morning.

HIGH HUMP

▶ Renowned for their speed, strength and courage, members of the Zaranique tribe in Yemen are the world's only professional camel jumpers. From a running start, jumpers attempt to clear as many camels as possible in a single leap. This champion, Bhaydar Muhammed Kubaisi, is sailing over three animals. Dating back 2,000 years, the sport is unique to the Tehama region of the country where tribesmen train all year round for competitions.

GOAL-KICKING ROBOT▶ A robot called Robo Dan proved itself as accomplished a goal-kicker as former New Zealand international rugby star Andrew Mehrtens, who scored 967 career points for the All Blacks between 1995 and 2004. The robot, built by Massey University Albany, matched Mehrtens' score of 11 successful kicks out of 12 in a special challenge.

BULL CHAMP▶ In more than two years, no U.S. rodeo rider managed to ride Bushwacker the bull for eight seconds—the minimum amount of time required to earn any points. During that period, the average time that professional riders managed to stay on the 1,600-lb (726-kg) beast was just 3.06 seconds.

CAPTAIN CANADA▶ In 2012, 65-year-old Canadian show-jumper Ian Millar—nicknamed Captain Canada—became the first person to compete in ten Olympics, having participated in the equestrian competition at every Games since 1972, except for the 1980 Moscow Olympics that Canada boycotted.

PLAIN NUTS▶ The beach volleyball competition at the 2012 Summer Olympics was disrupted because squirrels kept burying nuts and acorns on the sandy practice courts at London's St. James's Park.

▶ *French Jet Ski champion Franky Zapata demonstrates his invention, the Flyboard, a motorized device that allows him to fly up to 50 ft (15 m) in the air like Superman or to dive head first through the water like a dolphin. It is powered by a Jet Ski motor that generates a water jet connected via a long hose to a pair of jet boots and handheld stabilizers.*

DOLPHIN JETPACK

BODY ▶

GIRAFFE WOMEN

Kayan women of Burma are known as "Giraffe Women" because the custom of placing heavy brass rings around the neck makes it appear up to 15 in (38 cm) long—some five times the length of the average woman's neck.

This is achieved by the rings pushing down the collarbone to give the effect of an elongated neck. They are put around girls' necks from the age of five and are then added at regular intervals until adulthood. An adult may have as many as 25, weighing a total of more than 20 lb (9 kg). Long necks are said to be an indication of beauty for the Kayan and the metal adornments a sign of wealth.

▶ As well as wearing them around the neck, some Kayan women also have brass rings coiled around their legs and ankles.

▲ This Kayan woman has more than 20 brass coils placed around her neck to elongate it.

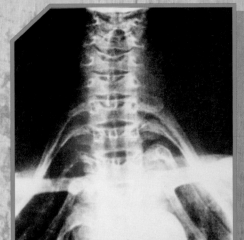

▲ This X-ray of a Kayan woman's neck shows how the practice earns the women the nickname "Giraffe Women."

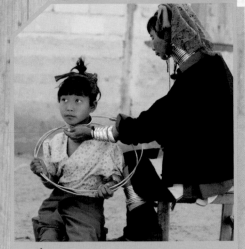

▲ Kayan girls are given their first coils when they are only five years old. The rings are added regularly as the girls grow up.

FISH SUPPER

▶ *A man suffering from the chronic skin disease psoriasis relaxes in a hot spa pool in Kangal, Turkey, while Garra rufa obtusas—or "doctor fish"—swim around his face and body nibbling away the diseased skin. Fortunately, the fish eat only the dead areas of flesh, leaving the healthy skin to grow, while the mineral-rich spa water helps the lesions to heal after the fish have had their lunch.*

Seventy-two-year-old farmer Chandra Bahadur Dangi from Nepal was named the world's shortest living man in February 2012 after his height was measured at just 21½ in (54.6 cm). Three of his brothers are less than 4 ft (1.2 m) tall, but his two sisters and his other two brothers are normal size.

SPEARED ALIVE ▶ Florida teenager Yasser Lopez survived after accidentally being shot through the head with a speargun. Miraculously, the 3-ft (0.9-m) spear went straight through his skull, narrowly missing the 16-year-old's right eye and every major blood vessel in his brain. Doctors at the Miami hospital had to saw off part of the spear so that he could fit into the scanner for an X-ray.

In August 2011, teachers at Totara North School in Northland, New Zealand, discovered that a skeleton model they had long assumed to be made of plastic was actually made of real human bone.

COOL HEADS ▶
When fire broke out on board their boat, forcing them to jump into Australia's Botany Bay, Scott Smiles, Rick Matthews and their respective 11-year-old sons Riley and Ryan saved themselves from drowning by clinging for 45 minutes to an ice box used to store their fishing equipment.

On June 14, 2012, in a ten-hour operation, doctors in Mexico City removed from a two-year-old boy a 33-lb (15-kg) benign tumor that weighed more than his body. Jesus Rodriguez weighed just 26 lb (12 kg), but the tumor grew to cover the entire right side of his body, from his armpit to his hip.

FALSE EYE ▶ The world's earliest prosthetic eye has been found by archeologists in Iran on a woman who lived 5,000 years ago. The false eyeball was made of a lightweight material that was a mix of natural tar and animal fat. It had a diameter of 1 in (2.5 cm) and a hole had been drilled on either side so that the eye could be held in place with thread.

Bolton Wanderers soccer player Fabrice Muamba was effectively dead for 78 minutes after collapsing during an FA Cup match at Tottenham on March 17, 2012. It took 15 defibrillator shocks to get his heart beating again, but just two weeks later he was sitting up in his hospital bed and smiling.

DIFFERENT COUNTRIES ▶
On July 1, 2012, Donna Keenan gave birth to twins less than two hours apart in two different countries. She went into labor at her home in Northumberland, England, and didn't have time to get out of the house and to hospital before her son Dylan was born; but then she was driven 40 mi (64 km) by ambulance to hospital in Melrose, Scotland, to give birth to daughter Hannah.

100 trillion good bacteria live in or on the human body, and weigh a total of up to 5 lb (2.3 kg) in an adult person.

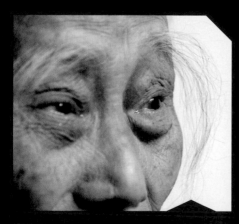

HAIR-RAISING

▶ Believe It or Not! 90-year-old Luo Zhicheng of Chengdu, China, has eyebrow hairs that measure more than 4 in (10 cm) long!

HUMAN CHECKERBOARD

▶ *Matt Gone from Portland, Oregon, has a staggering 98 percent of his body covered in tattoos, including his genitals and tongue, much of it in a distinctive black-and-white checkerboard design. He has even injected ink into the whites of his eyes, giving him one green eye and one blue. The only parts of his body that are not tattooed are the palms of his hands and the soles of his feet, and in some places there are seven layers of ink tattooed into his skin. He says: "I love the mathematical pattern of the checkerboard. Its symmetry makes up for my asymmetry, but the session to do the checkerboard hurt so much I was sick." Over a 17-year period, the Human Checkerboard, as he is known, has spent $65,000 on tattoos, with 80 different artists working on his body. He says his body feels ten degrees hotter than most other people's because tattooed bodies don't sweat as much and the ink attracts the sun's heat.*

IRON STOMACH▶ During his 60-year career as an iron-stomached stuntman, Branko Crnogorac from Apatin, Serbia, ate 25,000 lightbulbs, 12,000 forks, 2,000 spoons, 2,600 plates and nearly 6,000 vinyl LP records. He was finally forced to retire at age 80 after choking on a pedal when friends wagered him that he could not eat his entire bicycle within three days. He underwent emergency surgery, and when doctors opencd up his stomach they found 4 lb 6 oz (2 kg) of assorted metal, including two gold rings.

A 30-year-old woman from Atlanta, Georgia, accidentally swallowed a butter knife while laughing. The woman had put the knife near the back of her throat to impress her friends but sudden laughter caused it to slide down and lodge in her esophagus. She was rushed to a hospital where the knife was removed.

COVERED IN NAILS▶ Shanyna Isom from Memphis, Tennessee, suffers from a mystery illness, which causes the skin follicles on her body to produce human fingernails instead of hair. Her body first became covered in the hard scabs in 2009 after she appeared to suffer an allergic reaction to an asthma treatment. She lost all the hair on her head, and fingernails replaced the hair on her body, growing for a while and then falling off before growing all over again.

LONGEST BEARD

▶ Zach T. Wilcox from Carson City, Nevada, grew his beard for 41 years so that by 1922 it was 12 ft 9 in (3.9 m) long—making it a contender for the world's longest beard. He brushed and combed it regularly but it was so long that he had to carry it while walking.

LIVE GRENADE▶ When Karla Flores of Culiacán, Mexico, was shot by a grenade launcher, the grenade was embedded in her face but didn't explode. Aware that the deadly device could go off at any minute and kill everyone within 30 ft (9 m), doctors at Culiacán General Hospital took the patient to an open field and operated on her there, removing the live grenade from her face before it had a chance to explode.

OVERSIZED TONGUE▶ Wang Youping of Shaanxi, China, has been unable to close his mouth for more than 21 years owing to his massive tongue, which is 9½ in (24 cm) long, 4 in (10 cm) wide and 7 in (18 cm) thick. His tongue and face began to swell when he was six, and the enormous muscle has since forced his teeth to be squeezed horizontally, causing severe facial deformity.

TOUCHY-FEELY▶ Scientists at the University of Southern California have created a robot "skin" that has a superior sense of touch to humans. Fitted with special sensors and software, the robot hand is able to distinguish between 117 everyday materials solely by touch—a better performance than most humans would achieve.

NAIL IN BRAIN▶ Dante Autullo of Chicago, Illinois, accidentally shot a nail into the center of his brain, and didn't notice it until the next day. He thought he had merely cut himself with a nail gun while building a shed—until doctors showed him an X-ray of a 3¼-in-long (8.3-cm) nail lodged in the middle of his brain. The nail had come within a fraction of the part of the brain that controls movement. While being rushed to another hospital for surgery to remove the nail, Autullo still managed to post a picture of the X-ray on his Facebook page.

HORROR SHOW▶ Danielle Martin from Kent, England, quit university to join the Circus of Horrors, where she hammers nails into her nose, jumps on shards of broken glass, swallows razor blades, squeezes her 5-ft-6-in (1.67-m) frame into a 2-ft (0.6-m) jar and climbs a ladder barefoot with razor-sharp samurai swords as rungs.

YOUR UPLOADS

NO KNUCKLE

▶ Ripley's received this picture from Californian Isaac Burrier who is missing the knuckle on the ring finger of his left hand. The gap is visible only when he puts his hand into a fist and, he says, "the missing knuckle just looks like a 'trough' between my knuckle of my pinky finger and my knuckle of my middle finger."

BENCH BALANCE▶ Li Hongxiao balanced 23 wooden benches on his teeth for 11 seconds in Chongqing, China. Each bench was 3 ft 3 in (1 m) long and in total they weighed nearly 154 lb (70 kg).

BLACK TONGUE▶ When an excess of mouth bacteria prevents the tiny papillae nodules on a person's tongue from shedding properly and causes them to grow long—sometimes to 15 times their normal length—the result is an unsightly but harmless condition called black hairy tongue.

PLASTIC FORK▶ Lee Gardner from South Yorkshire, England, had a 9-in-long (23-cm) plastic fork stuck in his stomach for ten years. It was only when he started vomiting and experiencing stomach cramps that he remembered accidentally swallowing the fork a decade earlier.

KILLER DISEASE▶ Now in his seventies, British physicist Stephen Hawking has survived 50 years with a motor neurone disease that kills 90 percent of sufferers in less than a decade.

EYE WORM▶ Doctors in Mumbai, India, removed a 5-in-long (12.5-cm) live worm from the right eye of 75-year-old P.K. Krishnamurthy after he had complained of itching and irritation. The parasitic worm, which remained alive for 30 minutes following the surgery, may have entered the patient's bloodstream through a cut in his foot and made its way up to his eye.

▶This is not a trick photo! Australian performer Mr. Tetanus wears a homemade 0.4-in-thick (1-cm) metal spike through a hole above his ankle—and he uses the piercing to swing bowling balls and other heavy weights. He has had the extreme body modification, located just behind the Achilles tendon, for over 12 years. When the spike is taken out, the exterior hole closes up in a minute, and the inside begins to heal itself within half an hour.

CRYING SHAME▶ The average man cries 16 times a year—most commonly at weddings—whereas the average woman cries up to 64 times annually. Men usually cry for a maximum of two minutes at a time, but a woman's sobbing session often lasts for six minutes.

SPIKED ANKLE

MAN WITH TWO MOUTHS

Otto Tolpefer was born with two mouths—one that worked normally, and an extra mouth, through which he could neither speak nor eat, located just below his chin. When speaking, he used the top mouth and closed the second one, which was fitted with brass lips, with his fingers. "The Man with Two Mouths," as he was billed, appeared as an attraction at New York's Bowery in the 1880s, usually sitting on a platform, drinking water with one mouth while simultaneously smoking a cigarette or playing a musical instrument with the other. A *New York Times* reporter who saw Tolpefer's act wrote that "the leak in his tracheal bellows gives his voice a strange and unreal whispering sound like that of a sexton at a funeral... Otto is not a pleasant object to gaze at excessively." It was said that a two-headed cow, which shared the bill with Tolpefer, felt much better about its predicament following his arrival.

TITANIUM JAWBONE▶ Doctors in the Netherlands used a 3-D printer to custom-build a titanium jawbone, complete with screw-in teeth, for an 83-year-old woman patient. The implant, which was made from thousands of thin layers of laser-melted titanium powder, was then fitted to the face of the patient, who had developed a chronic bone infection.

DAILY HICCUPS▶ Lisa Doherty from Lincoln, England, has had hiccups for over five years, sometimes hiccupping 100 times a day. She has hiccupped through the births of two daughters and has even started hiccupping in her sleep.

GATOR GRAB▶ Attacked by an 11-ft-long (3.4-m) alligator on the Caloosahatchee River in Florida, 17-year-old Kaleb Langdale managed to save his own life by letting the reptile have his right arm. When the gator performed a sinister death roll, Kaleb offered up his arm, knowing that the animal would then spare his torso, and kicked his way free. He stemmed the bleeding by squeezing the stump of his arm and wrapping spider webs around the wound. The alligator was subsequently shot dead and Kaleb's arm was found inside its stomach, but it proved impossible to reattach the limb.

REMOTE CONTROL▶ Wearing an electrode-fitted cap, a severely paralyzed man in a Swiss hospital was able to send a mental command to a computer in his room, which transmitted it to another computer that activated a small robot nearly 40 mi (64 km) away.

TWO-HEADED BABY▶ At Anajas, Brazil, in December 2011, Maria de Nazare gave birth to a healthy baby—with two heads. The conjoined twins, named Jesus and Emanuel, were born with two functioning brains and two backbones, but only one heart.

Albinism affects just one person in 17,000. It is a genetic condition resulting from a lack of the dark melanin pigment, which gives color to the skin, hair and eyes and protects the body from the sun's rays. Albino people have a pink color to the iris of the eyes, and their skin and hair can be pure white. As their skin is unusually fair, it burns easily and is therefore susceptible to skin cancer. The eyes are sensitive to light, too, and there are often visual problems as well as involuntary eye movements.

▲ Two-year-old Dharamraj is the youngest albino member of the Pullan family.

▲ Rosetauri and Mani on their wedding day in 1983.

▲ Vijay, Pooja, Deepa and Shankar Pullan with their parents.

Seven members of the Pullan family—sons Shankar, Ramkishan and Vijay (back row) and daughters Deepa (left) and Pooja (right)—inherited the rare condition from their parents, father Rosetauri and mother Mani (center).

ALBINO FAMILY

The Pullan family from India certainly stand out in a crowd. No fewer than ten of them are albinos, making them the world's largest albino family. The six Pullan children—sons Shankar, Ramkishan and Vijay and daughters Deepa, Pooja and Renu—inherited the condition from parents Rosetauri and Mani, and when Renu married a man who had albinism, Rosheh, the couple's son, Dharamraj, inherited it, too.

The Pullans all live in a one-bedroom flat in Delhi, but with their pale skin, pink eyes and snowy white hair, they do not look like typical Indians. Rosetauri says: "I've heard people call us *angrez*, which means 'English.' It's hard for people to understand we're Indian."

Rosetauri and Mani had an arranged marriage in 1983 because their parents thought it best for them to marry as they were "the same." In South India, where they originally come from, marrying a person with albinism

is supposed to bring good luck and wealth, yet many people there, too, thought the couple had a disease and treated them like outsiders.

After her first child was born albino, Mani went to a hospital for a hysterectomy because she did not want to bring more albino children into the world. "But the doctor got scared just looking at me and sent me home. I never went back. Now I see it as a gift from God."

Their albinism means they can't stay out in the sun for long and they have bad eyesight. Two of the sons went to a school for the blind, and they all need a magnifier to read. Vijay, 26, is qualified to work with computers, but his poor vision makes it hard for him to find a job. Nevertheless, he is hoping one day to marry an albino woman and continue the family line.

SPADE SHAVE ▶ Teacher Alex Karpenko from Nizhny Novgorod, Russia, saves money on razors by shaving with a sharpened garden spade. Taught by his grandfather to shave with everyday objects, he had started with an ax before switching to using the spade.

AMERICA'S TALLEST ▶ Igor Vovkovinskiy of Rochester, Minnesota, stands 7 ft 8 in (2.3 m) tall and is America's tallest man. He has undergone 16 foot operations in six years and wears specially made size 24 shoes costing $15,000 a pair. The Ukrainian-born giant owes his excessive height to a childhood tumor in his pituitary gland that overwhelmed his body with growth hormones. At just seven years old, he was already more than 6 ft (1.8 m) tall.

TWISTED FACE

▶ *Champion gurner Tang Shuquan from Chengdu City, China, can twist and distort his face to such extremes that he can bite his own nose! Proud of his unusual ability, he even offered 100,000 yuan ($16,000) to anyone who could beat him in a face-off to find the ugliest face-puller.*

KEBAB TOURNIQUET ▶ James Hobbs of Somerset, England, used a meat kebab to stem the flow of blood from a knife wound to his neck. He successfully used the kebab in an attempt to seal the 5-in (13-cm) wound but still lost more than seven pints of blood.

SWALLOWED ITEMS ▶ A hospital in Sibenik, Croatia, has displayed a selection of swallowed objects that have been removed from patients' stomachs over the last 80 years—including needles, coins, animal bones, metal badges and buttons.

POWER OF THOUGHT ▶ Tim Hemmes of Connoquenessing Township, Pennsylvania, has been paralyzed since 2004 following a motorcycle crash. However, after only a month of practice with an experimental brain machine interface, in which electrodes were inserted into his brain, he is able to move his robotic arm using the power of thought.

SIXTH SENSE ▶ When Brenton Gurney of New South Wales, Australia, had an MRI scan after he started to get persistent headaches, doctors found nothing amiss, but they did discover a tumor in the brain of his identical twin Craig, whom Brenton had persuaded to have a scan, too. Brenton's good deed was payback for a previous occasion when Craig, from a distance of 1,678 mi (2,700 km), had divined that his brother had a mysterious and life-threatening rash.

CONCRETE CHEST ▶ Marek Barden of Bristol, England, had a 3-lb 5-oz (1.5-kg), melon-sized tumor removed from his ribs—and had his chest rebuilt with concrete. After he underwent a six-hour surgery to remove not only the tumor, but also the lining of his left lung, six ribs and part of his diaphragm, a cement panel 10 x 10 in (25 x 25 cm) was inserted to replace his ribcage.

VIOLENT SNEEZE ▶ Monique Jeffrey, 28, of Victoria, Australia, was almost left paralyzed by a sneeze. While sitting up in bed reading e-mails on her phone, she sneezed with such force that she dislocated two vertebrae in her neck.

LONG IN THE TONGUE

▶ Comedian Nick Stoeberl of Monterey, California, should never be short of something to say because he has a tongue that has been measured by a doctor to be a record-breaking 3.988 in (10.1 cm) long—big enough to hold five ring doughnuts.

LEG TUMOR ▶ On January 5, 2012, a team of surgeons led by American physician McKay McKinnon successfully removed a 198-lb (90-kg) tumor from Nguyen Duy Hai at a hospital in Ho Chi Minh City, Vietnam. The 32-year-old patient had suffered since childhood from a steadily growing leg tumor, believed to be the result of a rare genetic mutation. In 1997, his right leg was amputated at the knee in the hope that the tumor would stop growing. Following his latest operation he was able to walk for the first time in four years.

BULLET IN THE BRAIN ▶ Jim Saunders of Abilene, Texas, has lived with a bullet lodged in his brain since he was shot in the forehead on August 24, 1981. The 25-calibre bullet lies 3 in (7.5 cm) deep between two optic nerves and the two halves of his brain, but although it has left him virtually blind and without any sense of smell, doctors decided it was too risky to try to remove it.

MINI COP ▶ Although she stands only 2 ft 11 in (88 cm) tall, 31-year-old Aisha Al Hamoudi is a sergeant with Al Didya Police in Fujairah, U.A.E., making her the world's shortest policewoman.

VETERAN DOC ▶ At 100 years of age, Dr. Fred Goldman of Cincinatti, Ohio, was still working three eight-hour days a week, was still seeing 12 patients a day in his computer-free room and was still performing house calls—despite having had major heart surgery and a brush with prostate cancer. The veteran physician started practicing in 1935.

EYE POPPING

▶ *Could anything look more painful? Australia's Chayne Hultgren has pulled a world record weight of 908 lb (411.7 kg) with hooks attached to his eye sockets. Performing as the "Space Cowboy," Chayne has also swallowed a record 27 swords simultaneously and juggles razor-sharp axes, knives and even a running chainsaw while riding a 10-ft-high (3-m) unicycle. Sometimes he performs these feats blindfolded.*

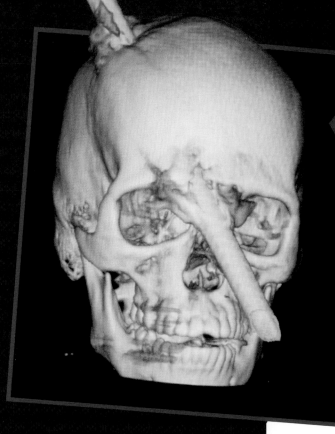

FRUIT PIT▶ While sitting in a car at a traffic light, Blanca Riveron, 62, from Seminole Heights, Florida, suddenly had a violent coughing fit, which regurgitated a fruit stone that had been sitting in her lung for 28 years. She had accidentally inhaled the nispero fruit pit in her native Cuba in 1984, and had spent much of the next three decades coughing and wheezing.

THIRD TIME LUCKY▶ Carpenter Li Xiangyang of Huangshi, China, swallowed the same 6-in (15-cm) nail three times! He was holding the nail between his teeth when he suddenly coughed and swallowed it. Finding the nail in his right lung, doctors fed a fiber-optic bronchoscope down his throat and pulled it out, but just as it was about to emerge through his mouth, he coughed again and sucked it back down his throat. With the nail now in his left lung, doctors repeated the procedure, but again Li involuntarily swallowed and this time the nail landed in his stomach, from where it was finally removed with a gastroscope clamp.

TURTLE BOY▶ Until it was removed in 2012, Didier Montalvo, a six-year-old boy from rural Colombia, had a giant growth that covered 40 percent of his body. The condition, known as congenital melanocytic nevus, was caused by an 11-lb (3.3-kg) mole and made it appear that Didier had a shell, which was why he was nicknamed "Turtle Boy." When he was born with the unusual dark stain on his back, his mother Luz was told it was her fault for looking at a solar eclipse while she was pregnant.

HOMEMADE HANDS▶ After losing both hands in an explosion, Sun Jifa from Jilin Province, China, was unable to afford the prosthetic limb replacements offered by a hospital, so he built his own from scrap metal. He spent eight years designing prototypes before finally creating a pair of metal hands that can grip and hold. They operate via a series of internal wires and pulleys and are controlled by his elbow movements.

LEFT BULLET▶ After New Yorker Ricardo Acevedo was shot by a gunman in March 2012, doctors released him from the hospital with the bullet still in his neck as it was not posing a danger.

EAR BUG▶ Danielle Eccles of Essex, England, lived with a ladybug in her right ear for three years. The insect, which was encased in wax, caused her to suffer deafness, swelling and ear pain before it was finally spotted and removed.

ARTIFICIAL HEART▶ Matthew Green from London, England, wears his heart on his back. While waiting for a donor heart to become available, he was fitted with a plastic heart powered by a machine that fits inside a shoulder bag and is light enough to be carried with him like a backpack wherever he goes.

▶ After accidentally cutting off his left thumb while sawing through a piece of wood, James Byrne of Bristol, England, had it replaced with his left big toe. Surgeons were unable to reattach the thumb so they suggested attaching his toe to his hand instead, and within two months it was working almost as well as a normal thumb.

TOE SWITCH

His big toe!

Ripley's Believe It or Not!®
www.ripleybooks.com

CAMERA SHY▶ Lotte van den Acker from Brunssum, Holland, has a permanent optical illusion on her skin. Her tattoo artist mother Helma inked a vintage Pentax camera onto her forearm in such a way that it looks like Lotte is setting up a snap shot when she covers her face with her arm.

CACTUS COLLAPSE▶ Workman William Mason of Yuma, Arizona, suffered a broken back and 146 needle wounds after he was crushed by a falling 16-ft (5-m) saguaro cactus. Other members of his work crew freed him and called 911.

EYE PULL▶ On April 28, 2012, Yang Guanghe of Anshun, China, pulled a 1.7-ton Mercedes Benz car with a rope attached by hooks to his eye sockets. Yang, who has been training his eyes for over ten years, weighs barely 100 lb (45 kg) himself.

PIERCED EYE▶ Two-year-old Wren Bowell from Somerset, England, had an amazing escape after falling on to a pencil that pierced her eye socket and penetrated almost 1.6 in (4 cm) into her skull. The pencil finished up just a fraction away from a major blood vessel, impact on which would have resulted in severe brain damage or even death. Surgeons had to remove part of her skull to get the pencil out before piecing her head back together with plastic plates and screws.

HAIR-BRAINED!▶ After letting his hair grow for more than three years, Josh Darrah, a graphic designer from Queensland, Australia, shaved it all off, then painstakingly glued the strands together to create a wig!

ROLLER-COASTER RIDE▶ Although she didn't know it at the time, schoolgirl Emma Bassett from London, England, was just hours from death with a brain tumor when she went on a theme park roller-coaster ride that saved her life. Emma, who had been complaining of headaches, had an undetected tumor so big it had stopped vital fluid moving around her brain, but the ride on the Nemesis Inferno roller-coaster at Thorpe Park, Surrey, relieved the buildup of pressure in her brain and bought her precious extra time. After a series of operations, she had to learn to walk and talk all over again, but she has stunned doctors by making a full recovery.

ANCIENT TATTOOS▶ The body of an ancient Siberian princess found high in the Altai Mountains of East-Central Asia has tattoos of a deer with a griffon's beak and a Capricorn's antlers—all preserved for 2,500 years in the icy permafrost.

▶ IN 30 MINUTES THE HUMAN BODY GIVES OFF ENOUGH HEAT TO BOIL HALF A GALLON OF WATER.◀

SEVERED THUMB▶ A thumb found in an Essex, England, parking lot in 2010 after it was seen falling from the sky was the only recovered body part ever of a murdered restaurant worker. The thumb appeared to have been severed by a butcher's saw and was probably dropped from the sky by a bird. It helped convict six people in connection with the killing.

NECK IMPALED▶ Julian Mattes of San Antonio, Texas, fell five stories from an apartment window and was speared through the neck by an iron fence as he hit the ground—but survived.

EYE BLING▶ Jewels in his wife's teeth inspired Dr. Chandrashekhar Chawan of Mumbai, India, to create a line of $15,000 contact lenses embedded with gold and diamonds. The gems do not touch the cornea of the eye, so are thought safe.

SPIDER LODGER▶ When a patient went to China's Changsha Central Hospital complaining of itching in her left ear, doctors found that a spider had been living inside her ear canal. Worried in case the spider burrowed deeper or bit the woman, they filled the ear with saline to flush it out.

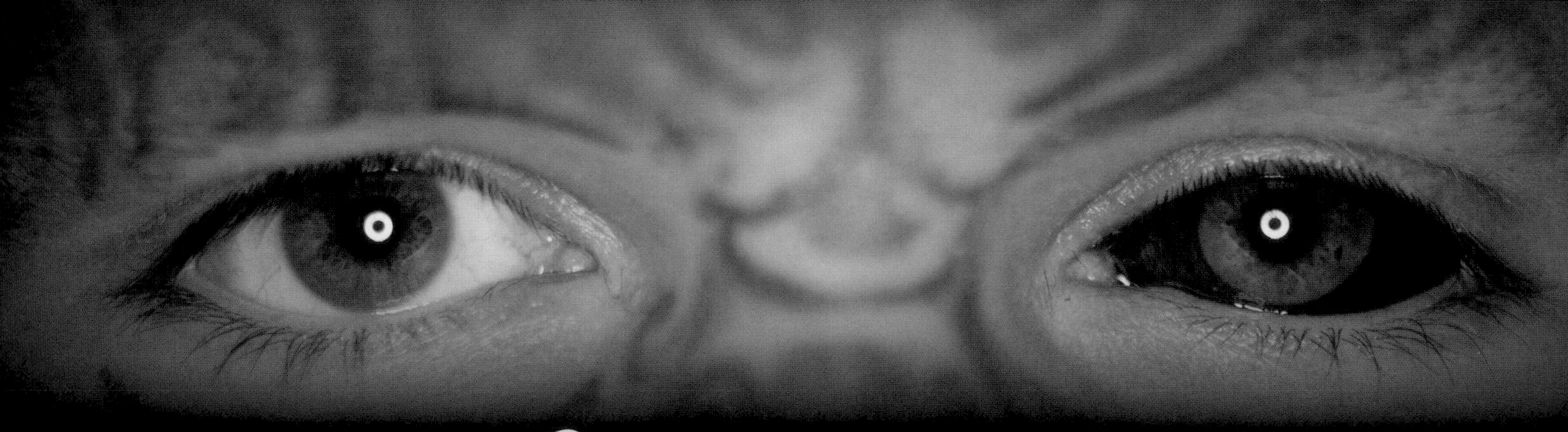

PROVISIONAL DRIVING LICENCE

PROVISIONAL
L

1. KING OF INK LAND KING BODY
2. ART THE EXTREME INK-ITE

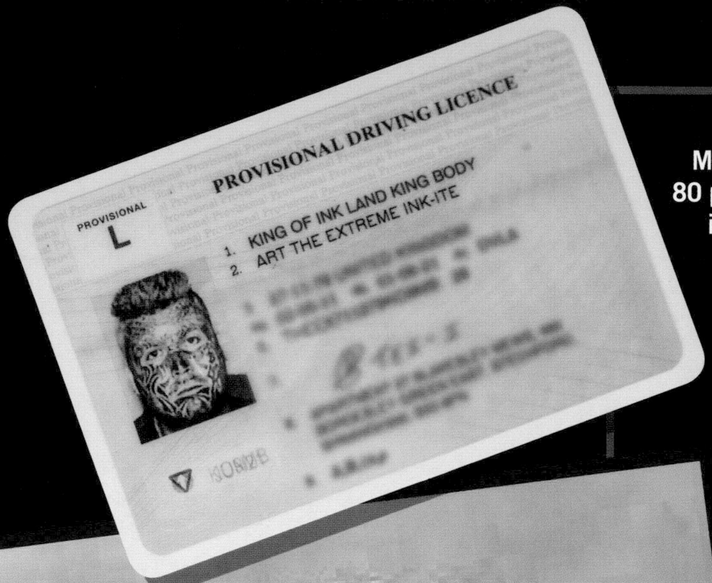

Mathew Whelan of Birmingham, England, has 80 percent of his body covered in tattoos—and is such a fan of tattooing that he has legally changed his name to the King of Ink Land.

The 33-year-old has spent £20,000 ($30,000) and 300 hours in the tattooist's chair turning his body into a colorful canvas. He even had the name of his favorite TV program, *The Jeremy Kyle Show*, tattooed on the back of his head specially for his appearance on the show in 2011.

He says: "My body art is so much more than just tattoos to me—it's a way of life. I am happy having changed the way I want to. My name is part of that change, too. I won't answer to my birth name now.

"I see the tattoos as extreme art—it interests people, they see it and go 'Wow!' Some of my family think I'm crazy but my body is a temple and these are the decorations."

A volunteer for the Liberal Democrats party, the King of Ink Land first became fascinated by tattoos as a child after admiring a small lion inked on his uncle's arm. He went on to have his first tattoo, on his arm, on his 16th birthday. He now has so much ink on his body that he has to undergo laser removal treatment to make room for any new designs.

He hopes that his artwork will even outlive him, like a famous painting. "After I die, taxidermists will strip my skin and carry out a preservation procedure, so that I go from Body Art in life to Skin Art in death."

KING OF INK LAND

▲ Mathew's first ever tattoo.

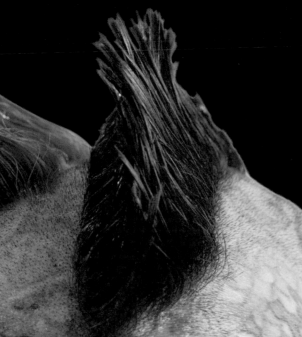

▶ Having changed his name to King of Ink Land King Body Art The Extreme Ink-Ite, he has now asked the U.K.'s postal service to recognize a change in his address from Birmingham, England, to Birminkham, Ink Land. The inking of his left eyeball was achieved through a dangerous surgical procedure.

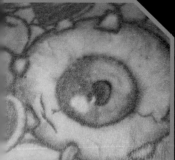

▶ Surgeons in the Netherlands removed **78 pieces of cutlery** from the stomach of 52-year-old Margaret Daalman.

▶ Doctors in Vietnam removed **119 rusty 3-in (7.5-cm) nails** from the stomach of a 43-year-old woman.

▶ A **10-lb (4.5-kg) hairball,** measuring 15 in (38 cm) long, was removed from the stomach of an 18-year-old woman in Chicago, Illinois.

▶ When a cockroach jumped into her mouth, an Israeli woman tried to dislodge it from her throat with a **fork.** In doing so she accidentally swallowed the fork, which ended up in her stomach... along with the **cockroach.**

▶ A 7-in (18-cm) **toothbrush** was retrieved from the stomach of a 15-year-old New Zealand girl who had tripped while running up some steps with the toothbrush in her mouth.

▶ Following an argument with her boyfriend, a woman from Foshan, China, swallowed **20 small cobblestones,** and needed surgery when they failed to pass through her body naturally.

▶ When doctors in India opened up the stomach of Kuleshwar Singh, they found **421 metal coins, 197 fishnet pellets, three keys and a bicycle chain.**

▶ Eight-year-old Haley Lents from Huntingburg, Indiana, had **20 steel balls and 10 magnets** removed from her stomach. She had eaten them because "they looked like candy."

BACK FROM THE DEAD

▶ Egyptian waiter Hamdi Hafez al-Nubi stunned his family by waking up at his own funeral in 2012.

▶ Declared dead after a highway accident in 2007, Venezuelan Carlos Camejo woke up in the morgue in extreme pain after medical examiners had started cutting him open as part of their autopsy.

▶ Suffering repeated cardiac arrests, Jim McClatchey died 100 times in an Atlanta, Georgia, hospital on November 20, 2004—but still came back to life.

▶ Despite being pronounced brain dead by four specialists following a 2008 car accident, 17-year-old Steven Thorpe from Warwickshire, England, recovered well enough to leave the hospital seven weeks later.

▶ Ninety-seven-year-old Dona Ramona from Sampues, Colombia, was wrongly declared dead on four separate occasions in 2005 after slipping in and out of a diabetic coma.

▶ Velma Thomas of Nitro, West Virginia, was taken off life support when she'd had no detectable brain waves for 17 hours, her heart had stopped beating three times and her hands and toes had started to curl up. She woke up ten minutes later.

▶ Eighty-one-year-old Feliberto Carrasco from Angol, Chile, woke in 2008 to find himself lying in a coffin at his own wake. Once he had been helped out of the coffin, he asked for a glass of water.

WEIRD MEDICAL CONDITIONS

▶ **Alien Hand Syndrome** A neurological disorder in which the afflicted person's hand appears to take on a life of its own as if it is "possessed" like something out of a horror movie. In extreme cases, the hand may even try to attack its owner.

▶ **Foreign Accent Syndrome** Following brain damage, a person may come round from surgery and start talking in a completely different accent—just like English woman Wendy Hasnip, who, after suffering a stroke, began speaking with a French accent.

▶ **Walking Corpse Syndrome** A rare mental disorder in which people are convinced they are dead or have lost their blood or internal organs, turning them into zombie-like creatures.

▶ **Sleeping Beauty Syndrome** Nicole Delian from North Fayette, Pennsylvania, has a rare neurological condition that causes her to sleep for more than 18 hours a day. She once slept for 64 days straight, waking only to eat—and even then she was actually in a sleepwalking state.

▶ **Exploding Head Syndrome** An anxiety-based hallucination in which the sufferer experiences a sudden, loud noise coming from within their own head, most commonly while asleep.

▶ **Alice in Wonderland Syndrome** A neurological condition that affects human perception, making objects seem much smaller or larger than they really are—such as mice or ladybugs as big as a house.

▶ **Capgras Delusion** A mental condition in which sufferers become convinced that someone close to them—usually a relative—has been replaced by an identical imposter.

▶ **Stendhal Syndrome** An anxious sensation—dizziness, confusion, sometimes even fainting—brought on by seeing beautiful works of art.

MEDICAL MIRACLES

▶ After spending 19 years in a coma following a car crash, Terry Wallis from Arkansas defied the odds by regaining consciousness and starting to talk again.

▶ Blind for ten years, New Zealander Lisa Reid suddenly regained her sight after accidentally bumping her head on the side of a coffee table.

▶ Technically decapitated in a car accident, nine-year-old Jordan Taylor, from Hillsboro, Texas, underwent surgery to reconnect his head to his neck and three months later he was able to leave the hospital.

▶ Emma Hassell from Southampton, England, suddenly went completely deaf after her ears popped—then nearly nine months later, excited at having just discovered she was pregnant, her hearing returned just as unexpectedly as it had vanished.

▶ Born with an aggressive tumor on his spine, two-year-old Brandon Connor from Atlanta, Georgia, was scheduled to undergo a risky operation that might have left him paralyzed—but on the eve of the planned surgery the tumor mysteriously vanished.

▶ Following a car accident in Curitiba, Brazil, a man lost both his memory and the power of speech—and, despite public appeals, he remained unidentified for another six years until he suddenly regained the ability to speak and gave his name as Amauri Calixto.

GREAT ESCAPES

▶ Sentenced to execution by firing squad during the 1915 Mexican Revolution, Wenseslao Moguel **survived despite being shot nine times,** the final coup de grâce bullet having been shot through his head by an officer to ensure death.

▶ Naked except for a T-shirt and with little food and water, American sailor Steven Callahan **drifted across the Atlantic Ocean for 76 days** and 2,071 mi (3,333 km) in 1982 in a small inflatable rubber raft after his boat sank in a storm.

▶ When her plane was struck by lightning and **crashed in the Peruvian rainforest** in 1971, Juliane Koepcke was blasted 2 mi (3.2 km) from the aircraft, still strapped to her seat. The only survivor among 92 passengers, she suffered a broken collarbone, a badly swollen eye and cuts and bruises, but despite her injuries she trekked for nine days to find help.

▶ Although both her parachutes failed, skydiver Joan Murray survived a **14,500-ft (4,400-m) fall over North Carolina in 1999 because she landed on a mound of stinging fire ants.** Doctors believe the 200-plus bites from the ants kept her heart beating and, despite spending two weeks in a coma, she was released from the hospital six weeks later.

▶ On a 1993 fishing trip in the Colorado Rockies, Bill Jeracki became **trapped after a boulder rolled onto his leg** and crushed it—but he survived by amputating the leg with a pocketknife. He then crawled to his truck and drove to the nearest town.

"EL FUSILADO" — THE EXECUTED ONE!

FACED A FIRING SQUAD — RECEIVED 8 BULLETS THRU THE HEAD AND BODY—AND THE COUP DE GRACE — YET LIVED

RIPLEY'S BELIEVE IT OR NOT PROGRAM

Wenseslao Moguel

FAT FANTASY▶ Drew Manning, a personal trainer from Eagle Mountain, Utah, deliberately gained 70 lb (32 kg) from overeating and inactivity, just so he could feel what it was like to be fat.

TEAR SALTS▶ Hoxton Street Monster Supplies of London, England, have produced a range of salts said to be collected from human tears. The range includes tears of sorrow, tears shed while sneezing, tears shed while chopping onions, tears of anger and tears of laughter.

SWALLOWED MAGNETS▶ When three-year-old Payton Bushnell of Portland, Oregon, complained to her parents about stomach pain, they thought she was suffering from flu—until an X-ray revealed she had swallowed 37 Buckyball magnets, a desktop toy. The high-powered magnets had forced her intestines to snap together and had punctured four holes in her lower intestine and stomach.

HAPPY GUY▶ After having hip surgery in the Netherlands in 2010, Huug Bosse can't stop laughing—at everything and everyone. The anesthetic he was under during the operation is thought to be the reason for his now uncontrollable laughter.

MONKEY RUNNER▶ For more than nine years, monkey-loving 30-year-old Kenichi Ito from Tokyo, Japan, has walked mainly on all fours. Modeling his running style on the African patas monkey, he has adapted so well that he can run the 100 meters on all fours in 17.47 seconds. He even performs household chores in a crawling position, but while walking in the mountains he was once almost shot by a hunter who mistook him for a wild boar.

FOOT FRACTURES▶ Tristan Stadtmuller of Los Angeles, California, fractured both of his feet during U.S. Marine Corps Infantry training but continued to serve with the Marines untreated for seven months.

CONSTANT SLEEP▶ Reece Williams, a schoolboy from Birmingham, England, suffered from such severe narcolepsy that he slept for up to 23 hours a day. When doctors monitored his sleep patterns, they found he was in a deep sleep after just 19 seconds, compared to 40 minutes for the average person. He also had cataplexy, a sudden weakening of the muscles triggered by strong emotions such as excitement, laughter and surprise, which meant that until he was diagnosed he used to fall over as many as 25 times a day. Just the excitement of kicking a ball was enough to cause him to fall over and doze off.

BROKEN NECK▶ Former soldier Philip Loveday of Bridgend, Wales, has lived with a broken neck for more than 40 years. He injured his neck playing rugby when he was 16, but the break was not discovered until 2012 when he went for a scan after dislocating his shoulder. In the meantime, he had actively served with the British Army in Northern Ireland and the Gulf, and continued playing rugby.

BILINGUAL BENEFITS▶ Bilingual people are better able to resist the dementia caused by Alzheimer's Disease than people who can speak only one language. People who speak more than one language can delay the onset of Alzheimer's by up to five years, as they need twice as much brain damage as unilingual people before they exhibit symptoms of the disease.

COPPER CURE▶ Just a month after gluing four copper coins to the insides of his shoes, 85-year-old Johnny Franks of London, England, cured the arthritis that had been plaguing him for 15 years. Some medical experts believe that putting copper next to the skin can help relieve the inflammation and pain of arthritis.

FETAL TUMOR▶ In a world first, surgeons at the Jackson Memorial Hospital in Florida removed a tumor from the mouth of an unborn baby to save its life. A prenatal scan on mother Tammy Gonzalez had showed a rare oral teratoma—only the second seen in 20 years at the hospital—and a laser was used to cut the tumor from the fetus's lips. Baby Leyna was born healthy five months later. Now the only sign of her life-saving surgery is a tiny scar on her mouth.

STICK TO HIS STOMACH▶ When doctors operated on Ove Sohlberg of Lycksele, Sweden, in 2011 they removed a sharp wooden stick that had been lodged in his abdomen causing stomach pain for 25 years. It is thought that the stick was originally left in his stomach following surgery he had had to remove stomach ulcers.

SPHERICAL CYSTS

▶ *These strange, perfectly round cysts were found in a larger cyst when it was removed from the abdomen of a 54-year-old woman, Wan Jiazhen, at a hospital in Chongqing, China.*

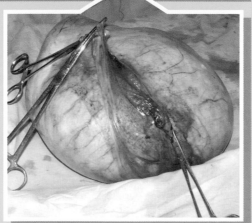

COMIC CUTS

▶ Artistic barber Radames Perez, from West Palm Beach, Florida, uses his razor and clippers to etch amazing likenesses of comic book characters and celebrities into the backs and sides of his customers' heads. His range includes P Diddy, Predator, Mickey Mouse and SpongeBob SquarePants.

ULTRA VISION▶ People suffering from aphakia have no lenses in their eyes—either due to a congenital defect or surgical removal—but can see ultraviolet (UV) light, which the lens had previously blocked to prevent the risk of snowblindness from exposure to high levels of UV. During World War II, aphakic observers were recruited by the military to watch the U.K. coastline for German U-boats signaling to agents on the shore with UV lamps.

TWIN FETUS▶ In January 2012, three-year-old Isbac Pacunda of Peru underwent surgery to remove a partially formed fetus—his twin—from his abdomen. The fetus weighed 1 lb 8 oz (680 g), was 9 in (23 cm) long and had bones, eyes and even hair. The condition is called fetus-in-fetu and occurs in about one in every 500,000 live births.

MOLECULAR BOMBARDMENT▶
Every single inch of your body is bombarded by more than a sextillion (1,000,000,000,000,000,000,000) air molecules every second.

BONE BREAKING▶ Your bones are four times stronger than concrete, and while babies are born with 300 separate bones, adults have only 206!

WHAT MOOSE?▶ After her car collided with a massive moose, Michelle Higgins of Norris Arm, Newfoundland, drove 25 mi (40 km) to work. She had fractured two bones in her neck, her face was bruised and bleeding, her windshield was smashed out and the car's roof was peeled back like an opened sardine can—but despite all this, she had no memory of the accident.

EXTRA GRIP
▶ British artists Mariana Fantich and Dominic Young replaced the traditional soles in a pair of size 15 men's black shoes with 1,050 teeth! The teeth, which were plastic rather than real, also included a few gold molars for extra impact. Sadly, the one-off Apex Predator shoes were not for sale.

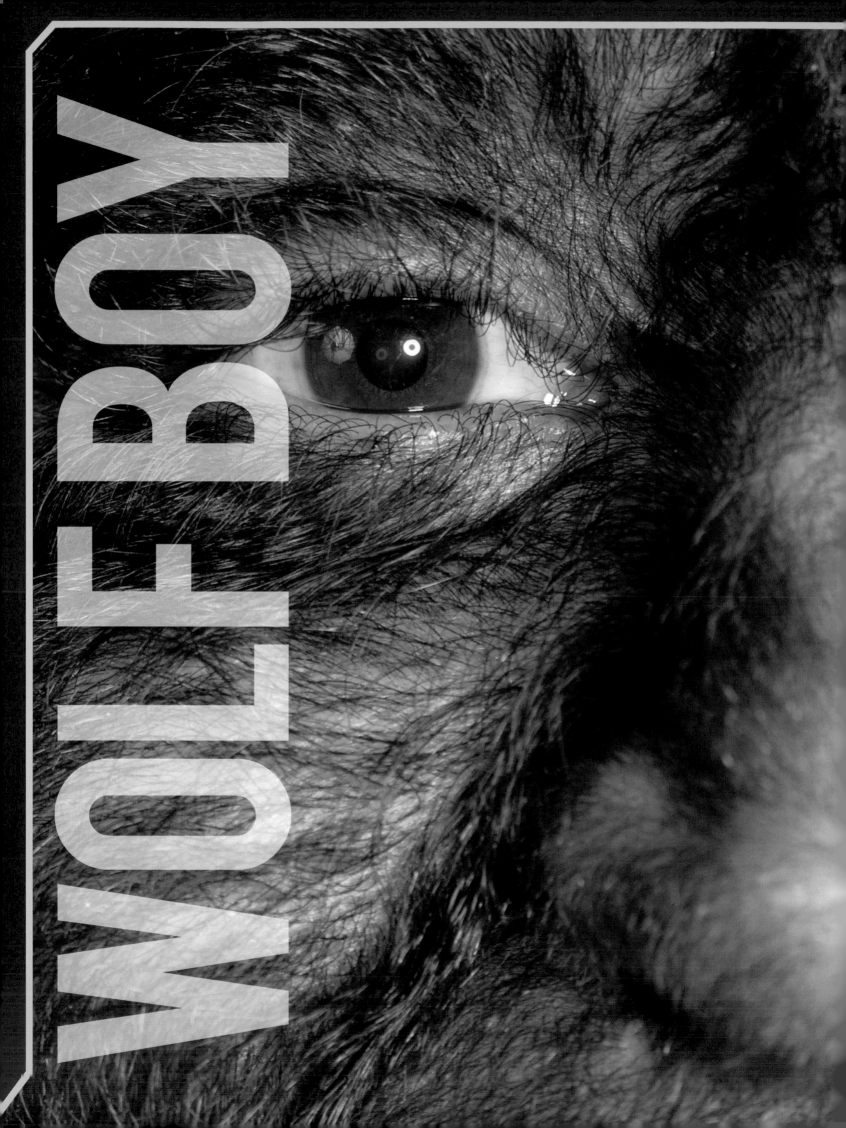

WOLFBOY

JESUS ACEVES
WOLF BOY

Jesus "Chuy" Aceves, from Loreto, Mexico, is known as "The Wolf Boy" because of a rare condition that has left his face completely covered in hair.

Chuy was born with a hereditary type of hypertrichosis—or "Werewolf Syndrome"—a condition that causes an abnormal amount of hair growth and affects just one in a billion people. There have been only 50 documented cases.

Fifteen members of Chuy's family have hypertrichosis, which was inherited from his great-grandmother three generations ago. Chuy's excessive hair growth exists only on his face. "The arms are more normal," he says. "Same thing with my legs, I don't have the excess hair. However, there are other members of the family, my cousins, who have more hair on the face, on the ears, over their chest and back. Some have more on their legs, others less, and others very little. That's how it is."

Chuy's sister Lili, who suffers from a less severe form of the condition, used to perform in a circus but quit to work as a police officer in Mexico. However, Chuy's cousins, Larry and Danny Ramos Gomez, who are as hirsute as he, have made successful careers in circuses and sideshows, and currently work as daredevil trapeze and trampoline artists.

▶ *Chuy is married with two daughters, one of whom has inherited the condition. He and his family experienced a lot of prejudice growing up in Mexico so, after some advice from a friend, when he was 12 he and his cousins and sister Lili joined a circus in Los Angeles. They instantly became the star attraction as hypertrichosis had never before been seen in the U.S.A.*

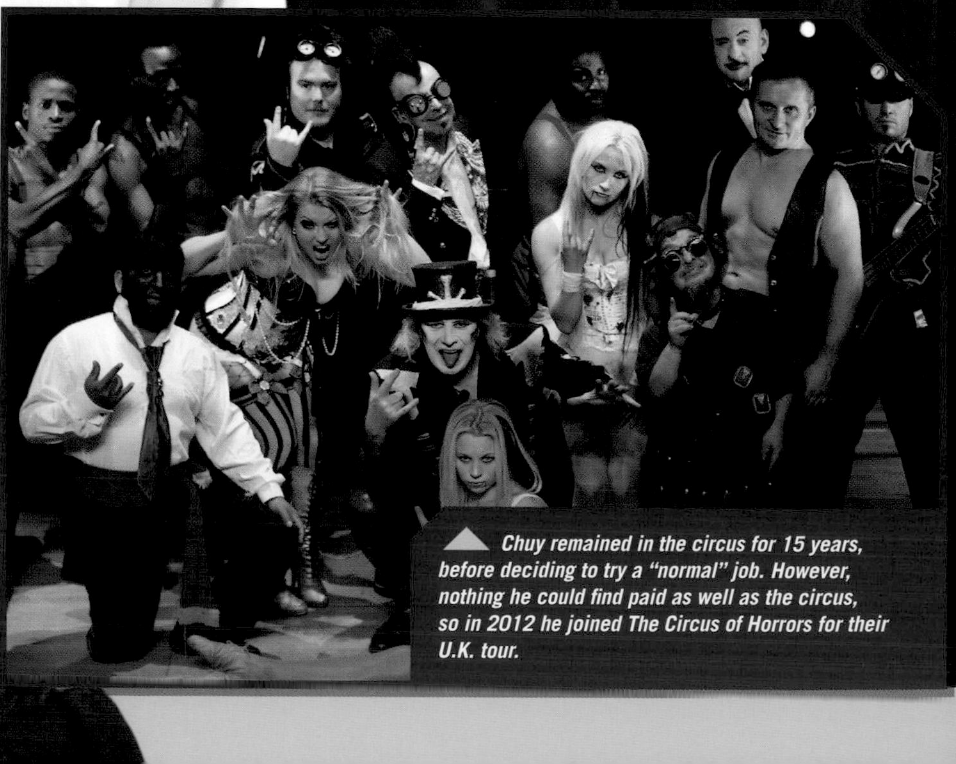

▲ *Chuy remained in the circus for 15 years, before deciding to try a "normal" job. However, nothing he could find paid as well as the circus, so in 2012 he joined The Circus of Horrors for their U.K. tour.*

Chuy considers his condition to be a "gift from God." He has to cut his hair every fortnight but has only ever shaved his face twice because he found it left the skin underneath sensitive and sore. "My face and eyes swelled up," he says. "It felt weird. I didn't like it. I feel better the way I am. One of my cousins did it, too, but he didn't like it either. He did not like how he looked, and he did not come out of his room during the entire time he was shaven until it grew out again. It just didn't feel right."

▲ Traveling with *The Circus of Horrors*, Chuy was the first person with *"Werewolf Syndrome"* to appear in Britain for over 30 years. For the tour he learned new skills, such as climbing a sword ladder and putting a spoon in his nose.

HEART ATTACKS ▶ Two men from Merseyside, England, saved each other's lives in the space of ten months after both suffered heart attacks while gardening. When Peter Smith collapsed in February 2011, he was given first aid by future son-in-law Tony Hopper before undergoing emergency surgery. Then in December 2011, Peter returned the favor after Tony's heart stopped twice.

NIGHTLY SERMON ▶ Following an illness in 1880, Hezekiah Perry of Saluda, North Carolina, delivered religious sermons in his sleep every night until his death in 1925.

LIFE-SAVING COUGH ▶ Claire Osborn of Coventry, England, saved her own life by coughing up an inoperable cancer tumor. After feeling a tickle in her throat, the 37-year-old mother of six coughed up a 0.8-in-long (2-cm) lump, which doctors said was an aggressive form of mouth and throat cancer. It had probably grown on a "stalk" at the back of her throat and become dislodged during the coughing fit. If she hadn't coughed it up, it would have grown and almost certainly spread to her other organs.

LUNG FISH ▶ Doctors in India operated to remove a live fish from the lung of 12-year-old Anil Barela. He swallowed the 3½-in-long (9-cm) fish as part of a game with friends on a riverbank in Madhya Pradesh state, but the fish went down the wrong way and entered the boy's left lung.

ACCENT CHANGE ▶ After having the flu, Debie Royston from Birmingham, England, suddenly started speaking with a French accent— even though she had never been to France. She suffered a series of seizures following the illness, and these caused her temporarily to lose the ability to speak. When her voice did come back a month later, her accent had completely changed.

TATTOOED LADY

▶ Isobel Varley, aged 75 and from Stevenage, Hertfordshire, England, has her entire body covered in tattoos, apart from her face, the soles of her feet and her ears. She has a group of tigers tattooed on her stomach, a pair of orangutans on her right calf, a spider in her left armpit, a cluster of strawberries on the left side of her neck, and a bunch of grapes on the right side of her neck. She even had her hair shaved off to add tattoos to the top of her head. She also has nearly 50 body piercings, including 29 in her ears.

TOUGH PEN ▶ A British woman accidentally swallowed a plastic felt-tip pen in 1986 while attempting to check her tonsils—and when it was finally removed from her stomach 25 years later, the pen still worked!

COSMETIC SURGERY ▶ Since 1988, when she was 32 years old, Kentucky-born Cindy Jackson has had 52 cosmetic procedures worth $100,000. They include 14 full-scale operations, five facelifts, two nose operations, jaw surgery, lip and cheek implants, eye lifts, chin bone reduction, Botox injections and liposuction.

HICCUP CURE ▶ Thirteen-year-old Mallory Kievman from Manchester, Connecticut, has set up her own company to market a product to cure hiccups. She devised Hiccupops—a lollipop containing apple cider vinegar and sugar—after curing her own bout of hiccups. She says the remedy over-stimulates the set of nerves in the throat that are responsible for hiccups and cancels out the message to hiccup.

HEAD REBUILT ▶ After a 25-ft (7.6-m) fall left him with a large dent in his head, Tim Barter of London, England, had his forehead rebuilt using his own body fat. His skull, cheekbone and eye socket were shattered in the fall, and titanium plates were then inserted through his cheeks to repair his skull before fat from his stomach was injected into his forehead to complete the reshaping process.

UNIQUE TWINS ▶ Sienna and Sierra Bernal of Houston, Texas, are the only identical twins in the world in which one is a primordial dwarf. The sisters were born three months prematurely with Sienna weighing just over a pound. Now at 13, she weighs half as much as her sister and stands just 4 ft (1.2 m) tall —the average height of a six-year-old—compared to her twin's 5 ft 1 in (1.5 m).

▶ Red Yao women from China cut their hair only once in their lifetime. They twist their hair so that they can loop it around the head to secure it in an up-do.

SHOULDER SQUEEZE

▶ Kathy Vick from Cedar Springs, Michigan, contacted Ripley's to let us know about her son's bizarre shoulder-blade stunts. Jean-Paul, aged 15, can squeeze his blades so tightly that he can hold a quarter between them for at least 2 minutes, and crush soda cans!

YOUR UPLOADS

HAIR PULL▶ Xu Huijun, a woman from Dalian City, China, who is just 5 ft 2 in (1.6 m) tall and weighs less than 112 lb (51 kg), pulled two jeeps with a combined weight of 5 tons—with just her hair! This means that she successfully used her hair to pull 90 times her body weight.

STRONG GIRL▶ Ten-year-old Naomi Kutin from Fairlawn, New Jersey, weighs slightly less than 97 lb (44 kg), but she can lift 215 lb (97.5 kg)—more than twice her body weight.

NO LAUGHING MATTER▶ Members of a "laughter yoga" club in Mumbai, India, have been ordered to curb their enthusiasm because neighbors say the sound of their therapeutic laughter amounts to "aural aggression."

MARATHON BIRTH▶ Amber Miller of Chicago, Illinois, gave birth to her daughter June just hours after completing the 2011 Chicago Marathon. She was nearly 39 weeks pregnant when she ran the 26.2-mi (42-km) race.

BALCONY FALL▶ Mikee Collins of Sydney, Australia, plunged eight floors from his balcony—and survived. An attempt to flip himself onto a concrete ledge below the balcony went horribly wrong when Mikee slipped on the wet railings. The 82-ft (25-m) fall broke all of his ribs, shattered his pelvis, bruised his brain, ruptured his spleen and fractured the base of his skull, his left foot and his lower vertebrae—but he didn't have a single bruise or scratch on his body.

HAIR VILLAGE

▶ The 120 ethnic Red Yao women from Huangluo village, China, have hair that is an average 5 ft 7 in (1.7 m) long. Believing that long hair is an indication of good fortune and wealth, the women can cut their jet black hair only once in their lives, when they turn 16. The snipped hair is turned into an ornamental headpiece, which is then presented to the woman's husband when she marries. Until recently, only a woman's husband and children were allowed to see her hair loose. If a passerby happened to stumble upon a Yao woman with her hair revealed, he had to spend three years with her family as their son-in-law.

POPULAR CULTURE ▶

HOBBIT HOLE

Lord of the Rings fan Jeremy Telford built his very own Hobbit Hole—out of 2,600 balloons. It took the professional balloon artist 40 hours over three days patiently inflating each balloon with a hand pump to re-create Bilbo Baggins' house Bag End in the living room of his own home in Pleasant Grove, Utah.

By carefully twisting differently colored balloons into shape, he built a staggering life-sized inflatable replica of J.R.R. Tolkien's famous fantasy creation.

THE HOBBIT MOVIE

- The first in a trilogy of movies, *The Hobbit: An Unexpected Journey* cost an estimated $270 million to make.

- It is the first feature film to be shot and projected at 48 frames per second, twice as fast as usual. The higher frame rate helps to synchronize the images for each eye when viewed in 3-D.

- Each of the 13 dwarf characters carries an average of nearly 176 lb (80 kg) of extra weight in the form of a fat suit, prosthetics and a large amount of facial hair.

- The dwarves' wigs and beards are made of imported yak hair, and in the course of the 18-month shoot, the production team went through 450 mi (720 km) of yak hair.

- Each dwarf has six wigs and eight beards, knotted one hair at a time, to accommodate stunt doubles and stand-ins.

- 5,000 prosthetic makeup costumes were constructed for the movie, altogether using 4 tons of silicon.

- A typical goblin grunt is composed of 16 layers of sound elements.

- More than 3,000 people turned up to a casting call in Wellington, New Zealand, where the movie was shot, in the hope of being chosen to play extras, forcing the police to cancel the call for safety reasons.

- From a first print run of 1,500 in 1937, *The Hobbit* novel has now sold more than 100 million copies and has been translated into over 50 languages. A signed first edition fetched $90,000 at auction in 2008.

- Working as a professor at Pembroke College, Oxford University, England, J.R.R. Tolkien wrote the first line of *The Hobbit*—"In a hole in the ground there lived a Hobbit"—as he doodled to relieve boredom while marking exam papers.

XXL JACKET ▶ Children from a school in Stockport, England, helped make a jacket that was big enough to cover more than half a tennis court. Made up of 8,832 knitted squares, the oversized jacket measured 42 x 18 ft (13 x 5.5 m).

SOUNDS FISHY ▶ Quintetto, a musical art installation by the Italian studio Quiet Ensemble, features five fish tanks that operate as five digital instruments, each playing differently depending on the position of the fish.

WEED FASHION ▶ Artist Nicole Dextras from Vancouver, Canada, has created a "Weedrobes" clothing line, with garments made from flowers, weeds, leaves and even thorns. She began by fashioning a coat from a bunch of laurel leaves she found in an alleyway but has since branched out to design everything from a pair of shoes cut from cabbage leaves to a beautiful evening gown adorned with camellia flowers.

NO FILM ▶ Germany-based director Jay Chung once produced, wrote and directed a 35mm movie with a crew of 20 over a period of two years—but with no film in the camera! He deliberately didn't tell the cast and crew that the nature of the project meant their efforts would never be seen.

CAMERA COSTUME ▶ When photographer Tyler Card of Grand Rapids, Michigan, needed a costume for a Halloween party, he turned himself into a fully functional Nikon camera. He made a working flash and shutter release button and attached it to his costume, which consisted of a black-painted cardboard box for the camera body and a paint bucket for the lens.

ZAPPA BUST ▶ Lithuania's capital, Vilnius, has a bronze bust of U.S. musician Frank Zappa built by members of the country's Cold War-era independence movement to celebrate his influence—even though he wasn't Lithuanian and had never even visited the country.

CONDENSED YEAR ▶ New York City-based animator Cesar Kuriyama filmed a second of his life every day for a year before editing the clips together in chronological order to create a six-minute video. His one-second snapshots, which ended with his 31st birthday in February 2012, included a marriage and a funeral.

FEEL THE PINCH

▶ Californian artist Laura Ann Jacobs has designed a bra that pinches—because it's in the shape of a crab, complete with claws. She has created dozens of wacky, brightly colored bras, incorporating everything from fish heads to fruit.

HOLY CATASTROPHE! ▶ A scientific study of Batman's ability to fly using only his rigid cape has concluded that he would be able to glide successfully for some distance over Gotham City, but would suffer serious injuries when trying to land. Physicists at the University of Leicester, England, calculated that his cape's 15-ft-5-in (4.7-m) wingspan—about half that of a hang glider—would keep him airborne for a while, but he would be hitting the ground at 50 mph (80 km/h)—too fast to avoid possibly fatal injury.

BAGGY DRESS ▶ Over the course of three months, 16-year-old Suraya Mohd Zairin of Shah Alam, Malaysia, created a floral pattern dress from 4,000 used tea bags.

CANINE CHANNEL ▶ In February 2012, a new cable TV channel solely for dogs was launched in San Diego, California. DOGTV aims to keep dogs relaxed and entertained in the home while their owners are out at work. The sound, colors and camera angles of the shows—most of which star animals—are all designed to have canine appeal.

SWEET MUSIC ▶ Croatian punk band Fon Biskich released a 2012 single made of chocolate. They used hard, bitter chocolate with a high-cocoa content to create a record that fans could eat when they got bored with the song.

COOKING WITH POO ▶ Saiyuud Diwong wrote a 2012 recipe book called *Cooking with Poo*, but it is not as gross as it sounds—"poo" means "crab" in Thailand and is also the chef's nickname.

UNFORGETTABLE AUDIENCE ▶ To celebrate his 50th birthday, Englishman Paul Barton dragged a piano up a mountain in Kanchanaburi Province, Thailand, to play Beethoven to blind elephants—he considered the feat a birthday present to himself. Barton, who has worked with blind elephants on the reserve for many years, sat at his piano just a few feet away from the animals.

PIE VICTIM ▶ U.S. comedian Soupy Sales (1926–2009) had an estimated 20,000 pies thrown both at himself and at the guests on his television shows in the 1950s and 1960s.

DUCT TAPE ▶ Brooke Wallace from Solomon, Kansas, made her prom dress completely out of duct tape. She used 42 rolls of duct tape to make a Western-style dress for herself and a suit for her date Mark Aylward and still had enough left over to create a purse and earrings. She spent more than 200 hours working on the outfits, hand-folding thousands of pieces of tape.

TIGHT FIT ▶ Andy Coyne of Greenville, South Carolina, wore 249 T-shirts simultaneously, the garments weighing a total of more than 200 lb (91 kg).

CORDUROY CLUB ▶ Founded by Miles Rohan, the Corduroy Appreciation Club of New York City, New York, boasts over 250 members. It meets twice a year—on January 1 and November 11 (1/1 and 11/11), on which occasions members must wear at least two items of corduroy clothing.

ICE BRA ▶ Lingerie manufacturer Triumph has created a bra containing built-in ice packs and a miniature fan to help women keep cool in summer.

Cecil Wigglenose

Created around 1938, Cecil Wigglenose has a nose that wiggles, eyes that cross, ears that wiggle, eyebrows that move, a tongue that sticks out and a fright wig. Made by the famous McElroy brothers, he is the only McElroy figure in the Vent Haven collection that is regularly demonstrated today.

CHAMPAGNE CHARLIE

Created by Frank Marshall
for W.S. Berger

Standing 5 ft 4 in (1.6 m) tall and built so that he could carry a cane, Charlie's walking mechanism was later remodeled by the McElroys as Berger struggled to master it.

JACKO

Created c.1940 by the McElroys
for W.S. Berger

Berger paid $125 for Jacko, who has simultaneously curling upper and lower lips, a stick-out tongue, sniffing nose, moving and crossing eyes and wiggling ears.

ROSITA

Created in 1943 by and for Bill Hume

Rosita was made in Panama out of wood salvaged from a torpedoed cargo ship during World War II. She switches effortlessly from Spanish to English, and was originally transported in a parachute bag.

Edgar Bergen ▶

Edgar Bergen was presented with an Honorary Oscar (in the form of a wooden Academy Award) for his creation of the inimitable Charlie McCarthy. An original wooden Charlie McCarthy is on permanent display at the Smithsonian Institution in Washington, D.C.

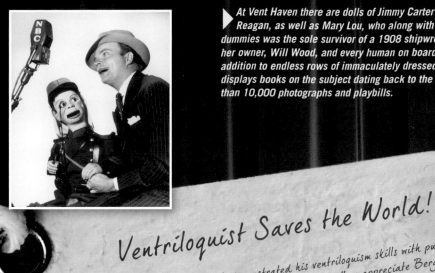

▶ At Vent Haven there are dolls of Jimmy Carter and Ronald Reagan, as well as Mary Lou, who along with three other dummies was the sole survivor of a 1908 shipwreck that killed her owner, Will Wood, and every human on board (far right). In addition to endless rows of immaculately dressed dolls, the museum displays books on the subject dating back to the 1700s, plus more than 10,000 photographs and playbills.

Skinny Hamilton ▼

Vent Haven founder W.S. Berger with his favorite figure, Skinny Hamilton. He said that if the museum were ever to fold, all the figures except Skinny should be sold and the proceeds given to charity. "Do not dispose of this figure as Skinny is part of me," he wrote, listing the dummy specifically in his will. In the final year of his life, he asked for Skinny to be brought to his nursing home where he proceeded to entertain nursing staff and his fellow patients.

Ventriloquist Saves the World!

For nearly 20 years, Edgar Bergen (1903–78) demonstrated his ventriloquism skills with puppet Charlie McCarthy on the radio. Since listeners could never see the doll or appreciate Bergen's expertise at throwing his voice, many thought Charlie was a real person.

The man who would go on to become the world's most famous ventriloquist was raised in Decatur, Michigan, and taught himself ventriloquism from a pamphlet when he was 11. A few years later, young Bergen commissioned Chicago woodcarver Theodore Mack to sculpt a likeness of a rascally Irish paperboy he knew, and Charlie McCarthy was born. Charlie was part of Bergen's act, and by 1936 was attired in his trademark top hat, tuxedo and monocle. His character was that of a mischievous, wisecracking little boy.

The pair made their radio debut on NBC's The Chase and Sanborn Hour in 1936, and the following year Charlie was joined by a dumber dummy, Mortimer Snerd. A feature of the show was Charlie's relentless baiting of comedian W.C. Fields.

On the evening of October 30, 1938, Bergen and Charlie were credited with saving the world. CBS was broadcasting Orson Welles' radio version of H.G. Wells' play War of the Worlds, which contained news reports stating that legions of Martians had landed and exterminated 7,000 U.S. soldiers. Although disclaimers were put out, many listeners thought the reports were genuine and carloads of residents fled New Jersey before the city could be overrun. Restaurants emptied, and people hid in cellars and prayed. The panic would have been worse had most of the population not been listening to Charlie McCarthy on the other station. Critic Alexander Woollcott wrote to Welles: "This only goes to prove that the intelligent people were all listening to the dummy, and that all the dummies were listening to you."

Welles subsequently became a guest on Charlie's show, along with Frank Sinatra, Henry Fonda, Roy Rogers, Groucho Marx, Rosemary Clooney and Liberace. Bergen's daughter, actress Candice Bergen, made her first appearances on the show. Bergen and Charlie were friends of Robert Ripley and also appeared on his radio show.

JOE FLIP
Created in the 1940s by Frank Marshall

Considered by Marshall to be his masterpiece, Joe was originally called Brewster but was later renamed after saxophone player Flip Phillips.

OSCAR
Created by Mack & Son

Oscar was used by magician and ventriloquist Howard Kingsley (real name Herman Schanbacher), who lived from 1885 to 1939 and wrote a book on the art of ventriloquism.

MAX
Created by Ramme for Charlotte Bern-Keller

Max cries, smiles, nods, winks, rolls his eyes, lifts his eyebrows, moves his right arm and leg, and can smoke a cigarette. He always wore makeup for his shows.

The World of Vent Haven

The Vent Haven Museum houses the world's biggest collection of ventriloquists' figures—around 800—ranging in height from 4-in (10-cm) miniatures to 5½-ft (1.7-m) life-size dolls that can walk. The oldest wooden doll at Vent Haven dates back to 1820, and some of the early models have glass eyes, human hair and real teeth— "accessories" that could be bought from barbershops.

Vent Haven was founded by William Shakespeare ("W.S.") Berger, who was a great lover of vaudeville. On a business trip to New York City in 1910, he bought his first figure, Tommy Baloney, so that he could try ventriloquism for himself. However, his interest wore off, and Tommy Baloney was put in storage for 20 years until Berger pulled him out to perform at a Christmas party at the Cincinnati tile factory where he worked.

The act went down so well that Berger began collecting ventriloquism memorabilia and soon dummies filled his house—before long he had to construct a second building in his backyard. Berger became President of the International Brotherhood of Ventriloquism from the late 1940s, and when he died in 1972, aged 94, his attorney helped to turn his private collection into a public museum—Vent Haven opened in 1974.

▲ **W.S. Berger with Tommy Baloney. Created by Louis Grannat in 1910, Tommy Baloney was the first of hundreds of figures owned by Berger and the one that inspired the whole Vent Haven collection.**

The Early Days

Ventriloquism first became popular in vaudeville in the late 19th century. Early dummies were often made of papier-mâché, had a string-and-loop system that operated the head and mouth, and manually controlled eyebrows. Later, eyebrows were sometimes moved by weight control (moving the head) and internal controls were on a stick, often made from ordinary household items.

Performers, such as Englishman **Jules Vernon** (1867–1937), liked to demonstrate their ability at seamlessly switching voices by conducting running dialogue with as many as seven different puppet characters, both male and female (right). Another Englishman, **Fred Russell** (1862–1957), was the first ventriloquist to have a single figure perched on his knee, a style copied by **The Great Lester** (1878–1956) (below), who is credited with developing the wooden dummy.

One of Lester's pupils was **Edgar Bergen,** who, with his doll **Charlie McCarthy,** starred throughout the golden age of ventriloquism—the 1930s and 1940s. Other performers of that era included **Max Terhune** and his puppet **Elmer,** who appeared together in western movies alongside a young John Wayne, and **Dick Bruno,** who spoke with a sophisticated French accent, while his doll, **Joe Flip,** wisecracked in a Brooklyn accent.

▼

Jules Vernon went blind at age 53, but he never revealed this publicly. The characters for his act were mounted on a bench, from which his wife ran a thread to guide him on from backstage. Once there, he knew where the controls were and performed as if he could see.

▲ *This 1937 signed photo to W.S. Berger from The Great Lester reads, "a real friend of all ventriloquists and a real deep student of the complete art of ventriloquism."*

▲ *A fake police record card belonging to Frank Byron Jr., which lists his crime as "Laugh Getter" and remarks how he has "a wonderful way with the ladies."*

The Great Lester & Frank Byron Jr.

Born Maryan Czajkowski, Lester used to drink a glass of water while his puppet, Frank Byron Jr., spoke. On one occasion, the show's musicians substituted whiskey for water as a prank. Lester downed the whiskey without any noticeable effect, but Frank started coughing and shaking as if he had drunk it! Lester also performed a routine where Frank blew out his matches while he tried to light a cigarette.

Behind the Scenes

Considerable work went into the creation of the dummies, some of which went on to achieve great success with their ventriloquist partners. The ingenuity and artistry of some of the dummy makers led to their work being in great demand.

The McElroys' figure Oscar was used by ventriloquist Harry Tunks who was a colonel in the U.S. Air Force. He performed shows after he retired from service after World War II.

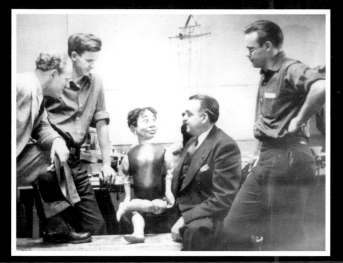

▲ George and Glenn McElroy worked as a team, with the elder brother, Glenn, doing the mechanics and George, a draughtsman by profession, concentrating on the artistic aspect, including the sculpting of the heads, painting the faces and hand-weaving the hair for the wigs.

The McElroy Brothers

George and Glenn McElroy of Harrison, Ohio, created the Rolls-Royces of ventriloquists' figures. Their dummies are generally considered to be the finest ever built, with a unique system of typewriter-like controls inside each one's body allowing for as many as 16 different facial functions.

McElroy figures could move their jaw, twitch their nose, curl their top lip, float their eyes from side to side, look down, cross their eyes, move their eyebrows, wink, stick out their tongue, wiggle their ears and even raise their hair in fright. The dolls were given exaggerated facial expressions so that they could be seen by people sitting in the back row of the theater.

The McElroys made fewer than 50 ventriloquists' figures before retiring, including **Cecil Wigglenose, Skinny Dugan** and **Oscar**. They also created a talking skull, a full-size human skull mounted on a short post and operated via a flatboard base, which the ventriloquist held.

For **W.S. Berger** they built **Jacko**, a 3-ft-tall (0.9-m) monkey whose body was covered in dyed rabbit fur and who had a movable upper lip made from a lady's kid glove.

Frank Marshall

Frank Marshall was the most famous and most prolific maker of ventriloquists' figures in history, carving hundreds of puppets, including such famous faces as **Danny O'Day, Jerry Mahoney** and **Farfel**.

He owed his success to the Mack & Son Woodworking Shop in Chicago, which originally specialized in carving doorframes and ornamental signs until ventriloquist **The Great Lester** asked the Macks to make him a new figure for his act. When word got out, many other ventriloquists approached the Macks, and business boomed.

▲ Frank Marshall kept refining his ventriloquist figures throughout his career, and today his creations are cherished by professionals and collectors alike. His human dolls are readily recognizable by their heavily lined eyes and smiling "cheeky boy" features.

After the Macks died, an industrial model maker named Alex Cameron purchased the shop. He didn't have the same skills as the Macks for making figures, so he hired Frank Marshall in 1925 to do the work. After a few years, Cameron contracted tuberculosis. Realizing he owed Marshall money for the work he had done making the figures, Cameron gave the business to Marshall as due payment.

One of Marshall's most ingenious models was **Champagne Charlie**, a life-sized walking figure made for **W.S. Berger** in 1938. Charlie had moving eyes, a smoking mechanism and a walking cane.

▲ Ventriloquist Jimmy Nelson with a range of puppets made by celebrated craftsman Frank Marshall. Left to right: Humphrey Higsbye, Danny O'Day, Farfel the dog and Ftatateeta the cat.

Marshall tailored his hand-carved dolls to suit the personality and appearance of the ventriloquist. So when ventriloquist **Jimmy Nelson** asked Marshall to make him a figure, Marshall watched Nelson's theater act and came up with a dummy that Nelson called **Danny O'Day** because the name, unlike "McCarthy" and "'Mahoney," contained none of the consonants that ventriloquists struggle to say without moving their lips.

Marshall later made Nelson another figure, **Farfel** the dog, which had ears that pulled up. For ten years from 1955, Farfel was the face of Nestlé chocolate drink commercials, but Nelson's nerves nearly blew the audition. As Farfel sang the last word "chocolate," Nelson's hand slipped off the control, causing the dog's jaw to snap shut. Luckily the executives loved it, told Nelson to keep it in, and it became Farfel's trademark.

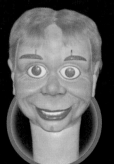

The inside of Cecil Wigglenose's head shows the intricate workings that were the trademark of ventriloquists' doll makers George and Glenn McElroy. The typewriter-like mechanisms allowed their creations a full range of facial expressions.

SUM DRESS ▶ Seventeen-year-old Kara Koskowich, who attended the Lethbridge Collegiate Institute in Alberta, Canada, made her graduation dress from her old math homework. She crafted the one-shouldered dress from 75 pieces of algebra formulae and neon Post-it® notes.

BODY PARTS ▶ London, England-based jewelry designer Percy Lau has introduced a range of pieces that looks like miniature body parts. Handcrafted in clay, the jewelry items include earrings in the shape of a human ear, finger rings in the shape of a closed mouth, and a necklace with a human nose on the end.

WRITE ON ▶ American author John Green autographed each of the 152,000 books in the first printing of his 2012 novel *The Fault in Our Stars* by signing his name for 12 hours a day, every day, for a month.

TONGUE INSURED ▶ At the height of the band's success, Kiss front man Gene Simmons had his trademark extra-long tongue insured for $1 million.

CELEBRITY TREE ▶ The daughter of Beyoncé and Jay-Z was named an honorary citizen of the Croatian town of Hvar because they named her Blue Ivy after a local tree. The celebrity couple had been impressed by the tree, which was wrapped in blue ivy, during their visit in September 2011.

SPARKLING NAILS

▶ Priced at $250,000 for a tiny bottle, Azature Black Diamond is the most expensive nail polish ever produced. Created by Los Angeles-based luxury jeweler Azature, the polish contains 267 carats of precious black diamonds and is so exclusive that only one bottle has been made.

AZATURE
black diamond

TOILET PAPER DRESS ▶
In June 2012, Susan Brennan of Orchard Lake, Michigan, won an annual toilet-paper wedding dress contest for the second year in a row by rustling up a modern dress made out of ten rolls of toilet paper, held together with glue, packing tape and thread, in just a week. She called her creation "Bohemian Cupcake," with the skirt part looking like layers of delicious cake frosting.

GOOD VIBRATIONS ▶ The Royal Philharmonic Orchestra played a three-hour concert in Cadogan Hall, London, England—to an audience of more than 100 plants and bulbs. The concert was to test whether musical vibrations can help stimulate plant growth.

COMEDY ORDER ▶ In addition to food and drink, customers who ordered room service at the Hotel Indigo in Edinburgh, Scotland, in April 2012 could order a 10-minute stand-up comedy routine by Janey Godley, who would come to their room and tell jokes.

BALLOONING BRIDES ▶ Thelma Levett from Leicestershire, England, made a replica of Kate Middleton's wedding dress from more than 5,000 balloons. The balloon artist, whose other balloon creations include a pink Cadillac and a bicycle, used both inflated and non-inflated balloons for the special wedding dress, which took more than four days to blow up.

DEEP VOICE ▶ The voice of U.S. singer Tim Storms can go so deep that the human ear is unable to hear it. Blessed with vocal chords twice the length of the average person's, he has a vocal range of ten octaves and can hit the note G7 (0.189Hz), the lowest note ever recorded by a human.

HAIR-RAISING

▶ Six employees and students from South Gloucestershire and Stroud College, England, created the longest hair extension in the world, an attachment stretching a hair-raising 1,185 ft (361.4 m)—that's the length of four soccer fields! The record-breaking extension, worn by Jade Bryer, took seven hours to make.

GUMSHOES

▶ *Israeli designer Kobi Levi creates handmade women's high-heeled shoes in quirky sculptured shapes—including a partly peeled banana, a slingshot, a sticking-out tongue, a shark, an elephant, and sneakers with fake chewing-gum heels—that sell for more than $2,000 a pair.*

BEATLES LOOK-ALIKES ▶ Each year the English city of Liverpool hosts a Beatles Week, which attracts more than 200 Beatles look-alike bands from around the world.

MILK FABRIC ▶ A young German designer with a passion for fashion and a degree in biology has combined the two to create a range of clothes made out of milk. Anke Domaske discovered a way of mixing powdered organic milk with other ingredients to weave a special fabric for her Qmilch line.

ROTTEN TOOTH ▶ Dr. Michael Zuk, a dentist from Red Deer, Canada, paid $31,000 in 2011 for former Beatle John Lennon's rotten molar tooth that had been extracted in the 1960s.

BOSS SILENCED ▶ Shortly after welcoming Sir Paul McCartney on stage at the 2012 Hard Rock Calling festival in Hyde Park, London, England, Bruce Springsteen and 80,000 fans were silenced when the concert was cut short for breaching a council late-night noise curfew. Springsteen's three-hour gig was supposed to have finished at 10.15 p.m. but when it overran to 10.38—eight minutes beyond the curfew—officials pulled the plug.

POLICE RESCUE ▶ Blind novelist Trish Vickers of Dorset, England, spent months painstakingly writing a book in longhand, only to be told one day that 26 pages were blank because her pen had run out of ink. However, local police officers were able to retrieve the missing words by using forensic technology to study the indents made by her pen.

KLINGON MASTER ▶ Even though he is dyslexic and had always struggled to read English, 50-year-old Star Trek fan Jonathan Brown of Milton Keynes, England, spent 12 years learning how to speak Klingon—and was so successful that he became the chief linguist on a CD teaching others how to master the alien language.

▶▶ THE HOWLING NOISE MADE BY CHEWBACCA IN STAR WARS CAME FROM AN ANGRY CAMEL. ◀

TV BANNED ▶ Bhutan was the last nation in the world to have television—as recently as 1999. Previously, it was banned, but then Bhutan's rulers decided that the country should be less isolated.

GRASS SHOES ▶ Australian footwear company KUSA has launched a range of flip-flops with fake turf stitched into the soles to give the wearer the experience of walking barefooted on grass.

OLDEST CLOWN ▶ Floyd Creekmore from Billings, Montana, was still performing as Creeky the Clown at age 95, making him the world's oldest clown. He has been entertaining crowds at fairs and rodeos since he was ten but it was not until 1981 that the former rancher became a full-time clown, in which guise he often performs with his grandson Tom McCraw.

GIANT DRUMSTICKS ▶ A concert at the Warren Amphitheater, Ohio, unveiled two 900-lb (408-kg) drumsticks carved from poplar logs in honor of hometown boy Dave Grohl, frontman of the Foo Fighters and formerly drummer with Nirvana. The giant drumsticks were engraved with feathers to represent Grohl's tattoos.

ROYAL UNDERPANTS ▶ A large pair of silk bloomers worn by Queen Victoria of England more than 100 years ago sold at an auction in Edinburgh, Scotland, in 2011 for nearly $15,000.

ABBA TRIBUTE ▶ On November 17, 2011, at Kew Primary School in Melbourne, Australia, 368 children turned into "dancing queens" to set a new record for the largest gathering of Abba impersonators.

LITTLE FEET ▶ K.B. Shivshankar displays more than 170 homemade pairs of miniature shoes, ranging from stiletto heels to gum boots, in his shoe shop in Bangalore, India. A cobbler by trade, he began making miniature shoes with the leftover materials and can handcraft a pair in just an hour. The smallest pair in his collection is 0.7 in (1.75 cm) long and the largest is 2 in (5 cm).

JUSTIN BRIE-BER

▶ British food artist Faye Halliday has created a portrait of Justin Bieber out of soft cheese spread. She uses around three pots on each of her cheesy images, which also include Barack Edam-a, Marilyn Mon-zzarella and Irish singing twins Ched-ward. She occasionally adds roasted garlic dip and sour cream and chives dip for extra texture.

ODD TITLES ▶ Contenders for *The Bookseller's* Oddest Book Title for 2012 included *A Century of Sand Dredging in the Bristol Channel*, *The Mushroom in Christian Art* and *Estonian Sock Patterns All Around the World*.

SAME SONG ▶ Alan St. Louis of Nashua, New Hampshire, performed the U.S. national anthem at special events 217 times in one year, singing for audiences as small as five at a college softball game and up to 12,000 at a New England Revolution soccer match.

THE NAME'S BOND ▶ British author Ian Fleming was an avid birdwatcher and his fictional British super-spy James Bond was named after an American ornithologist, the author of *Birds of the West Indies*, first published in 1936.

DOG STAR ▶ In December 2011, canine actor Danny, a soft-coated wheaten terrier, retired after ten years of playing Sandy, Orphan Annie's faithful pet companion in the U.K. production of the long-running stage musical *Annie*. Danny, who joined the cast as a seven-month-old puppy, traveled the length of the country with owner and trainer Rita Mansell and notched up 1,400 performances, each rewarded with a dish of cheese and sausages.

BLOOD COMIC ▶ A 1977 comic book featuring U.S. rock band Kiss was printed with red ink that had been mixed with the band members' blood.

CRAZY HORSES ▶ German designer Iris Schieferstein has created a range of shoes from dead animal parts, including high-heel horse hooves, sandals sculpted from deceased doves, and snakeskin stilettos with a replica pistol as a heel. She collects the dead animals from her butcher in Berlin, then removes the meat and bones from her chosen animal's foot before fitting the preserved skin, with the fur still in place, around a shoe model. Her shoes sell for nearly $6,000 a pair, and she has designed a pair of horse hooves for Lady Gaga.

ONE-TAKE MOVIE ▶ Indian filmmaker Haroon Rashid shot a 140-minute Bollywood thriller, entiled *One Shot Fear Without a Cut*, with a crew of 17 on a single camera, in one take, without a single cut. He rehearsed the action for five months before setting the camera rolling.

FERMENTED FASHION

▶ Scientists from the University of Western Australia have teamed up with designer Donna Franklin to create the world's first dress made from red wine. By adding bacteria to the wine, it ferments into vinegar and a thin, cottonlike microbial skin gradually forms on the surface. The skin is then harvested and dried on an inflated mannequin, where it shrinks to fit. When the dummy is deflated, the seamless garment retains the body's shape and is ready to wear like a second skin.

DEATH OF A PRESIDENT

On Friday, November 22, 1963—John Fitzgerald Kennedy, aged 46, the 35th President of the U.S.A., was assassinated while traveling in a motorcade alongside his wife Jacqueline through the streets of downtown Dallas, Texas.

He was shot with a rifle from a sixth-floor window, apparently by a lone gunman, former U.S. Marine Lee Harvey Oswald. Oswald was arrested within 40 minutes, but was himself shot and killed by local nightclub owner Jack Ruby two days later while being transferred to Dallas County Jail.

Since Kennedy's death there have been many conspiracy theories surrounding the assassination, with most Americans refusing to believe that Oswald acted alone. The events of that day remain a defining moment in 20th-century history, and spawned some incredible facts of their own.

LATE NEWS▶ Within 30 minutes of J.F.K.'s shooting, TV and radio reports relayed the news to more than 75 million Americans—but 12 jurors in a murder trial in Milwaukee, Wisconsin, did not hear about it until the evening of November 23. They had spent four days behind locked doors, and it was only when they reached their verdict on the Saturday night that the judge told them about Kennedy's assassination.

GRIEVING LETTERS▶ J.F.K.'s widow Jackie received more than 1.5 million condolence letters following her husband's assassination, 45,000 arriving at the White House on one day alone. Around 200,000 pages of letters were subsequently stored at the John F. Kennedy Library in Boston, Massachusetts, where they filled 170 ft (52 m) of shelf space.

COVER-UP?▶ A 2009 opinion poll found that only 10 percent of Americans believe that Lee Harvey Oswald acted alone in killing J.F.K. Seventy-four percent believe there was an official cover-up to keep the truth about the President's killing from the public.

MOVIE CAMERA▶ Dallas clothing manufacturer Abraham Zapruder captured the J.F.K. assassination on his home movie camera. He had arrived at the office that morning without it, and his secretary, Lillian Rogers, persuaded him to go home and fetch the camera, saying "How many times will you have a crack at color movies of the President?" The Zapruder Film, as it became known, was sold two days later to *Life* magazine for $150,000—the equivalent of more than $1 million in today's money.

PINK SUIT▶ The pink suit that Jackie Kennedy wore on the day of the assassination is kept in a secret vault in the National Archives and Records Administration's complex in Maryland, where the temperature is kept at between 65 and 68°F (18 and 20°C), the humidity is 40 percent, and the air is changed six times an hour. The blood-splattered suit has never been cleaned, and only a handful of people have been allowed to see it since 1963.

FINAL FILM▶ In his final movie before entering politics, future U.S. President Ronald Reagan was filming *The Killers* with Lee Marvin and Angie Dickinson at Universal City in California when production was halted because of J.F.K.'s assassination. As President, Reagan himself survived an assassination attempt in 1981—the first sitting President to survive being shot by a would-be assassin.

CASKET RESTING PLACE▶ The casket that contained Kennedy's body on the flight to Washington, D.C., in preparation for his burial was later weighted and dropped by a U.S. Air Force plane into the Atlantic Ocean in an area where the disposal of test weapons left the seabed littered with munitions, making it too dangerous for anyone to try to recover it.

CHILD SUPPORT▶ After President Kennedy was killed, 11-year-old Jane Dryden from Austin, Texas, was so upset that she sent one condolence letter a week to the White House for the next six months.

KENNEDY MUSEUM▶ Located in the former Texas School Book Depository building from which Oswald fired the fatal shot, the Sixth Floor Museum in Dallas contains over 40,000 items relating to Kennedy's assassination.

HAT AUCTION▶ The gray fedora hat worn by Jack Ruby when he shot Lee Harvey Oswald was sold at auction in 2009 to an anonymous buyer for $53,775.

CONSPIRACY THEORIES▶ Numerous conspiracy theories surround J.F.K.'s assassination, alleged culprits including the C.I.A., the Cubans, the Russians, Vice President Lyndon Johnson, and U.S. mobsters. One theory even suggested that Kennedy was killed by an accidental discharge from the rifle of a Secret Service agent traveling in the car behind the President's limousine.

FOUR DEATHS▶ West Virginian Perry Gum's life spanned the deaths of all four assassinated U.S. presidents. He celebrated his 99th birthday on the day Kennedy was shot, and wrote in his letter to the White House that he had also lived through the assassinations of Abraham Lincoln (1865), James Garfield (1881) and William McKinley (1901).

KENNEDY AND LINCOLN

A series of spooky coincidences link the assassination of President Kennedy with that of President Abraham Lincoln almost 100 years earlier.

- Lincoln was elected to Congress in 1846, Kennedy in 1946.
- Lincoln was elected as President in 1860, Kennedy in 1960.
- Both were assassinated on Fridays in front of their wives.
- Lincoln was shot in Ford's Theatre; Kennedy was shot in a Lincoln, made by Ford.
- Both Presidents' wives lost a child while living in the White House.
- Both assassins, John Wilkes Booth and Lee Harvey Oswald, were killed before facing trial.
- The surnames of both Presidents have seven letters.
- The names of both assassins have 15 letters.
- Their successors as President were both named Johnson.
- Andrew Johnson was born in 1808, Lyndon Johnson in 1908.
- Both assassinated Presidents were shot in the head.
- Both Presidents were particularly concerned with civil rights.

▶ Among the J.F.K. related exhibits in the Ripley collection is a lock of Lee Harvey Oswald's hair and his body identification (toe) tag. Ripley's also own the car in which Oswald traveled on the way to assassinate Kennedy.

TWILIGHT ZONE

▶ Cathy Ward from Berkshire, England, is such a huge fan of the *Twilight Saga* series of books and movies that she has had images of the cast tattooed over her entire back. She spent £2,000 ($3,000) and 22 hours in the artist's chair to have tattoos of Robert Pattinson, Kristen Stewart and Taylor Lautner inked on to her skin—and they were her first-ever tattoos!

TRUE FANATICS

has seen the original *Star Wars* trilogy over 300 times. He also had a Star Wars-themed wedding and named his two daughters Emily Rose Princess Leia and Bethany Violet Skywalker.

have collected more than 4,670 items of *Conan the Barbarian* memorabilia since the 1970s.

has read each *Harry Potter* book over 100 times and has spent $13,000 turning his home into a Potter shrine. He also has four *Harry Potter* tattoos, including the Hogwarts crest on his shoulder and Sirius Black's prison numbers on his neck.

is such a massive *Superman* fan that he named his son Kal-El, Superman's birth name.

LONDON TOUR▶ Leo Ihenacho (aka Leo the Lion), a former member of U.K. hip hop band The Streets, played 24 gigs in 24 hours in London, England, from July 11–12, 2012. Venues included the London Eye, a prison cell and a meat market.

WASHBOARD MUSIC▶ Logan, Ohio, is home to an annual washboard music festival celebrating the use of laundry equipment as musical instruments.

PIANO PRODIGY▶ At age nine, piano player Ethan Bortnick of Pembroke Pines, Florida, became the youngest musician to headline a solo concert tour. After begging his parents for piano lessons, he started playing the piano at the age of three and was composing music by the time he was five. In July 2011, he headlined a show in Las Vegas, Nevada, at age ten, and has shared a stage with a host of stars from Elton John to Beyoncé.

MOBILE BAND▶ A three-piece Russian band, the Bremen Town Musicians, played a gig while speeding down a highway on a motorbike fitted with a drum kit and guitar amp. One member steered, one played guitar and one played drums.

GUITAR TOWER▶ The Experience Music Project in Seattle, Washington State, features a 60-ft (18-m) tower made up of over 500 guitars.

GUITAR SOLO ▶ On May 14, 2012, David DiDonato performed a mammoth guitar solo when he played for 24 hours 55 minutes at the Red 7 club in Austin, Texas.

SHORTEST ANTHEM ▶ Uruguay's national anthem has 105 bars of music and is 6½ minutes long, while the national anthem of Uganda is only nine bars and lasts just 18 seconds.

DEAF DRUMMER ▶ Scotland's Evelyn Glennie was the world's first full-time solo percussionist even though she has been deaf since age 12. She has learned to "hear" through her feet and often plays barefoot in order to feel the music better.

BEARD HAT

▶ A Canadian company has designed the ultimate fashion line to keep people warm in winter—a woolly hat with an attached beard. The acrylic Beardo is adjustable and makers Beardowear claim it can fit any face. It can also be tucked away inside the hat for occasions when a knitted beard might not be appropriate. The beard hats were the brainchild of Jeff Phillips, a Canadian snowboarding enthusiast.

LIGHTNING CONCERT

▶ *Wang Zengxiang is no ordinary electric guitarist. When he plays, a million volts of electricity surge through his body as he generates lightning bolts over 13 ft (4 m) long. Wearing special protective suits of metallic silk thread, which insulates him from the current, Wang and his band, Thunderbolt Fan, from Fujian Province, China, are rigged up to a Tesla coil, a transformer that acts as a giant lightning conductor. It produces vast amounts of voltage at high frequencies and creates spectacular bolts of electricity that arc through the air.*

TRANSPORT ▶

MINI MAGIC

Artist Ian Cook has more fun than should be legal, spending his days messing around with toy cars and pots of paint. When he composes one of his original artworks, instead of applying paint to the canvas with brushes, he uses remote-controlled toy cars. For bigger pieces, he has painted with real cars, motorbikes, go-karts and even a six-ton truck!

Ian, from Birmingham, England, discovered his unique style after a trip to Latvia, where he was struck by the sheer diversity of cars. Afterward, his girlfriend of the time bought him a remote-controlled toy car, warning him not to take it down to his art studio or it would be ruined. So naturally that was the first thing he did!

MINI COOPER

At Ripley's we were so impressed with Ian's finished artwork that we bought it! The Ripley's Believe it or Not! Odditorium in London, England, displays the unique piece as part of a special multimedia exhibit showing the painting and how it was created.

MINI COOPER

SEE MORE AMAZING EXTRA STUFF!!

Simply download our APP & try out

ODD SCAN

Watch Ian's remote controlled cars skidding in wet paint!

AUTO MISSILE▶ Paul Stender of Indianapolis, Indiana, strapped a cruise missile engine to the roof of a 1967 Chevrolet to create a crazy car that could do 300 mph (480 km/h) and fire out 30-ft (9-m) flames from the rear. The 10,000 bhp engine on his Jet-Impala 67 is the equivalent of ten high-powered Bugatti Veyron sports cars. He has previously built a jet-powered toilet and a jet-powered school bus featured in *Ripley's Believe It or Not! Strikingly True.*

OLD FAITHFUL▶ Rachel Veitch of Orlando, Florida, drove 567,000 mi (912,500 km) over a 48-year period in the same car. She bought her Mercury Comet Caliente in 1964, and it went on to outlast three marriages and 18 battery changes. The 93-year-old grandmother finally had to give up driving it in March 2012 because she had been declared legally blind.

TIGHT SQUEEZE▶ In Beijing on May 21, 2012, Chinese stunt driver Han Yue parallel-parked his Mini in a space just 6 in (15 cm) longer than his car—in less than two seconds!

GHOST TRAINS▶ A group of U.K. rail enthusiasts ride on special "Parliamentary trains"—or "ghost trains"—services that are often otherwise empty, and are run just once a week and only in one direction. Train operators run these ghost trains to keep small routes open because it is cheaper and less time-consuming than closing them down.

COLD COMFORT▶ The NS *Yamal*, a Russian icebreaker ship, will never sail out of the Arctic Sea because its design means it requires the cold waters to cool the two nuclear reactors that power it.

BIGGEST FLOTILLA▶ Queen Elizabeth II helped set a new world record for the largest parade of boats after leading a 1,000-strong flotilla along London's River Thames on June 3, 2012, as part of her Diamond Jubilee celebrations.

SWEET RIDE▶ Fritz Grobe and Stephen Voltz of Buckfield, Maine, built a single-seat rocket car powered only by soda and candy. They used the chemical reaction—a process called nucleation— that occurs as a result of mixing 54 bottles of fizzy Coke Zero and 324 Mentos to propel the car a distance of 239 ft (73 m).

BRIDGE FIRE

▶The 100-car Union Pacific coal train was traveling from Denver, Colorado, to Chicago, Illinois, when a wheel bearing on the train overheated and melted, causing white hot molten metal to fall down onto the rail. Spotting the smoke coming from the 57th car, the alert crew immediately stopped the train but unfortunately the hot wheel was directly over Turkey Creek Bridge near Sharon Springs, Kansas. As the wooden structure caught fire, the crew saved the rest of the train by unhooking it from the cars that were stopped on the bridge, but the accident still caused $2 million damage.

HEAVY PENALTY ▶ In January 2012, railroad officials in Indonesia began suspending weighted balls over railroad tracks to discourage "train surfing"—the practice of commuters riding on train roofs without paying a fare.

POOP POWER ▶ On March 22, 2012, the Denver Zoo in Colorado demonstrated a three-wheeled motorized rickshaw—or tuk tuk—that runs on a mixture of trash generated by zoo visitors and employees and animal poop.

DESERT REPAIRS ▶ When Frenchman Emile Leray crashed his Citroen 2CV car into a rock in the middle of the Moroccan desert, leaving it undrivable, he reached the safety of a village some 20 mi (32 km) away by building a makeshift motorbike out of the wrecked car. Using the limited tools he had with him, the 43-year-old retired electrician began by removing the Citroen's body, which he then used as a shelter for sleep. To build the bike, he shortened the car's chassis before reattaching the axles and two of the wheels, as well as installing the engine and gearbox in the middle. After 12 days, by which time he had just one pint of water left, he was ready to ride off to the village, but even then he kept falling off the bike's seat, which was made from part of the car's rear bumper.

SUBWAY SYSTEM ▶ New York City has a land area of 302.6 sq mi (784 sq km)—but its subway system has 842 mi (1,355 km) of track.

FRENCH LESSON ▶ A confused driver drove down the steps of a Paris Metro station after mistaking it for an underground parking lot. He managed to brake in time to stop the car on the steps of the Chaussée d'Antin-La Fayette station but left the back wheels sticking out on the sidewalk.

FISHY PASSENGER

▶ This successful fisherman in Jinja, Uganda, decided there was only one way to take his monster catch home—on the back of his motorcycle.

BAD IDEA ▶ A drunk driver caused a railway in Wuhan, China, to be closed for five hours when he tried to drive home along the tracks. The man told police he didn't know the area and blamed his "misleading" GPS system. He made it about 100 yards when the metal rails shredded his tires and his car became stuck. Luckily, he was spotted before passenger trains started moving the following morning.

ROCKET MAN ▶ In June 2012, daredevil Swiss rocket man Yves Rossy dropped from a helicopter and deployed his four-engined Jetwing flying suit alongside a vintage Breitling passenger plane at an altitude of 4,500 ft (1,370 m) over Lake Lucerne, Switzerland. He flew for seven minutes at 128 mph (205 km/h) until his fuel ran out and he parachuted safely to the ground.

CHIPPED BODYWORK ▶ Zhang Lianzhi of Tianjin, China, has covered a brand new Range Rover in 10,000 pieces of broken antique porcelain. He spent nearly 20 years collecting porcelain chips from all corners of China before sticking them to the vehicle. Even though they are broken, the bits of ceramic are worth an estimated $157,000.

This is the moment when the wooden railroad bridge burst into flames and collapsed in a freak accident that sent six 280,000-lb (127,000-kg) train cars crashing into the creek below.

BONE
◄IDOL

▶ Biker Phil Boxall has ridden more than 32,000 mi (51,000 km) around the U.K. on his 1200cc Yamaha V-Max with a human skeleton as his passenger! Bought on eBay, "Sid Bones" has ridden everywhere with Phil for more than four years. The pair even once reached a bone-rattling 120 mph (193 km/h) in just 12 seconds on a drag strip.

PRIZE CRASH▶ Truck driver David Dopp of Santaquin, Utah, won a $300,000 Lamborghini sports car in a competition in November 2011, but within six hours of driving it away, he crashed it.

The MV Liemba, a ferry that runs across Africa's Lake Tanganyika, was originally built in 1913 as a warship for Imperial Germany.

TOY STORY▶ In April 2012, two-year-old Noah Joel pedaled his toy bicycle over 3 mi (4.8 km) across the busy town of Hamelin, Germany, to visit his grandmother in the hospital, while his mother thought he was playing in his room.

Pete Golsby from Suffolk, England, spent nearly five years building a sports car from scratch—even though he is blind and cannot drive it. He put it together using an engine from an old motorbike, piping from a shower and car parts donated by friends.

RICKSHAW RACE▶ In October 2011, 66 people from 12 countries raced from Jakarta, Indonesia, to Bangkok, Thailand, in auto rickshaws, each with a half-horsepower engine. They covered the distance of 1,864 mi (3,000 km) in two weeks.

INVISIBLE BIKE▶ Artist and designer Joey Ruiter of Grand Rapids, Michigan, has created a street-legal motorbike that looks invisible and appears to make the rider float silently along the road. "Moto undone" has a quiet, electric engine and is encased in a shiny metal box that conceals the bike's framework. It has no speed dial or other gauges—they are all viewed through a downloadable smartphone app.

PEDAL FLIGHT▶ A pedal-powered helicopter, the Gamera II, designed by students from the University of Maryland, successfully hovered in the air for 50 seconds in June 2012. Although it is 105 ft (32 m) wide and each of its four rotors has a span of 42 ft 7 in (13 m), the helicopter weighs just 71 lb (32.2 kg).

NEON TRUCKS▶ Enthusiasts of Japan's Dekotora art form decorate their cargo trucks to extremes—with shiny metallics, lavish paint jobs and so many neon lights that the rigs aren't street legal when they are turned on.

BIKER BIRD▶ At New Hampshire Motor Speedway, Loudon, on June 17, 2012, Myles Bratter rode his motorcycle at a speed of 78 mph (125 km/h) with Rainbow, his pet Macaw parrot, perched on his shoulder, thereby setting a world speed record for riding a motorbike with an untethered bird. Bratter and Rainbow have been riding together for more than 17 years. "I raised her from an egg," he says. "The first thing she saw when she hatched was me."

SNAKES ALIVE!

▶ A Brazilian motorcyclist doing 164 mph (262 km/h) on an open road had the shock of his life when a yellow snake suddenly lunged at him from near the right handlebar and came to rest on his hand. Luckily, the biker kept his cool and pulled over to the side of the road. The snake had probably been hiding in the bike's engine to keep warm.

AIR MILES▶ Ron Akana of Boulder, Colorado, spent 63 years as a flight attendant, during which time he flew an estimated 20 million mi (32 million km)—the equivalent of more than 800 trips around the world. He retired in 2012 at age 83 after completing a United Airlines flight from Denver, Colorado, to Kauai, Hawaii.

CRASH LANDING▶ Shortly after an airplane took off from Opa-Locka Executive Airport, Florida, its door became detached in flight and crashed down onto a golf course in Broward County. Luckily, the course was closed at the time for maintenance and the plane was able to land safely at nearby Fort Lauderdale-Hollywood International Airport.

GOLD CAR▶ In 2011, Indian car manufacturer Tata created a Nano car covered in gold, silver and jewels worth $4.6 million—the price of more than 1,500 standard model Nanos. Thirty craftsmen worked on the creation of the one-off model, using 176 lb (80 kg) of 22-carat gold, 33 lb (15 kg) of silver and around 10,000 assorted gemstones.

GHOST CAR▶ Sci-fi fan Paul Harborne from the West Midlands, England, spent £50,000 restoring a battered 1959 Cadillac into an exact replica of Ecto-1, the *Ghostbusters* car from the 1984 movie. Available to hire, the car makes a big splash with its replica lightbars and rotating beacons.

SADDLE SOAR▶ Felix Guirola rides a 13-ft-high (4-m) homemade, super-tall bicycle through the streets of Havana, Cuba. He pedals around at eye-level with second-story apartments, peering over pickup trucks and buses, and wears no helmet or other protective gear to break a fall.

TOILET BEST▶ At a stunt show in Sydney, Australia, on May 2, 2012, stuntwoman and former motocross champion Jolene Van Vugt from Ontario, Canada, set a new land speed record for a motorized toilet of 46 mph (74 km/h). Her contraption resembles a go-kart but has a porcelain toilet in place of a driver's seat.

BEE-LEAVE IT!▶ Interstate 15 in Utah was closed for several hours after a truck carrying 25 million bees overturned. Beekeepers worked overnight to recapture the insects—worth more than $100,000—which were being transported from South Dakota to California.

◀TRUCK PILE UP

▶ Traffic cops in Laian, China, thought they had probably seen everything until they spotted these three flatbed trucks piled on top of each other driving erratically along the highway. Having just bought the trucks, cargo firm boss Sun Lin wanted to save money on drivers' and toll fees, so he asked the seller to stack them up by crane ready to be driven more than 100 mi (160 km) to his yard. He was fined $750 for his crazy idea.

SCHOOLBOY HERO▶ When the driver of his school bus suffered a heart attack on the morning of April 9, 2012, quick-thinking 13-year-old Jeremy Wuitschick of Milton, Washington State, grabbed the steering wheel, directed the bus safely toward a curb and pulled the key from the ignition. He then began performing chest compressions on the unconscious driver.

ALTERNATIVE HEATER▶ When the heater in his Volvo broke, Pascal Prokop of Mettmenstetten, Switzerland, overcame the bitter cold of the Swiss winter by installing a functional wood-burning stove in the car. He removed the passenger seat in order to accommodate the stove and also installed a chimney to get rid of the carbon monoxide and smoke. Swiss officials had no objection to his unconventional modifications.

LONG RIDE▶ Paul Archer, Johno Ellison and Leigh Purnell from the U.K. traveled a mind-boggling 43,320 mi (69,716 km) on a 15-month journey around the world in a black London taxi cab. They racked up almost $120,000 on the meter during a trip that took them to four continents and 50 different countries. They were arrested in Moscow and were nearly kidnapped in Pakistan, but also achieved the highest taxi ride ever when they drove up to the Mount Everest base camp, which lies 17,143 ft (5,225 m) above sea level.

FREE TRAVEL▶ After running away from his mother during a shopping trip, 11-year-old Liam Corcoran-Fort was able to fly from Manchester, England, to Rome, Italy, despite not having a ticket, a boarding pass or a passport.

SPEED SLIDE▶ A Swiss motorcyclist set off a police speed camera, while sliding along the ground having fallen off his bike. After losing control of his machine, Boris Maier from Bern, was clocked hurtling helplessly at 67 mph (108 km/h) in a 50-mph (80-km/h) zone while the riderless bike's speed went unrecorded.

FARE POINT▶ For a $5,000 fare, New York City cab driver Mohammed Alam took John Belitsky and Dan Wuebben on a six-day, 2,800-mi (4,500-km) drive to Los Angeles, California—with a stopover in Las Vegas, Nevada, for a night of gambling where they won $2,000. A first-class return air fare was just under $4,000, but Belitsky wanted to prove that his father, a former New York City cab driver, was wrong when he said no cabbie would take them all the way to L.A.

ROAD LEGAL▶ Engineer Russ Bost from Essex, England, has created a road-legal Formula-1 look-alike car out of spare parts. His custom-built machine has a motorcycle engine and a top speed of 170 mph (274 km/h). It only costs $15,000 and does 30 miles per gallon (10.6 km/liter), compared to an F1 car's miserly 3.8 miles per gallon (1.3 km/liter). It also has a rear seat for carrying groceries back from the supermarket in style.

LUXURY HEARSE▶ Italian custom builder Biemme Special Cars created a $600,000, 23-ft-long (7-m), stretch hearse, made entirely from aluminum and constructed from more than 600 assembled parts and 660 ft (200 m) of welding. The coffin compartment of the Rolls-Royce Phantom Hearse B12 features high luminescence LEDs to illuminate the casket.

HELPING HAND▶ A giant green hand protruding from a large manhole in the road startled drivers in Tianjin, China. With the manhole missing its cover for more than a month, local residents stuffed an abandoned hand-shaped sofa down it to warn motorists of the hazard ahead.

CRAZY BIKE▶ Zhang Yali from Jilin City, China, built a larger-than-life bike—more than 10 ft (3 m) high and 18 ft (5.5 m) long—for his cartoon-crazy son. It cost him $3,000 to create the one-ton bike, which has two huge wheels taken from an excavator. The seat is made from old sofas, and can sit up to eight people in two rows.

MASS BURNOUT

PAINTED BENTLEY

▶ British artist Paul Karslake created his artwork *Empire*, by painting a Bentley Mulsanne with scenes of the British Empire. Featuring portraits of former Prime Minister Winston Churchill and Queen Elizabeth II, as well as famous British military victories including Trafalgar and Waterloo, the car was unveiled outside the Ripley's museum in London, England, in June 2012 to celebrate the Queen's Diamond Jubilee.

SCRAP BATPOD▶ Batman fan Vu Tung Lam from Lang Son, Vietnam, built his own version of the Caped Crusader's motorbike, the Batpod, from scrap metal and an old Suzuki engine. It took him two months and $450 to build, but although the machine has a top speed of 56 mph (90 km/h), he is not permitted to ride it on Vietnamese roads.

BEE SWARM▶ A flight from Pittsburgh, Pennsylvania, to New York City was delayed at Pittsburgh International Airport on August 1, 2012, after a swarm of thousands of honeybees suddenly gathered on the airplane's wing.

OLDEST BACKPACKER▶ Keith Wright from Queensland, Australia, loves traveling around the world with his backpack—even though he is 95 years old. He took up backpacking when he was 85, and has visited more than 20 countries and 100 foreign cities.

SPEED SAIL▶ A sailing boat traveled at an astonishing speed of 43.2 mph (69.5 km/h) over one nautical mile in San Francisco Bay on August 31, 2012. Designed by French yachtsman Alain Thébault, *L' Hydroptère* rises up out of the water on hydrofoils as it picks up speed.

TWO-WHEEL DRIVE▶ British stunt driver Terry Grant drove a Nissan Juke over a 1-mile (1.6-km) course at the 2011 Goodwood Festival of Speed in 2 minutes 55 seconds—driving sideways on only two wheels. His average speed was just over 20 mph (32 km/h).

FLYING SAUCER▶ Intrepid farmer Shu Mansheng successfully flew his homemade flying saucer at an altitude of 6 ft (1.8 m) or more for over 30 seconds in Wuhan, China. He spent $4,500 building the 18-ft-diameter (5.5-m) octocopter, which is powered by eight motorbike engines with propellers.

DOZED OFF▶ Patrice Christine Ahmed, a French woman flying from Pakistan to Paris, slept through the landing at Charles de Gaulle Airport and didn't wake up until she was on the way back to Lahore!

HOMEMADE PLANE▶ Retired pilot Patrick Elliott and his wife Linda, from Surrey, England, circumnavigated the globe in a tiny homemade airplane, which they had spent 16 years building. The couple took off around the world in the 16-ft-long (5-m) Rutan Long-EZ in September 2010, flying a total of 37,398 mi (60,186 km) before returning home a year and a day later. In the course of their epic journey, they made 99 flights, visited 23 countries and used $18,000-worth of fuel.

FAKE FERRARI▶ The Fahrradi Farfalla FFX looks like a new Ferrari, but it is actually a quad-cycle with a top speed barely any faster than that of a pedestrian. Created by Austrian artist Hannes Langeder using plastic and lightweight steel, the unique cycle, based on the exterior of a Ferrari FXX, weighs just 220 lb (100 kg) and is steered using pedals that control 11 different gears.

▶ At Australia's biggest horsepower party, the Summernats 26 festival in Canberra, 69 cars revved up furiously for 30 seconds, creating billowing clouds of red and white smoke and black rubber to set a new world record for the largest simultaneous burnout.

NEAR MISSES

BALANCING ACT

▼ Shan Dan avoided disaster by a matter of inches after mistaking the gas pedal for the brake while reverse parking and leaving her BMW hanging precariously over the edge of an elevated parking garage in Changchun, China. She calmly climbed out but said: "I was terrified when I got out and saw the position of the car."

AMAZING ESCAPE

▼ Driver Yang Junsheng incredibly escaped with barely a scratch after dozens of steel bars crashed through the windshield of his car in Taizhou, China. He smashed into the back of a pickup truck carrying the metal rods but instinctively ducked as they flew toward him, and somehow they all missed him.

NEAR MISS

▲ A driver in Zhenjiang, China, had a lucky escape after he drove into a metal road barrier, which speared through the front of his van and straight out of the back, missing him by inches. He suffered nothing worse than a scratch on his left leg, but passed out due to shock.

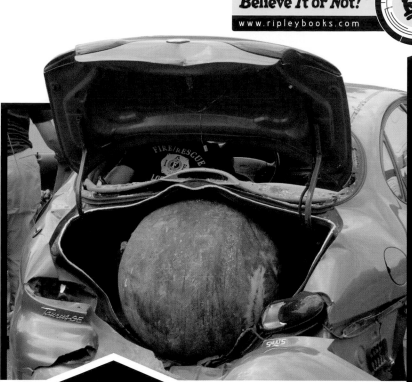

CAR WRECKER

▲ Alex Habay was sitting in his car at a traffic light in Meadville, Pennsylvania, when a 1,500-lb (680-kg) wrecking ball suddenly smashed into the rear with such force that it pushed his vehicle into the two cars in front of him. The runaway ball had broken loose from a demolition crane and careened down the street hitting nine parked cars before crashing into Habay's trunk where the presence of eight soccer balls may have lessened the impact and saved him from serious injury.

CLIFF HANGER

◀ This BMW car finished up just a few feet from the edge of a steep cliff and a 100-ft (30-m) drop to the sea below after hurtling down a grassy bank at Flamborough Head in Yorkshire, England. The driver was winched to safety by rescue helicopter.

CRAZY CROSSING

▶ This car driver had an unbelievable escape after sneaking over a level crossing in Carmarthenshire, Wales, just a split second ahead of an oncoming train. The driver, who had his wife and young son in the car at the time, later admitted dangerous driving. He said he had not seen the flashing warning lights at the crossing.

FEATS ▶

VOLCANO CHASER

Photographer and thrill-seeker Geoff Mackley stood on a spot where no human has ever been before—just 100 ft (30 m) above a boiling lake of 2,100°F (1,150°C) lava in an active volcano. Even though he was wearing a special fire suit and breathing apparatus, just one slip or a sudden surge of the bubbling lava would have turned him instantly to ash.

Geoff, from Christchurch, New Zealand, specializes in photographing spectacular natural phenomena, including hurricanes, cyclones and tornadoes, but this ultimate quest to reach the Marum Volcano on one of the Pacific islands of Vanuatu, 1,200 mi (1,900 km) off the northeast coast of Australia, took him 15 years of planning.

"You had to dodge rocks big enough to kill you that are moving at terminal velocity past you every few minutes."

◀ On his first day, Geoff climbed down toward the volcano. When he reached the rim he stood without his protective suit, but the heat was so intense that he had to cover his face and run back after just six seconds. All too aware that over 200,000 people have died from volcanic eruptions in the past five centuries, he knew that just one gulp of the superheated air coming off the lava would kill him instantly.

◀ With its lava lake the size of 2½ football fields, the Marum Volacno emits heat that is as fierce as that from the flame of a blowtorch, nearly five times hotter than the maximum temperature of a conventional oven, and more than 20 times hotter than the record temperature at Death Valley, California. A volcano's lava tubes are so efficient in containing heat that lava flowing as far as 6 mi (9.6 km) from the center of a volcano cools only by about 18°F (10°C).

◀ Just to reach the edge of the lava pit, Geoff had to climb down a 1,200-ft (366-m) vertical drop—that's almost the height of New York City's Empire State Building. He donned the suit and breathing apparatus and descended again to create history by standing next to the volcano for 40 minutes. He was so focused on what lay before him that his colleagues eventually had to warn him that he was running out of air in his breathing gear.

CHURCH LICKER

▶ To win a bet with a friend, Lawrence Edmonds of London has licked all 42 of England's Anglican cathedrals. His 17-month, 5,000-mi (8,000-km) tour saw him place his tongue on the stonework of cathedrals that included Durham, York, Canterbury and Winchester.

JUMP FLIP▶ Hollywood stuntman Robert Souris set a record-breaking longest forward jump flip when he achieved a leap of 19 ft 11½ in (6.08 m) at Davie, Florida, on July 4, 2012. He celebrated by doing four backflips.

Ralf Esslinger, Thomas Hinte and Guido Verhoef created 2,335 balloon flowers in eight hours on May 13, 2012, at a garden show in Nagold, Germany. Each flower consisted of at least two balloons.

BOTTLE CAPS▶ Pupils at Ambrosoli International School in Bugolobi, Uganda, strung 34,149 bottle caps into one continuous chain measuring 508 ft (155 m) long.

PAPER PLANE▶ On February 26, 2012, former football quarterback Joe Ayoob threw a paper airplane a world-record distance of 226 ft 10 in (69.1 m) inside a hangar at McClellan Air Force Base near Sacramento, California. Built by John Collins, who has designed real airplanes for many years, the paper missile was made from A4 paper and a small piece of sticky tape.

YOUNGEST COWBOY▶ Aged just 2½, Royce Gill from New South Wales is a regular on the Australian rodeo circuit, riding against cowboys more than seven times his age. Royce, the world's youngest rodeo star, rides a six-year-old miniature pony called Maybelline and is the seventh-generation rodeo rider in his family.

MARATHON RIDE▶ Californian Gus Martinez rode for 25 hours, with just a five-minute break each hour, aboard the 130-ft-tall (40-m) Ferris wheel at Santa Monica Pier's Pacific Park—even though he doesn't like heights.

FLYING HIGH

▶On July 28, 2011, children in Gaza, Palestine, flew a record number of 12,350 kites simultaneously along a 1.2-mile (1.9-km) stretch of beach in an event organized by the United Nations Relief and Works Agency. It was the seventh world record that children from Gaza had broken in two years.

FEATS

BIONIC WOMAN▶ 32-year-old Claire Lomas from Leicestershire, England, who was left paralyzed from the chest down following a horse-riding accident in 2007, became the first person to complete a marathon in a bionic suit when she finished the 2012 London Marathon in 16 days. Hundreds of people lined the streets as she made her final steps to cross the line.

OLDEST SHOPKEEPER▶ After 78 years of standing behind the counter of his haberdashery store at Greater Manchester, England, Britain's oldest shopkeeper, Jack Yaffe, finally retired in 2012 at age 103.

LIFT OFF▶ At the 2011 Albuquerque International Balloon Festival, a world record 345 hot-air balloons were launched in a single hour.

PERIODIC TABLE▶ Scientists at the Nanotechnology and Nanoscience Centre from the University of Nottingham, England, used an electron microscope and an ion beam writer to carve the periodic table of elements onto a single strand of hair—belonging to chemistry professor Martyn Poliakoff. The world's smallest periodic table, measuring just 89.67 by 46.39 microns, it is so tiny that a million copies of it would fit on a standard-sized Post-it note.

SHOULDER STRENGTH

▶ A stuntman in Nanning, China, demonstrates his incredible shoulder blade muscles by using them to pull a cart containing ten women and by gripping an iron between them (below).

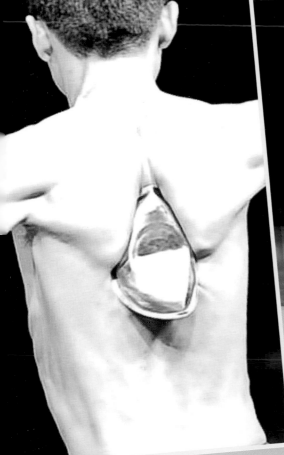

EGG BALANCING▶ A total of 4,247 eggs were stood upright simultaneously on individual tiles during the 2012 Dragon Boat Festival in Hsinchu City, Taiwan. The tradition of balancing eggs at noon on the day of the festival supposedly guarantees a year of good luck.

NAKED ROWERS▶ In January 2012, the British quintet of Debbie Beadle, Julia Immonen, Katie Pattison-Hart, Kate Richardson and Helen Leigh rowed across the Atlantic Ocean in a record 45 days and, to avoid friction burns from clothing, they made most of the trip naked. Their 2,600-mi (4,184-km) crossing took them from the Canary Islands to Barbados—the first all-female crew to complete the voyage.

VERTICAL DIVE▶ A total of 138 skydivers broke the world record for vertical skydiving—beating the previous best by 30—when they flew headfirst in a snowflake formation over Ottawa, Illinois, falling at speeds of up to 220 mph (354 km/h).

QR MAZE▶ The Kraay family designed a huge, 312,000-sq-ft (29,000-sq-m) corn maze on their farm near Lacombe, Alberta, Canada, to operate as a fully functioning QR (Quick Response) code. When scanned from the skies—the test flight went as high as 14,000 ft (4,260 m)—with a smartphone, the code sent the user to the website for the Kraay Family Farm. The Kraay family have been carving corn mazes into their crops for more than 13 years.

WHEELCHAIR JUMP▶ Paraplegic bungee jumper Christine Rougoor plunged 150 ft (46 m) from a bridge into a ravine at Whistler, Canada, while in a wheelchair. The chair actually provided more stability for the bungee jump, stopping blood from rolling around her body too fast and preventing blackouts.

LEAP

ONE GIANT

"Standing there on top of the world, you become so humble."

SEE MORE AMAZING EXTRA STUFF!!

Simply download our APP *Ripley's Believe It or Not!* & try out

ODD SCAN

See Felix in action, jumping an incredible 127,852.4 ft, feet first!

ZENITH
SWISS WATCH MANUFACTURE
SINCE 1865

The Red Bull Stratos Mission provided science with the first data showing what happens to the human body during supersonic freefall.

From the very edge of space, daredevil Austrian skydiver Felix Baumgartner hurtled 24 mi (39 km) to Earth at speeds of up to 843.6 mph (1,357.6 km/h)—faster than the speed of sound—and amazingly landed safely on his feet.

In doing so, the then 43-year-old veteran of more than 2,500 parachute jumps became the first person to break the sound barrier in freefall while setting numerous other world records. These included the highest-ever manned balloon ascent and the highest-ever parachute jump—an incredible 127,852.4 ft (38,969.4 m), more than four times the height of Mount Everest.

Felix was in touch with the Red Bull Stratos mission control throughout and took instructions from his mentor, Col. Joe Kittinger, then 84, who acted as capsule communicator.

Felix's death-defying leap, which had taken seven years to plan, took place on October 14, 2012, in the skies above New Mexico. Wearing a pressure suit able to withstand temperatures as low as −95°F (−70°C), he ascended for 2 hours 36 minutes in a tiny capsule carried upward by a giant helium balloon. Filling almost 30 million cubic ft (850,000 cubic m), the balloon was nearly three times larger than any balloon previously used to hoist a human being.

▼ After 4 minutes 20 seconds of freefall, Felix opened his parachute. His descent took a total of 9 minutes 18 seconds, and he finished it with a textbook landing. Felix's capsule landed about 12 mi (19 km) east of where he finally touched down.

There was a last-minute scare when Felix's helmet visor seemed to fog up, causing the team to consider aborting the mission. Instead Felix decided to press ahead and, sliding out of the capsule door, he hauled himself up on to an outside platform a little bigger than a skateboard. He then jumped out into the stratosphere—feet first in an attempt to avoid falling into a flat spin where blood might rush to his head with possible fatal consequences.

Felix went from 0 to supersonic— 693 mph (1,115 km/h)— in just 34 seconds, and he reached his top speed 16 seconds later. He went into a flat spin and noticed some pressure in his head, but not enough to pass out. While he could have pressed a button to release a stabilization chute which would have pulled him out of the spin, that would have slowed him down. Felix wanted to go as fast as he could, so he fought to get control using arm positions, and it worked. Only an expert like Felix could stop such a spin using skydiving skills alone.

◀ Felix drops from his capsule 24 mi (39 km) above the Earth.

ALTITUDE COMPARISON

■ Mount Everest	29,029 ft (8,848 m)
■ Jet airplane cruising	35,000 ft (10,700 m)
■ Concorde cruising	56,000 ft (17,000 m)
■ Felix Baumgartner	127,852.4 ft (38,969.4 m)

MOUNTAIN SKATER

French daredevil Jean-Yves Blondeau built his incredible Buggy Rollin' suit in 1995 as part of his graduation project at a Paris industrial design school. His aim was to create a wearable speed machine that would enable the human body to move freely in every direction. The body armor suit is equipped with 31 skateboard wheels on the torso, back and most joints, allowing him to ride in every conceivable position—upright, on hands and knees, lying back luge-style or racing downhill face-first with his nose 4 in (10 cm) from the ground. He can now reach 70 mph (112 km/h) and leap over 18½ ft (5.7 m) while wearing his suit.

▶ Wearing his special 31-wheel roller suit, Jean-Yves skated down a Chinese mountain road containing 99 hairpin bends at speeds of up to 70 mph (112 km/h). During his descent of the 6.7-mi-long (10.77-km) road on Tianmen Mountain, he even completed a series of jumps over pits of sharp spikes.

YOUNG SCIENTIST ▶ At 17, Taylor Wilson of Reno, Nevada, was asked to advise the U.S. Department of Energy on nuclear fusion research, making him the world's youngest nuclear scientist. He has also built a functioning device that can detect nuclear weapons smuggled by would-be terrorists in cargo containers. At age seven, he had memorized every rocket made by the U.S. and Soviet governments from the 1930s onward, and by 14 he had built his own nuclear fusion reactor.

TIGER SUIT ▶ Wearing a 9-ft (2.7-m), 28-lb (13-kg) tiger suit strapped to his back, Paul Goldstein from London, England, ran the Brighton and London marathons and climbed Africa's highest mountain, Kilimanjaro—all in eight days.

CANYON RIDE ▶ Sideshow performer Dextre Tripp from Minneapolis, Minnesota, entertains tourists by unicycling around the rim of the Grand Canyon above a 6,000-ft (1,800-m) vertical drop. As part of his act, the versatile artist can also walk uphill along a flaming tightrope 20 ft (6 m) in the air, juggle burning torches while standing on a person's shoulders and slice an apple in his mouth with a chainsaw inches from his face.

BACKWARD SPELLER ▶ Shishir Hathwar of Bangalore, India, can spell 30 randomly chosen words backward in one minute. He can also pronounce words backward and can even spell the longest word in the Oxford English Dictionary—the 45-letter "pneumonoultramicroscopicsilicovolcanokoniosis" (a lung disease)—forward and backward.

WACKY WHISKERS

▶ More than 150 competitors exhibited their carefully crafted facial hair at the 2012 European Beard and Mustache Championships in Wittersdorf, France. There were 18 different categories, including "Imperial Mustaches," "Dali Mustaches," and "Chin Beard Freestyle."

TIME TEAM▶ Roy and Pauline West have collected clocks for over 25 years and now have more than 4,000 crammed into their apartment near Southampton, England. The clocks cover every wall in their two-bedroom home—including 60 in the bathroom—and when the clocks change for British Summer Time, it takes the couple three days to reset them all.

TOY ARMY▶ The Museo de los Soldaditos de Plomo in Valencia, Spain, displays a collection of more than 85,000 toy soldiers and miniature figures—and keeps a million more in storage. The collection was started in 1941 when museum director Alejandro Noguera's father received a set of toy soldiers for his second birthday.

HUMAN DOMINOES▶ In just under ten minutes, 1,001 people were knocked backward in sequence onto mattresses in Shanghai, China, in July 2012 in an enormous chain of human dominoes.

FIGHTING FIT▶ In 2012, at the age of 73, boxing grandfather Paul N. Soucy of Livonia, Michigan, became a four-time Ringside World Champion—an incredible feat considering he has undergone heart bypass surgery, has metal plates in his ankle and neck and is diabetic. Paul, who has been boxing since he was 19, won his age group in the 165-lb (75-kg) weight class at Kansas City, Missouri, by defeating Bill Cruze, also 73, in the third round. He had previously won the title in 2005, 2006 and 2008.

OLDEST SIBLINGS▶ In June 2012, 108-year-old Dorothy Richards and her sister, 105-year-old Marjorie Ruddle, became the world's oldest siblings. The sisters, who were raised in Northampton, England, clocked up a combined total of 213 years.

SPEEDY WHEELIE▶ A professional stunt rider for more than ten years, Ian Drummond, from Tyne and Wear, England, performed a 100-meter (330-ft) bicycle wheelie in the lightning fast time of 13.7 seconds on August 27, 2012.

TEDDY TREASURE▶ The town of Hill City, South Dakota, has more teddy bears than human residents. That's because one of the 1,000 people living there is Jackie Miley who has a collection of over 7,800 teddies. Her house is filled from top to bottom with all types of bears, including Beanie Babies, Care Bears and porcelain teddies.

BLIND LINGUIST▶ At the age of ten, Alexia Sloane, a blind schoolgirl from Cambridge, England, who is fluent in four languages, became the youngest interpreter to work at the European Parliament. Alexia, who lost her sight when she was two after being diagnosed with a brain tumor, can speak English, French, Spanish and Mandarin, and is learning German. She has been tri-lingual since she learned to talk, as her mother is half French and half Spanish and her father is English.

WIRE WALK▶ In August 2011, Chinese acrobat Saimaiti Aishan walked 50 ft (15 m) across a thin metal wire strung between two hot-air balloons floating 100 ft (30 m) above the ground in Hunan Province.

BOLD JUMP▶ On May 23, 2012, British stuntman Gary Connery became the first person to jump out of a helicopter and land without using a parachute. Using a special wingsuit, which he has developed to help him glide through the air and dramatically reduce speed on descent, he jumped from 2,400 ft (732 m) above Oxfordshire, England. He descended at 80 mph (128 km/h) before landing on a special runway that was made up of 18,000 cardboard boxes.

PLUCKY GUY
▶ This talented street performer in Guangzhou, China, makes sure he gets himself noticed by playing the guitar and singing while standing on his head!

BUNGEE JUMP▶ Frances Gabe of Fresno, California, celebrated her 91st birthday by bungee jumping at the local fair—a tradition she began on her 82nd birthday after overcoming a serious illness.

BRIDGE JUMP▶ To celebrate Bridge Day, every year more than 400 daredevil base jumpers leap off the New River Gorge Bridge in Fayetteville, West Virginia, and plunge 876 ft (267 m) into the river below. The festival, which has been running since 1980, is the only time when it is legal to base jump off the bridge.

BIKE CLIMB▶ On January 30, 2012, Polish cyclist Krystian Herba climbed the 2,040 steps of the 68 floors of the Rose Rayhaan by Rotana Hotel, Dubai, U.A.E., in 1 hour 13 minutes 41 seconds on his bike—a record for the most steps climbed on a bicycle.

DOMINO CHAIN▶ After weeks of hand-assembling hundreds of thousands of dominoes into a series of elaborate constructions, the Sinners Domino team toppled 127,141 of them in just seven minutes in Büdingen, Germany, in August 2012.

FAST WORKER▶ Brewery worker Benjamin Pilon of Blanco, Texas, is able to open 110 bottles of beer in 60 seconds—that's nearly two bottle caps every second.

SMASHING TIME

▶ *A Belarussian soldier has a solid concrete masonry block on his chest smashed by a flaming hammer as part of the annual week-long Maslenitsa celebrations in Minsk, which showcase feats of strength.*

BOTTLE BALANCE▶ Seven-year-old Romanian gymnast Giuliano Stroe can perform eight push-ups while balancing his hands and feet on four glass bottles. He has been lifting weights and practicing gymnastics since the age of two.

HUMAN TOWER▶ A 150-strong Catalan performance troupe, the Castellers de Vilafranca, built the first-ever eight-level human tower, or castell, on June 20, 2012, when they gathered on the roof deck of a skyscraper on New York City's 5th Avenue.

CHAINSAW JUGGLER▶ Ian Stewart of Nova Scotia, Canada, made 94 catches while juggling three chainsaws—all with razor-sharp teeth and the motors running—at the Hants County Exhibition in 2011. He has been juggling chainsaws for more than 15 years.

HUMAN TORCH▶ In Hamburg, Germany, in 2011, Denni Duesterhoeft ran for 393 ft (120 m) while on fire! Wearing fire-resistant clothing, the stuntman completed the record-breaking run as flames raged around his body.

HELD BREATH▶ German free diver Tom Sietas held his breath underwater for a world record 22 minutes 22 seconds at Changsha, China, on May 30, 2012. His lung capacity is 20 percent larger than average for his size. When preparing for a record attempt, he does not eat for at least five hours beforehand in order to slow his metabolism. He fills his lungs with pure oxygen to help him hold his breath for an extra 10 minutes.

FOOD FIGHT▶ On December 2, 2011, a total of 473 students and adults of Eisenhower Junior High School, Taylorsville, Utah, took part in the world's largest marshmallow fight, throwing more than 140,000 marshmallows at each other.

JOGGING RECORD▶ On July 27, 2012, 20-year-old Matthew Feldman, a student at the University of Florida, broke a 23-year-old record when he jogged one mile (1.6 km) while simultaneously juggling five balls in 6 minutes 33.6 seconds.

CLEAN GETAWAY

▶ Chained and handcuffed to the roof of an SUV as it went through a car wash in Winnipeg, Manitoba, and battered from head to toe by brushes, soap, water and hot wax, Canadian escape artist Dean Gunnarson still managed to break free from his shackles before the vehicle reached the massive blow-dryers at the end of the wash cycle.

URBAN

▶Young people in Moscow are playing a game that is every bit as scary as Russian roulette. It is called "extreme urban climbing" and it involves scaling as high as 1,000 ft (300 m) up the sides of the city's tallest structures—without wearing any kind of safety equipment. Up to 200 "roofers," some masked to conceal their identity from the police, have taken up the daredevil pursuit just to have their picture taken above a death-defying drop.

CLIMBING

TRIATHLON JUGGLER ▶

BATHTUB PADDLE ▶ Rob Knott from Somerset, England, paddled down the River Avon from Bath to Bristol in a bathtub, covering the 17 mi (27 km) in 13 hours 45 minutes.

FULL HOUSE ▶ Lawrence Cobbold has more than 20,000 bird ornaments in his home in Devon, England. He has been acquiring them for over 25 years, and his collection is now so big that he has to go to his parents' house for meals and to store his clothes because there is no room at his own home.

PENNY PYRAMID ▶ Tom Haffey of Denver, Colorado, used 626,780 pennies to build a pyramid weighing about 4,000 lb (1,814 kg).

MOUNTAIN KING ▶ Since 1989, when he was 29 years old, Nepalese climber Apa Sherpa has reached the summit of the world's highest mountain, Mount Everest, 21 times.

ROBOT RACER ▶ A four-legged robot called Cheetah set a new land speed record for legged robots on March 5, 2012, by running at 18 mph (29 km/h) on a treadmill at a laboratory in Massachusetts. The robot, designed by robotics specialists Boston Dynamics, mimics the running pattern of a real cheetah, stretching out and increasing its speed by flexing and unflexing its back with each stride.

OLDEST BARTENDER ▶ In April 2012, 97-year-old Angie MacLean became the world's oldest bartender when she celebrated nearly 20 years behind the bar at Panama Joe's Café in Bridgeport, Connecticut.

FREQUENT FLYER ▶ Tom Stuker, a sales consultant from Bloomingdale, Illinois, has collected ten million airline frequent-flyer miles. He has made over 6,000 flights in the past 30 years, clocking up enough air miles to have flown to the Moon and back 20 times. United Airlines has even named an airplane in his honor.

HEAD FOR NUMBERS ▶ On December 8, 2011, China's Wang Feng accurately recited a 500-digit number after memorizing it for just five minutes at the World Memory Championships in Guangzhou.

CAR CRAZY ▶ Charlie Mallon of Downingtown, Pennsylvania, has more than 2,100 items of Chevrolet memorabilia acquired over 40 years, including signs, racing flags, soda cans, books, hats, belts, shirts, miniature cars, drinking glasses and playing cards.

UNDERWATER MARATHON ▶ Running on an underwater treadmill in a pool at Salem, Oregon, on September 9, 2012, Mike Studer completed a 26.2-mile (42-km) underwater marathon in 3 hours 44 minutes 52 seconds.

CONCERT IN THE CLOUDS

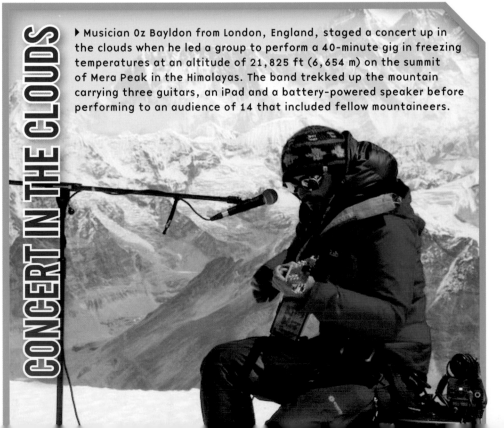

▶ Musician Oz Bayldon from London, England, staged a concert up in the clouds when he led a group to perform a 40-minute gig in freezing temperatures at an altitude of 21,825 ft (6,654 m) on the summit of Mera Peak in the Himalayas. The band trekked up the mountain carrying three guitars, an iPad and a battery-powered speaker before performing to an audience of 14 that included fellow mountaineers.

▶Joe Salter of Pensacola, Florida, completed a triathlon—while juggling balls the whole way. He swam 0.25 mi (0.4 km) backstroke while juggling three balls, cycled 16.2 mi (26 km) juggling two balls in one hand and ran 4 mi (6.4 km) also while juggling—and still finished the event in under two hours, beating 99 non-juggling competitors. He completed the last two sections without dropping a ball, making more than 15,000 successful catches. A pioneer of joggling (juggling and running), Joe is the first person to be able to swim and juggle proficiently. He says: "I came up with the techniques. I wanted to achieve the goal of juggling a triathlon because it was unexplored territory. Swimming was the hardest part because I had to swim just using my legs. Cycling was also quite a challenge. I was going about 17 mph (27 km/h), was surrounded by other competitors and had to toss the balls from one hand to the other when it was time to switch gears."

DISABLED DIVER

▶Despite having no arms and no legs, French athlete Philippe Croizon became the first disabled person to dive to a depth of 108 ft (33 m) when he achieved the feat in a special diving pool in Brussels, Belgium, on January 10, 2013. When he swims, Philippe (left), who had his arms and legs amputated following a 20,000-volt electric-shock accident in 1994, uses specially adapted prosthetic limbs that have fins attached.

OTHER ACHIEVEMENTS

■ In 2010, Philippe became the first quadruple amputee to swim across the English Channel, between England and France, covering the 21 mi (34 km) in less than 14 hours.

■ During 2012, Philippe swam four inter-continental straits—Oceania to Asia (Papua New Guinea to Indonesia), Africa to Asia (Egypt to Jordan), Europe to Africa (Spain to Morocco) and North America to Asia (Alaska to Russia)—a total of 35.6 mi (57.3 km).

PINNED SKIN

Kelvin Mercado from Puerto Rico smashed his way through the pain barrier to pin a new Ripley record 161 clothes pegs to his face—and he did it in the dark!

Kelvin flew to Ripley's Orlando headquarters for the attempt in 2013. With his first try he attached 173 clothespins to his face, but was disqualified because some pegs were pinned to his neck. On the second attempt he had to quit at 157 because of the pain. Finally, on his third attempt of the day, and using glow-in-the-dark pegs, he pinned 161—more than anyone has ever done before!

Kelvin is helped by having particularly elastic skin, and each challenge takes him around 15 minutes to complete. He usually adopts the same pattern when placing the pegs because at some point he knows he will be unable to see anything due to the number of clothespins. He starts under his ear and follows the jawline until he gets to his chin, then clips another row below that. Next he does the high cheekbone area and forehead. Last, he pins the areas around the eyes, nose and mouth. He has to keep a straight face to avoid pegs falling off.

Despite the pain, Kelvin's ambition is to become the first person to clip thousands of clothes pegs onto his entire body.

▶ Kelvin really suffers for his art. "It hurts my skin and leaves marks on my face, like small contusions. It usually takes me one or two days to get better. That's why I don't practice often!"

RECORD-BREAKING

161 PEGS!!

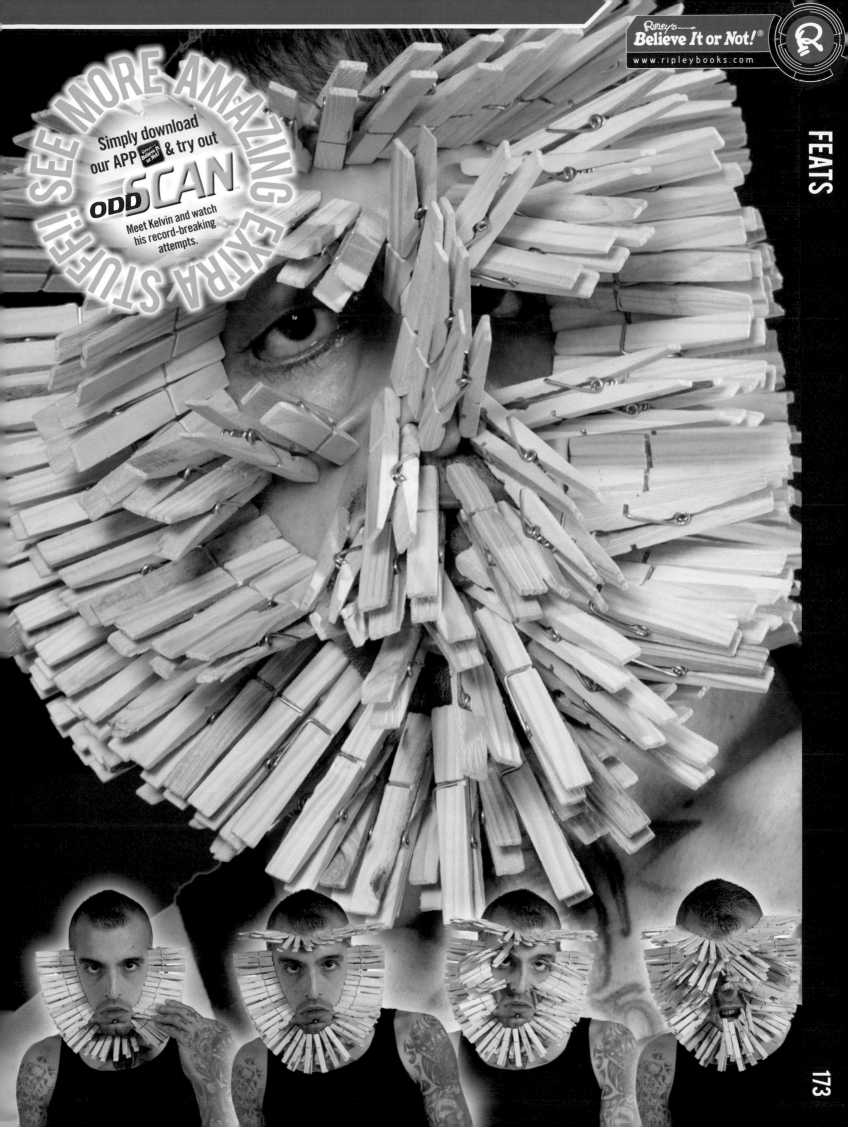

Rathakrishnan Velu

RAW STRENGTH

▸ **Kevin Shelley** of Carmel, Indiana, broke 46 wooden toilet seat lids in 60 seconds—with his head.

▸ **Steve Carrier** from Dallas, Texas, broke 30 baseball bats over his leg in under 60 seconds.

▸ **Kevin Taylor** of Clinton Township, Michigan, broke 584 cement bricks in 57.5 seconds with his hand.

▸ **Indian strongman Manoj Chopra** tore through fifty 2,000-page phone books in three minutes with his bare hands.

▸ **Larry Fields** of Kansas City, Kansas, smashed 354 cement patio blocks in one minute with his elbows.

▸ **Minoru Yoshida** of Japan once did 10,507 push-ups nonstop.

▸ **Rev. Les Davis** of Headland, Alabama, can bend steel bars in his teeth.

▸ **John Wooten** of West Palm Beach, Florida, has back-lifted a 7,000-lb (3,178-kg) elephant.

▸ **Iranian-German strongman Patrik Baboumian** can lift a 13-gal (50-l) beer keg weighing 330½ lb (150.2 kg)—that's around 15 lb (7 kg) heavier than he is—over his head.

BODY PULLING

▸ **Rathakrishnan Velu of Malaysia** (*above*) pulled a 327-ton train with his teeth.

▸ **Wang Ying of Jiangsu, China,** lifted 14 bricks with ropes attached to a 2-in-long (5-cm) tumor that had grown on his forehead.

▸ **Zhang Xingquan of Jilin, China,** pulled along a family car with his ear and while walking on raw eggs, none of which he broke during the feat.

▸ **Shailendra Roy of India** pulled a train engine and four coaches—a combined weight of over 44 tons—using only his hair, braided into a ponytail.

▸ **Ashok Verma of Agra, India,** lifted three 50-fl-oz (1.5-l) bottles of cola with a string attached to his eyelashes.

▸ **China's Fu Yingjie** pulled a 1.7-ton van and its driver more than 40 ft (12 m) with his nose.

▸ **Siba Prasad Mallick of Balasore, India,** pulled two motorcycles 1¼ mi (2 km) with his mustache.

QUICK OFF THE MARK

Paul Blair

▸ **John Cassidy of Philadelphia, Pennsylvania,** inflated and sculpted 747 balloons in one hour.

▸ **Claude Breton** picked 30,240 apples in eight hours at an orchard in Dunham, Quebec, Canada.

▸ **Basketball-crazy Mike Campbell of Denver, Colorado,** made 1,338 free throws in an hour—faster than one throw every three seconds—achieving a success rate of almost 90 percent.

▸ **Garry Hebberman of Jamestown, Australia,** sheared 1,054 sheep in 40 hours—that's one sheep every 2 minutes 17 seconds.

▸ **Paul Blair** (*right*) **of San Francisco, California,** can run a mile in under eight minutes while twirling a hula hoop.

▸ **Germany's Christopher Irmscher** completed the 100-meter hurdles in 14.82 seconds—while wearing swim fins on his feet.

▸ **Ashrita Furman of New York City** hopped a mile on one leg in 27 minutes 51 seconds.

▸ **Jill Stamison of Grand Haven, Michigan,** ran a 150-yard (137-m) sprint in 21.95 seconds while wearing 3-in (7.6-cm) high heels.

Milan Roskopf

EXTREME JUGGLING

▶ Kyle Petersen juggled three knives for 1 minute 2 seconds while riding a unicycle in New York City.

▶ With a single breath, Merlin Cadogan from Devon, England, juggled three objects underwater for 1 minute 20 seconds.

▶ Spain's Francisco Tebar Honrubia can juggle five Ping-Pong balls, using only his mouth and sending them up to 50 ft (15 m) in the air.

▶ Hanging from scaffolding and wearing special gravity boots, Erik Kloeker of Cincinnati, Ohio, juggled three balls upside down for over four minutes.

▶ Slovakia's Milan Roskopf (*left*) juggled three bowling balls, each weighing 12 lb (5 kg), for 28 seconds.

▶ While juggling chainsaws on July 28, 2008, Aaron Gregg of Victoria, Canada, achieved 88 catches.

▶ Australian performer Marty Coffey juggles an apple, a bowling ball and an egg simultaneously, and during the stunt he even eats the apple.

▶ David Slick juggled three balls for 12 hours 5 minutes at North Richland Hills, Texas, in 2009.

MARATHON EFFORTS

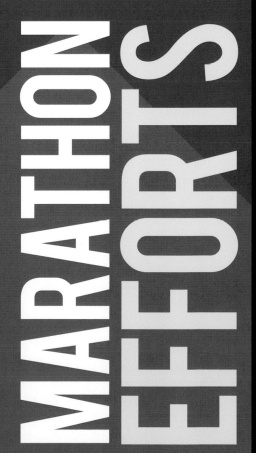

▶ Anthony Thornton **walked backward for 24 hours** around Minneapolis, Minnesota, covering a distance of 95.7 mi (154 km).

▶ Josef Resnik **skied** the same Austrian piste **for 240 consecutive hours**—that's 10 days—taking only short breaks for the toilet and food.

▶ Adrian Wigley from the West Midlands, England, **played an electric organ nonstop for two hours—with his tongue.**

▶ Tony Wright of Cornwall, England, **stayed awake for over 11 days and nights** in 2007—a total of 266 hours.

▶ India's Jayasimha Ravirala **delivered a speech lasting 111 hours.**

▶ Joseph Odhiambo **dribbled a basketball** through the streets of Houston, Texas, **for 26 hours 40 minutes,** during which time he bounced the ball an estimated 140,000 times.

▶ Rafael Mittenzwei **roller-skated backward for over 129½ mi** (208.4 km) in 24 hours around a track in Germany, completing 685 laps.

STRONG SKIN Chinese kung fu performer Huang Yao, 63, can carry heavy objects—such as two buckets of water—suspended from needles inserted through the skin of his neck and arms. He can also swallow solid steel balls and stand barefoot on two razor-sharp knife blades. As a boy Yao was unable to walk until he was six or talk until he was eight, so to improve his education his parents sent him to the Wenshu Temple, where the monks also taught him to perform his eye-watering stunts.

Pinned through the skin!

CHILLED OUT Wearing only shorts and braving a temperature of 23°F (-5°C), Cui Deyi and Wang Baoyu spent 24 hours inside specially built giant ice cubes in Changsha, China, without food, water or sleep. Wang passed the time inside his ice prison by squatting down to rest his legs and by performing a series of slow, exaggerated movements.

SHARED NAMES Alex Nunn of Ipswich, England, spent more than ten years visiting seven other places around the world also called Ipswich. His 61,000-mi (98,000-km) odyssey took him to Ipswiches in Massachusetts, South Dakota, New Hampshire, Jamaica, Queensland (Australia) and Manitoba (Canada), plus Ipswitch, Wisconsin.

NUN PARADE In June 2012, 1,436 men and women dressed as nuns and paraded through the town of Listowel, County Kerry, Ireland.

BUSY BUS On April 20, 2012, a total of 246 students from a school in Kielce, Poland, squeezed into a single-decker city bus, setting a new world record for the most people crammed in a bus.

JAW DROPPING! Martial arts teacher Dragon Jetlee broke 150 eggs with his chin—one egg at a time—in 60 seconds in Tiruchirappalli, India.

SPEED SKIPPER Army Major Leticia Walpole skipped rope 9,335 times in an hour at Fort Leavenworth, Kansas, on May 10, 2012—that amounts to 155 skips per minute, or 2½ per second!

OLDEST CLIMBER Following a six-day trek, 84-year-old Richard Byerley from Walla Walla, Washington State, became the oldest person to climb the 19,340-ft-high (5,895-m) Mount Kilimanjaro in Tanzania on foot. He reached the summit on October 6, 2011, with his two grandchildren, Annie, 29, and Bren, 25.

BIRTHDAY TO REMEMBER To celebrate her 101st birthday, great-grandmother Mary Allen Hardison of Ogden, Utah, went paragliding. She made the flight because she was determined not to be outdone by her 75-year-old son Allen who had recently taken up paragliding.

AUTO FLIP Aaron Evans of Milwaukee, Wisconsin, does death-defying somersaults over cars that are moving at speeds of 30 mph (48 km/h). Inspired to take up gymnastics after watching a Bruce Lee movie when he was five, he tackles the cars head on. He takes a short run-up, leaps into the air a split second before the front bumper is about to hit him, then performs a full flip in midair and lands well behind the car. In 2011, he jumped over three moving cars in just over a minute.

GIANT SKATEBOARD▶ A team of six U.K. engineers took 300 hours to build a giant skateboard measuring 22 ft (6.7 m) long, 8 ft (2.4 m) wide and weighing 560 lb (254 kg)—big enough to hold 30 children at once and weighing as much as a baby African elephant.

CARD SHARP▶ Ye Tongxin from Nanjing, China, can slice 12 cucumbers in 47 seconds by throwing playing cards at them ninja-style.

RUBIK ROBOT▶ A robot made out of LEGO® blocks and powered by an Android smartphone has broken the record for the fastest time to solve a Rubik's Cube. In London, England, on November 11, 2011, CubeStormer II, invented by David Gilday and Mike Dobson, solved the puzzle in just 5.27 seconds—faster than any human. The robot uses a cell-phone camera to take images of each face of the Rubik's Cube, then analyzes the images and sends instructions via Bluetooth to four Lego arms, which rotate the cube at high speed.

POLE SKI▶ In December 2011, 16-year-old Amelia Hempleman-Adams, daughter of British adventurer David Hempleman-Adams, became the youngest person to ski to the South Pole. She skied 97 mi (156 km) to the Pole and she and her father spent 17 nights on the ice, enduring sub-zero temperatures, whiteouts and 24-hour daylight.

GLACIER PLUNGE▶ Californian thrill-seeker Ben Stookesberry became the first person to kayak down a glacial waterfall when he plunged over the 65-ft-high (20-m) Braswell Glacier in Svalbard, Arctic Circle, and into the icy waters below.

WALKING DEAD

▶ Nearly 10,000 people wearing ghoulish makeup and ragged clothes splattered with fake blood shambled in a trance-like state through the streets of Mexico City on November 26, 2011, in what was the world's biggest zombie walk. Since the first recognized zombie parade was staged in Sacramento, California, in 2001, similar walks have taken place all over the world—including in Australia, Canada and Argentina.

09

DIGITAL ▶

CHANGING FACES

Creative Director Dominick Reed from Cambridge, England, transformed his face every day for two whole years to create a series of wacky self-portraits, using a mix of computer wizardry, makeup, wigs and props.

Better known to his online fans as his alter ego, Mr. Flibble, Dominick spent a total of 3,650 hours compiling his pictorial portfolio, and usually needed two to three hours a day to prepare for each picture, although it once took him an entire day when he had to bury himself in compost in his living room. Mr. Flibble often finds himself in strange predicaments, such as unlocking the secrets in his head, growing mustaches from his eyes, or getting addicted to laughter pills at clown school. He has such a large Internet following that, despite the crazy disguises, Mr. Flibble/Dominick gets recognized in the street!

SMART FEEDER▶ Pet owners can now feed their animals remotely—using a smartphone. Carlos Herrera from Los Angeles, California, has invented the Pintofeed, an automated feeder that connects to an app enabling owners to hit the feed button on their phone from anywhere in the world to ensure their pet never misses a meal. The feeder even tweets owners afterward to let them know how much the animal has eaten.

CAT APPEAL▶ A U.S. company has developed a series of iPad apps for cats. Little Hiccup's first app features a fast-moving virtual mouse to appeal to cats' hunting instincts as they try to catch it, and it proved so successful that a sequel was launched called "Paint For Cats," where the cat makes a colorful paw imprint every time it touches the screen.

BALANCING DOG▶ Nick Johnson of Norfolk, England, spent up to five hours a day teaching Ozzy, his chocolate Border collie-kelpie cross, to balance on all four paws on a thin metal chain attached to two posts and then to stand on his hind legs without falling off. Filmed by a stunned passerby on his cell phone, the footage was uploaded to YouTube, where it attracted more than 80,000 hits on its first day.

PRIEST'S CONFESSION▶ Father Massimo Donghi, a priest from Besana in Brianza, Italy, had to explain to parishioners how he came to be rescued from the wreck of luxury cruise ship *Costa Concordia* in January 2012 after originally telling them he was taking time off to spend a couple of weeks at a spiritual retreat. His deception was uncovered when his niece Elisabetta, who was with him on the cruise, posted on Facebook that she and all her family "including Uncle Massimo" were safe.

RECORD GAME▶ In an event that took place simultaneously in New York and London on June 26, 2012, Kathleen Henkel of Oakland, New Jersey, and Laura Rich of Cardiff, Wales, both played the video card game Solitaire Blitz on Facebook for a record 30 hours straight, in total playing more than 1,500 hands.

MANY MONSTERS▶ In March 2012, U.S. pop star Lady Gaga became the first person to rack up 20 million Twitter followers. She calls her fans "little monsters."

TALKING TO HIMSELF▶ Filmmaker Jeremiah McDonald of Portland, Maine, produced a YouTube video—20 years in the making—in which he interviewed his 12-year-old self. Editing together interview footage of himself at age 12 and, in 2012, at age 32, he makes it appear as if he is talking to his child self about a range of subjects including *Star Wars*, *Doctor Who* and dead pets.

STOLEN CAR▶ In 2012—42 years after it had been stolen—Bob Russell of Dallas, Texas, tracked down his 1967 Austin Healey in Los Angeles, California, when the car was put up for sale on eBay.

TRUE BELIEBERS▶ Canadian pop star Justin Bieber's charity rallying call on his 18th birthday on March 1, 2012, attracted a world record 322,224 tweets and re-tweets from his fans.

DIGITALLY ALTERED

▶ An artist from Bologna, Italy, using the pseudonym Dito Von Tease ("dito" is Italian for "finger") converts the tip of his index finger into famous faces by creating different skin colors and features and adding hairstyles and makeup. Each face takes him up to 16 hours to make, and his portfolio includes such diverse characters as Star Trek's Mr. Spock, a Kayan woman with a brass-ringed neck, Steve Jobs, Sherlock Holmes, the Dalai Lama and Mickey Mouse. He had the idea when looking for an original avatar for his profile picture on Facebook, and he chose a finger portrait in order to conceal his identity.

Mr. Spock

Kayan woman

Steve Jobs

SHELL SHOCK

▶ *Maia, a grieving chicken owned by Ashley Wood of Somerset, England, was coaxed into laying eggs again by watching videos of other birds on an iPad. She had stopped producing eggs after her companion chicken, Baba, was eaten by a fox, but with the help of the iPad she was soon laying five a week.*

NEW SPIN▶ Design student and games enthusiast Lee Wei Chen from London, England, combined a washing machine with a video game console, the progress of the washing cycle being dependent on the success of the person playing the game.

STATUS UPDATE▶ When Facebook founder Mark Zuckerberg got married to longtime girlfriend Priscilla Chan in a surprise ceremony on May 19, 2012, his status update on his Facebook Timeline received 1,045,272 likes, appropriately setting a new record for most likes on a Facebook item.

▶ MORE PEOPLE ON THE PLANET OWN A CELL PHONE THAN A TOOTHBRUSH. ◀

WRONG MAP▶ A group of schoolchildren from Normandy, France, who were on an exchange trip to the town of Ipswich in Suffolk, England, were hopelessly lost until they were told by a local tourist information office that the maps they had downloaded from the Internet were of Ipswich, Queensland, Australia, 10,000 mi (16,000 km) away.

FACEBOOK RESCUE▶ Waking up paralyzed and with the battery in his cell phone dead, Peter Casaru of Brecon, Wales, received quick medical treatment thanks to his friends on Facebook. He managed to crawl to his laptop and post that he was unable to move his legs or call for an ambulance. Friends from as far away as New York and Vancouver offered to help, but it was Juliet McFarlane from 6 mi (9.6 km) away who was first to call an ambulance.

RECYCLED TREE HOUSE▶ Joel Allen built an egg-shaped tree house in the woods near Whistler, Canada, from thousands of dollars of recycled materials donated through Craigslist over several months.

TEEN EXCELS▶ Fifteen-year-old Rebecca Rickwood of Cambridgeshire, England, beat 228,000 international rivals to be crowned the world champion user of Microsoft's Excel 2007 spreadsheet software in a timed contest in San Diego, California.

LAPTOP COMPUTER

▶ Dutch computer experts Erik de Nijs and Tim Smit have designed a pair of jeans with a full-size Bluetooth keyboard integrated into the upper leg. The $375 jeans, which give the wearer freedom of movement around a room while still being in control of the computer, operate via a USB device plugged into the computer port and also feature speakers and a wireless mouse.

WEDDING INVASION▶ Bride Lee Su and groom Ming found what they thought was a quiet woodland clearing in Nanjing, China, for their romantic wedding photos—but seconds later it was invaded by hundreds of computer game fans playing a real-life reconstruction of *Counter Strike*.

TECHNO CAT▶ A cat named Tiger Lily regularly plays with her owner's iPad for up to 15 minutes at a time. The cat is so fascinated by the technology that Anne Druais of Sydney, Australia, has to keep a plastic screen guard over the iPad to protect it from Tiger Lily's claws.

FACE SPOOK

▶ In January 2012, Ripley's employee Charlotte Howell of Essex, England, took a seemingly uneventful photograph at Highgate Cemetery in North London. When she uploaded the image to Facebook, the automatic recognition software picked out something nobody had noticed: a ghostly face among the headstones, which the site tried to tag as a real person. Charlotte testifies that nobody else was in the area when the photo was taken.

WALKING WEBSITE▶ Patrick Vaillancourt from Montreal, Canada, has more than 15,000 Internet addresses tattooed all over his body. With profits going to charity, he charges sites $35 to have their URL permanently inked into his skin, the price rising to $500 for prime positions and large tattoos. He hopes eventually to have 100,000 URL tattoos on his body, which would take at least 10,000 hours of inking to create.

BANK CRISIS▶ When British bank NatWest suffered a major computer glitch in June 2012, hundreds of Twitter users voiced their frustration to @Natwest, unaware that it was the Twitter account name chosen by Natalie Westerman, a 22-year-old schoolteacher from Newcastle upon Tyne.

PIANO BOY▶ Ethan Walmark, a six-year-old autistic boy from Westport, Connecticut, became an Internet sensation with his YouTube version of Billy Joel's "Piano Man," racking up 640,000 hits in just five days. He learned to play the piano at age four—by ear.

CUTTING EDGE▶ A video of an Ecuadorian man using a piranha as a pair of scissors went viral on YouTube. Taken in the Cuyabeno Rainforest, the clip shows the fish, held tightly in the man's hand, using its razor-sharp teeth to slice instantly through a twig placed in its open jaws.

ANGRY BRIDES▶ Inspired by the popular Angry Birds game, a new Indian online game called Angry Brides seeks to highlight the practice of illegal dowry demands in India. In Angry Brides, players attack prospective dowry-hungry grooms—an engineer, a doctor and a pilot—with a variety of weapons, including a brick-red stiletto shoe and a broomstick.

VIRTUALLY MARRIED▶ On Valentine's Day 2012, 21,879 marriages took place in the online role-playing game Rift, setting a record for the most in-game marriages in 24 hours.

BEYOND THE GRAVE▶ An Israeli-produced app, "If I Die," allows people to compose their final Facebook update, which is then posted after their death. Three Facebook friends are nominated as trustees to guard the posthumous text or video message before hitting the publish button once the person has died.

POPULAR POST▶ Led by Tracey Hodgson of the U.K. and Cathy Matthews of Sacramento, California, 107 people—mostly fans of the game FrontierVille—joined forces and posted a record 1,001,598 comments on a single Facebook item. Each person commented on the original post an average of about 9,350 times.

FATAL FRIEND▶ After defrauding banks in Seattle, Washington State, Maxi Sopo fled to Mexico where he boasted about his freedom on Facebook. Then he made the mistake of adding a former Justice Department official to his list of friends, a move that landed him in a Mexican jail and led to his extradition back to the U.S. where he was eventually sentenced to 33 months in prison.

DARING JUMP▶ A YouTube video captures the moment a daredevil young Russian BASE jumper had a miraculous escape when his parachute failed to open after he had jumped from a 400-ft-high (120-m) pylon. Although snow cushioned his fall, he still suffered fractured vertebrae, pelvis and legs and could not walk again for three months.

ROBBERY FOILED▶ A man from Essex, England, foiled a raid on his home by shouting at burglars via a webcam from Turkey 1,500 mi (2,400 km) away. The man, who was attending a funeral abroad, was talking to his family back home in England via Skype when he spotted two strangers in the hallway after his wife had briefly left the room. He yelled at them to get out of his house and they fled empty-handed.

VIDEO GLASSES▶ Skydivers jumped from a blimp above San Francisco wearing new Google glasses that video everything they see—and a live camera feed from the glasses meant that people on the ground were able to watch footage of the jump from the skydivers' perspective.

APE PADS▶ Orangutans at Jungle Island Zoo in Miami, Florida, are being encouraged to use iPads in the hope that they will eventually be able to communicate with keepers and visitors. The younger apes, in particular, have taken to the handheld computer tablets, and enjoy drawing and playing games on them.

GOOGLE HUNT▶ An Indian boy who became separated from his mother in 1986 found her 25 years later from his new home in Tasmania, Australia, after using Google Earth to trace her. Saroo Brierley was five when he got lost on a 14-hour train journey. He ended up in Calcutta, where he was taken in by an orphanage and eventually adopted by a couple from Tasmania. Years later, through satellite computer images, he managed to identify his Indian hometown of Khandwa and when he traveled there he was reunited with his birth mother.

PHONE INTERRUPTION▶ After a member of the audience forgot to switch off a cell phone during a solo classical music concert, interrupting the concert with a distinctive ringtone, Slovakian violinist Lukas Kmit took his opportunity to highlight the unfortunate incident by pausing for a moment and then continuing his performance with an improvised version of the ringtone.

STREET LIFE
▶ Google Street View has thrown up some bizarre images in Tokyo, Japan, including a seemingly headless pedestrian walking down the street toward a burst of white light.

GAMING LIZARD▶ Crunch, a bearded dragon lizard owned by Philip Gith of Brisbane, Australia, uses her tongue to "eat" on-screen insects in the Ant Smasher game on Gith's smartphone. She is so fast that a clip of her gaming soon attracted more than six million views on YouTube.

PHONE COSTUMES▶ To raise money for charity, 330 people dressed up as cell phones at Caterham School in Surrey, England, in July 2012.

LIFE SALE▶ So that he could start a new life, weathy businessman Shane Butcher from Tampa Bay, Florida, put his old life up for sale on eBay for $3.5 million. He sold off his chain of computer game shops, two waterfront homes, three cars and even his pet dog.

TWEET LIFE▶ Just 0.5 percent of Twitter's total population attracts nearly 50 percent of all attention on the microblogging site. In fact, a quarter of Twitter users have no followers at all. Of the 400-million tweets that are sent every day, more than 70 percent gain no response and 40 percent of Twitter users never tweet at all.

COMPUTER KID▶ Born in 2006, Wasik Farhan-Roopkotha of Bangladesh began to master complex video games aged just two, and knew how to program and download games at the tender age of four. Wasik says he now has ambitions to be a computer expert and to work for a large computer company in the future.

MOO-BILE PHONES

▶ To encourage visitors to learn more about cows, dairy farmer Jane Barnes from Leicestershire, England, painted the side of Lady Shamrock, her eight-year-old Friesian, with a QR code. When people scan the cow's digital bar code with their smartphones, they are directed to a blog that details her lifestyle and also the farmer's daily routine.

CRASH LANDING ▶ To test the durability of iPad cases, skydivers in the United States started playing movies on iPads, then zipped them into protective cases and dropped them from a height of 1,300 ft (400 m) to see if they could survive the fall. When retrieved after their crash landing, the iPads were still playing the movies.

BINOCULARS BUILDING ▶ the Binoculars Building in Venice, California, one of the Google offices, gets its name from the giant pair of binoculars—45 ft (13.7 m) high and 44 ft (13.4 m) wide—that links the two disparate parts of the Frank Gehry-designed building. The entrance to the parking garage is between the lenses of the binoculars, which were created by artists Claes Oldenburg and Coosje van Bruggen.

ROBOT HUMMINGBIRD ▶ Japanese scientists are developing a robot hummingbird that will one day save lives by searching for survivors in wreckage and other areas not easily accessible to humans. The tiny, flying robot, fitted with a minute camera, flaps its wings 30 times per second—just like a real hummingbird—and researchers hope to use infrared sensors to get it to hover in mid-air.

FACEBOOK HUGS ▶ Scientists at Massachusetts Institute of Technology have invented the Like-A-Hug—a wearable social media vest that enables people to give hugs to their friends and family on Facebook. The vest inflates whenever friends "Like" a picture, video or status update, translating their virtual thumbs-up into a real hug.

FRIED GADGETS ▶ To link the consumption of gadgets and the consumption of fast food, Brooklyn, New York-based artist Henry Hargreaves photographs deep-fried iPads, MacBooks and Game Boys. However, he doesn't cook real gadgets—instead he uses fakes made from a material called foamcore.

TELLTALE SIGNAL ▶ After a 76-year-old woman fell 12 ft (3.6 m) through an uncovered manhole in Palatine, Illinois, rescuers were about to call off the search when dispatchers managed to use her cell phone signal to pinpoint her location.

FREE BOAT ▶ To avoid paying a $2,400 salvage fee after his 16-ft (5-m) fishing boat capsized in the Gulf of Mexico, owner Jack Roberts, from Fort Walton Beach, Florida, put the boat, plus its contents of $2,000 worth of fishing gear and $800 cash, up for sale on Craigslist for free—provided the buyer could first haul the vessel up from the seabed.

HEALTHY APP ▶ An app called "SkinVision" monitors the moles on your skin for signs of skin cancer. It photographs each mole and builds a structural map, which reveals the different growth patterns of the tissues and alerts you to any abnormal development that could be an indication of melanoma.

DOOR CLIMBER ▶ "Spider-Girl" Sofya Dickson, age 3, from Leicestershire, England, can climb a 6-ft (1.8-m) doorframe—several times her own height. Her dad Peter only uploaded the video of her acrobatics to YouTube so that her aunt could see it, but it became a worldwide Internet hit and led to requests from American TV shows.

ZOMBIES INJURED ▶ Emergency medical crews called to an accident on a movie set in Toronto, Ontario, were alarmed to find the actors covered in blood and gore. They then realized that most of it was makeup because the actors were dressed as zombies for the movie *Resident Evil: Retribution*.

FIRST APPLE ▶ One of the still-functioning Apple 1 computers—the first product built by Apple Computer Inc. in 1976—sold at an auction on June 15, 2012, for $374,500.

ROCKING CHARGER ▶ A Swiss company has invented the iRock, a rocking chair that charges iPads and iPhones. The $1,700-wooden chair generates enough power from its rocking motion to recharge an iPad 3 to 35 percent in an hour.

FACEBOOK WINDFALL ▶ When graffiti artist David Choe was asked to paint the office walls at Facebook's first HQ in Palo Alto, California, in 2005, he was offered payment of a few thousand dollars or the equivalent in shares. Despite thinking then that Facebook was "pointless," he took the stock and when the company was floated seven years later he stood to pocket an estimated $200 million.

HUMAN FLOWERS

▶ Take a close look at these beautiful flowers and plants—the petals and stems are made from naked human bodies! They are the work of Los Angeles, California-based artist Cecelia Webber who takes pictures of naked people and, with the help of a digital photo editing application, turns them into magical blooms. She was inspired to create the images after noticing that in a photo her own back looked like a flower petal.

AGE RESTRICTION▶ When centenarian Marguerite Joseph from Grosse Pointe, Michigan, joined Facebook in 2011 she couldn't type in her real age. Whenever she entered her year of birth as 1908, Facebook automatically changed it to 1928, making Marguerite, who has over 1,750 followers, 20 years younger than her then 102 years of age.

LAURA UNSAFE▶ Laura Safe, a newsreader on the Capital FM Breakfast Show, was so engrossed in texting her boyfriend that she walked straight into a freezing canal in Birmingham, England. She was rescued from the icy water by a passerby, but not before the drama had been captured on CCTV, ensuring that on this occasion she made the news!

MARCHING GAMES▶ During the half-time break at a university football match against Nebraska in June 2012, a total of 225 members of the Ohio State University Marching Band recreated images from Space Invaders, Pokemon, Tetris, Halo, The Legend of Zelda and other classic video games.

SHINING LIGHT▶ A farmer in Devon, England, damaged his iPhone by accidentally inserting it into the rear end of a cow while attempting to use it as a flashlight during calving.

DONALD DUCK▶ A lawyer in Zadar, Croatia, complained that Judge Domagoj Kurobasa was not serious-minded enough to try an important libel case because the judge used a picture of Donald Duck for his Facebook profile.

BIRD TWEETS▶ British ornithologist and broadcaster Bill Oddie translated the different calls of tropical birds at the London Zoo and tweeted each interpretation out on Twitter in a maximum 140 characters.

SACRED COMPUTERS▶ In January 2012, the Swedish government formally recognized the Church of Kopimism, a religious group that promotes distribution of knowledge and claims that computer file sharing ("kopyacting") is a sacred act.

COMPUTER WEDDING▶ When web designer Miguel Hanson married Diana Wesley in July 2011 in Houston, Texas, the wedding ceremony was conducted by a computer. Unable to get a friend to officiate, the groom programed a computer to perform the role instead, creating on a 30-in (75-cm) monitor the face of a virtual minister, Rev. Bit, who recited instructions such as "You may kiss the bride" in a robotic voice.

▶Students from Newcastle upon Tyne, England, pour 4-pint (2-l) containers of milk over their heads in public as part of an Internet craze called "milking," a new rival to "planking." A YouTube video, created by 22-year-old Tom Morris, quickly went viral with its clips of students drenching themselves in milk in shopping malls, in the middle of busy traffic islands, outside bars and even up a tree.

MILKING

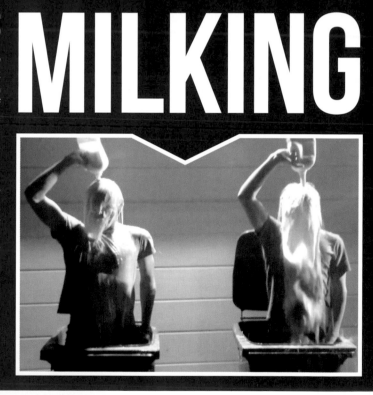

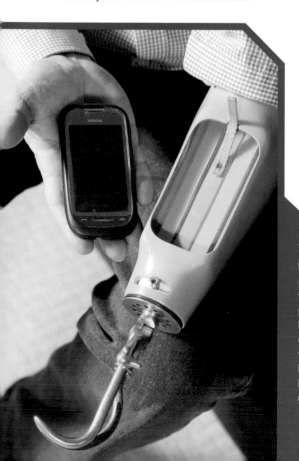

SMART ARM

▶ Trevor Prideaux from Somerset, England, became the first person to have a smartphone built into his prosthetic arm. Born without a left arm, he used to have to balance his phone on the false arm or on a flat surface to use it, but now that a Nokia C7 has been embedded into the fiberglass and laminate limb, he simply calls and texts using his right hand.

WRONG BOX▶ After ordering a 39-in flat-screen TV from Amazon, Seth Horvitz opened the parcel at his Washington, D.C., home and found that it contained a high-powered, military-grade assault rifle instead of his TV.

VIDEO CHARACTERS▶ In New Berlin, Wisconsin, in 2011, 425 people dressed as characters from video games including Angry Birds, Super Mario Bros, Halo 3 and Pac-Man.

VIRTUAL BRIDESMAID▶ Stranded 1,600 mi (2,575 km) away in Virginia, Renee Armstrong still managed to take part in the wedding of her best friend Jamie Wilborn by following her down the aisle in Denver, Colorado, on an iPad. An usher carried a white iPad connected to Armstrong's webcam and the absent bridesmaid even made it into the wedding photos.

SOCCER TWEET▶ Fernando Torres' last-minute goal for Chelsea in the Champions League semi-final second leg against Barcelona on April 24, 2012, attracted 13,684 tweets per second, breaking the sports tweets record of 12,233 during the climax of the 2012 Super Bowl between the New York Giants and New England Patriots.

MAGIC POTIONS▶ Online auction site eBay banned the sale of potions and spells in 2012 after buyers kept complaining that the products failed to bring them instant wealth or make them stunningly beautiful.

TWISTED VISION▶ Lithuanian photographer Tadas Cerniauskas invited 100 people to his studio in Vilnius to have their faces blasted with a high-powered jet of air from an industrial leaf blower so that he could capture the effect it had on their mouths, eyes and hair. When posted on his Facebook page, the pictures got three million views in just a week.

WI-FI DONKEYS▶ Kfar Kedem, an Israeli tourist attraction dedicated to showing how people lived in Old Testament times, fitted its donkeys with Wi-Fi routers so that visitors dressed in biblical robes and headdresses could have Internet access at all times.

▶▶ THE AVERAGE CELL PHONE CONTAINS AT LEAST 18 TIMES MORE BACTERIA THAN A TOILET SEAT. ◀

BADLY STUFFED▶ A Facebook page dedicated to bizarre or incompetent taxidermy has attracted some 13,000 likes. "Badly Stuffed Animals" includes such strange items as a dead dog riding a tricycle, a camel in a suitcase, and a dog leap-frogging a globe.

TIME-LAPSE TRIP▶ Photographer Brian Defrees from Syracuse, New York State, made a time-lapse video of his 12,225-mi (19,560-km) trip around the U.S.A. and posted the result on YouTube in a five-minute film that he made from more than 200,000 individual photos. Mounting a camera on his car, he set it to take a picture every five seconds as he crossed more than 30 states in 55 days.

HOMER BLOB▶ While cleaning out a cupboard, Christopher Herbert from London, England, discovered a blob of dried glue that his girlfriend said resembled Homer Simpson—and when he put it up for sale on eBay, it sold for a staggering £152,200 ($236,000) after attracting 85 bids.

MISTAKEN IDENTITY▶ At the height of the 2010–11 Ashes cricket series between England and Australia, Ashley Kerekes of Westfield, Massachusetts, received dozens of unwanted tweets simply because her Twitter account was named @theashes. When she protested that she was not a cricket match, her follower count jumped from 300 to 13,500 and she was offered a free trip to Australia.

IRAN BAN▶ Protests by young gamers in Iran persuaded the country's government to ban the bestselling U.S. video game Battlefield 3, which depicts American soldiers invading Iran in search of missing nuclear warheads in 2014.

MONEY FACING▶ There are Facebook groups dedicated to an Internet craze called "Money Facing" in which people have their photo taken with a folded banknote in front of their face. Hundreds of people have created facial hybrids of themselves with the likes of Queen Elizabeth II and Charles Darwin by posing with banknotes from all over the world.

FISHY
BUSINESS

▶ *Nearly 10,000 people used a website's online tool to design colorful sneakers that, it was claimed, would be grown to order by mixing and matching stingray DNA—unaware that the whole enterprise was an elaborate hoax. Advertised as a Thai company, Rayfish Footwear attracted widespread media coverage but was actually created by a team of Dutch designers. Far from being genetically modified, the beautifully patterned shoes were dyed with simple paint.*

ART ▶

BIZARRE BODY PAINT

In the bizarre world of 19-year-old Japanese artist Chooo-San, the skin on human feet is laced together, a belly has real buttons and a zipper runs up the length of a person's back. It's enough to send shivers down your spine, yet she achieves these creepy creations without any digital enhancement—just by applying acrylic body paint to the naked skin of her models.

A student at Musashino Art University, Tokyo, Chooo-San (whose real name is Hikaru Cho) discovered her talent after doodling eyes on the back of her hand during study breaks. She developed this theme by painting a spooky extra pair of eyes onto a person's face or adding a second mouth in an unusual place.

Now she has gone even further, painting buttons and zippers on to friends' bodies to make it look as though they are literally bursting at the seams. Her artwork is so lifelike that the buttons, laces and zippers actually appear to be attached to the skin.

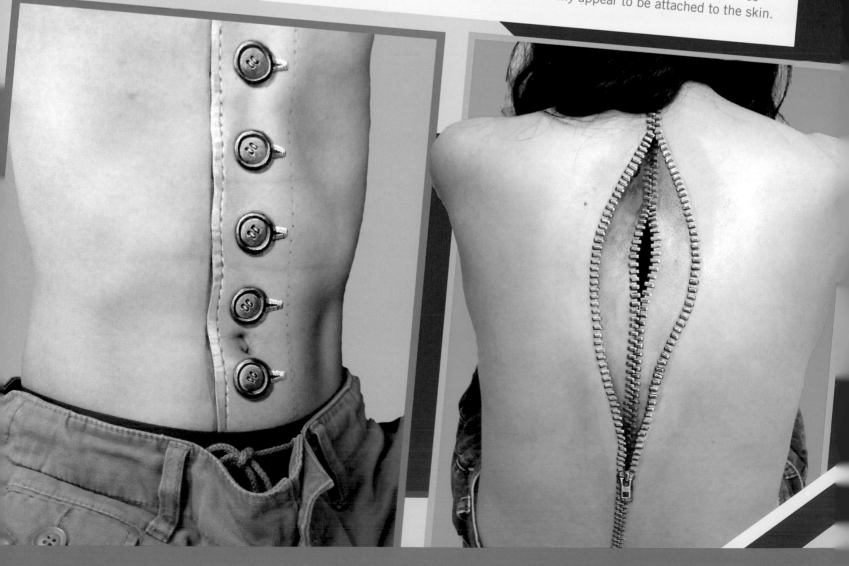

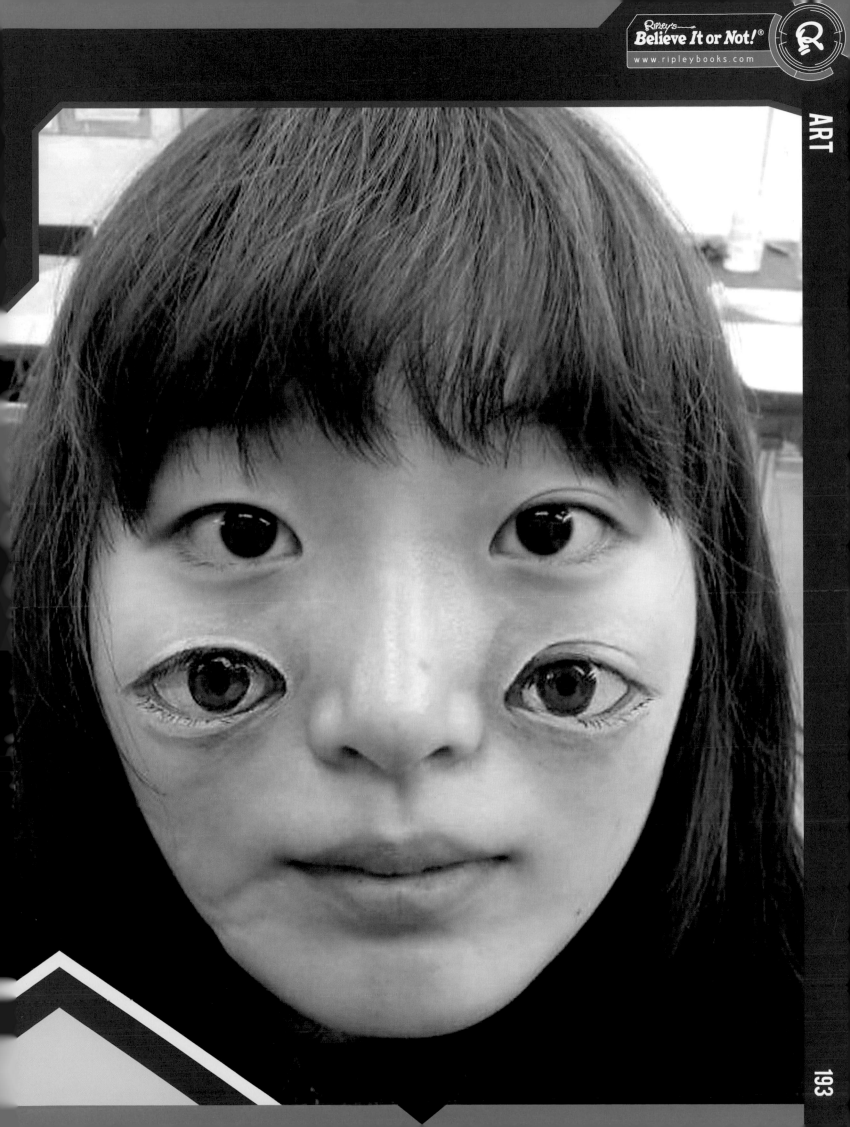

HEALTHY PROFIT▶ A chipped 15th-century Ming Dynasty rice bowl, bought for just £65 ($100) in 1948 by a London collector, sold at a U.K. auction in 2012 for £1.6 million ($2.5 million).

BUILDER'S BLUNDER▶ "Parachuting Rat," a valuable piece of street art by British graffiti artist Banksy, was destroyed when a builder in Melbourne, Australia, drilled a hole through it to install a bathroom pipe.

CARDBOARD ARCADE▶ At his father's shop in Los Angeles, California, nine-year-old Caine Monroy built his own games arcade out of cardboard—complete with a range of games, prize displays, a security system and one-month fun passes. Filmmaker Nirvan Mullick was so captivated by Caine's creation that he made a short movie about it, and a flashmob organized on Facebook led to hundreds of people lining up at the arcade to play the homemade games.

SPANISH STEPS
▶ Walking along a street in Madrid, a woman is dwarfed by a giant shoe figure, which was part of a 2012 exhibition called *Shoe Street Art*, designed to promote Spanish footwear.

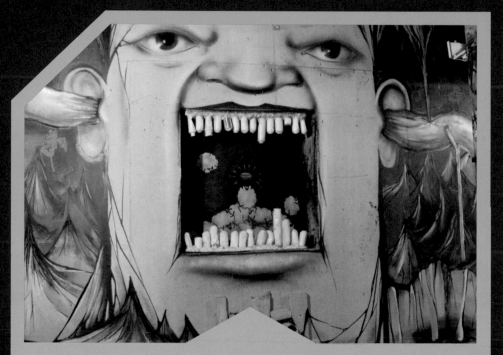

LIVING WALL
▶ For his *Living Wall* series, Russian street artist Nikita Nomerz makes the country's derelict structures come alive by adding facial features. He has painted eyes and a nose on to this crumbling wall and given it white spray cans for teeth. He has also painted water towers to make it look as if they're laughing and put faces on dilapidated buildings, using the broken windows as eyes.

JUBILEE YARN▶ Great-grandmother Sheila Carter from Southampton, England, spent over 500 hours and used 4,500 ft (1,372 m) of wool knitting her own version of the Diamond Jubilee of Queen Elizabeth II. She used an estimated 1.8 million stitches for her royal tribute, the centerpiece of which was a 3.3-ft-long (1-m) woolen barge carrying woolen likenesses of the royal family along London's River Thames toward a woolen Tower Bridge. In 2011, she had knitted a 3-ft (0.9-m) wedding cake with woolen figures of Prince William and Catherine Middleton on top.

MARMITE NATIVITY▶ Nathan Wyburn, an art student from Ebbw Vale, Wales, created a Nativity scene from 120 slices of toast coated with Marmite savory spread. His Marmite portfolio also includes portraits of Simon Cowell, Amy Winehouse and Australian-born entertainer Rolf Harris.

DREAM CAR▶ Unable to afford the real Ferrari that he had always wanted, Chris Smart of Hampshire, England, settled for a highly realistic one that he painted on his garage door instead.

COFFEE CREATION▶ In June 2012, Russian sculptor Arkady Kim used 397 lb (180 kg) of coffee beans to produce the world's biggest coffee bean painting. Titled *Awakening*, it measured 323 sq ft (30 sq m), took two weeks to create and was made from around one million coffee beans.

JUST A-MAZE-ING▶ Japanese artist Motoi Yamamoto creates vast intricate mazes made entirely of salt. He works by filling a plastic bottle, usually used for machine oil, with white salt and then sprinkling it on the floor. Some of his larger designs can take him up to two weeks, working 14 hours a day.

GOLD RUSH▶ Visitors to an art gallery in Bangkok, Thailand, were challenged to search through *Sickness*▶, an installation filled with knee-deep yarn, in the hope of finding ten gold necklaces worth hundreds of dollars. The necklaces had been planted there by the artist, Surasi Kusolwong. Anyone who found a necklace was permitted to keep it.

CLOSE-KNIT COMMUNITY▶ A team of more than 50 knitters from Poole, England, worked for nine months to produce a 10-ft-tall (3-m) Christmas tree consisting of 1,200 individual 8-in (20-cm) green woolen squares. They hung the squares on a metal frame and completed the tree with the addition of 200 knitted decorations, including Santas, snowmen and reindeer.

CLAY FIGURES▶ Using around 30 tons of clay, British sculptor Antony Gormley encouraged ordinary people to create 40,000 small terracotta humanoid figures for his piece *Field for the British Isles*. It took five days to position the characters when they were exhibited at Barrington Court, Somerset, England, in 2012.

PICTURE DIARY▶ Angie Stevens of Swansea, Wales, drew a picture of her son Gruff almost every day for the first two years of his life—a total of more than 700 drawings—and she's still going. Doodlemum, as Angie is known, sketches a picture each evening to document things that happened to Gruff and the rest of her family that day.

SATELLITE IMAGES▶ German artist David Hanauer created a line of elaborately patterned rugs based on satellite imagery of Earth. Inspired by the uniform layout of the streets of Las Vegas, Nevada, he used aerial images from Google Earth as prints for his modern Persian carpets, mirroring the images in four directions to give the rugs the familiar symmetrical Persian look.

SILENT PROTEST▶ In July 2012, St. Petersburg artist Pyotr Pavlensky sewed his mouth shut with thin red string in a special performance to protest against the Russian trial of three women from the Pussy Riot punk group.

GREAT STINK▶ A 13-ft-high (4-m) sculpture of a nose, *The Great Stink*, appeared on a bridge in London, England, in August 2012. It was promoting an exhibition to remember the terrible stench of untreated waste in the summer of 1858, which led to new laws being introduced to clean up the British capital.

FALLEN HEROES

▶*It looks as though Ernie has fallen upon hard times, but the depiction of the Sesame Street character as a down-and-out is all part of a German art exhibition, Broken Heroes, by Patricia Waller. Her series of hand-crocheted, childhood iconic figures in peril also features Winnie the Pooh as a suicide victim, Spider-Man trapped in his own web and Superman meeting his death by flying into a wall.*

STREET ART

▶ In the summer of 2011, a row of condemned, dilapidated houses on Bellevue Avenue East in Seattle, Washington, were transformed for three weeks into some of the weirdest dwellings in America. Fourteen local artists were set loose on the empty homes and were briefed to convert them into a public art experience. Sutton Beres Culler used 12,000 ft (3,660 m) of bright red ratchet straps to tie two of the houses together, knocking holes in the walls in the process. Luke Haynes decorated one of the buildings with 1000 lb (454 kg) of old T-shirts. One of the deserted family homes was completely wrapped in household plastic wrap and fitted with a barcode, as if it were for sale. After three weeks the street of art was knocked down to make way for a new development.

BLANK CANVAS▶ In 1969, British minimalist artist Bob Law created a "painting" that consisted of nothing more than a large blank canvas with a hand-drawn black marker pen border and the date in the bottom right-hand corner—and it has been valued at nearly $100,000.

INVISIBLE EXHIBITION▶ The Hayward Gallery in London, England, exhibited 50 "invisible" works by people such as Andy Warhol, Yoko Ono and Yves Klein for an exhibition of art that nobody could see. Featured artworks included invisible ink drawings, a piece of paper that U.S. artist Tom Friedman stared at for 1,000 hours over a period of five years, and a plinth once stood on by Andy Warhol.

PAPER MUSTANG▶ Canadian artist Jonathan Brand has built a life-sized 1969 Mustang automobile—entirely from paper. The replica car started out as a 3-D model on a computer. Every piece of the digital model was then printed out on paper, cut by hand, folded and then glued in place. The paper model is authentic down to the last detail, with a paper steering wheel, paper rear-view mirror and even a paper engine housing paper spark plugs.

TINY DRAGON▶ To welcome the Chinese year of the dragon in 2012, Taiwanese miniature artist Chen Forng-shean spent three months creating a dragon sculpture that was just 0.5 in (1.2 cm) long—so small that it could fit on a coin and had to be viewed under a microscope. The incredible detail on the dragon included claws and whiskers.

▶▶ **AS A LABORER, FRENCH ARTIST PAUL GAUGUIN HELPED BUILD THE PANAMA CANAL.◀◀**

LITTLE LANDSCAPES▶ In March 2012, Kelowna Art Gallery in British Columbia, held a display of 4,154 standard postcard-sized (6 x 4 in/15 x 10 cm) original, landscaped-based works of art by local artists.

MAD HOMES • JULY 2011
723

WEATHER OR NOT?

▶ Dutch artist Berndnaut Smilde's *Nimbus* artworks bring the weather indoors. His incredibly convincing homemade clouds, created with a standard smoke machine and water spray, are photographed in the few seconds before they dissipate, so the final images show the miniature clouds floating in empty rooms, as if by magic. No computer trickery or cotton wool is involved!

STREET WISE▶ Michael Wallace uses his bicycle as a pencil and the streets of his home city of Baltimore, Maryland, as his canvas to create giant GPS images of assorted shapes, including an owl, an elephant, the Manhattan skyline and a train. After studying the street map to see if any interesting shapes jump out at him, he plots his riding route, even if it means going the wrong way down a one-way street to finish his GPS artwork.

ART BATEAU▶ A boat made from 1,200 pieces of wood, including fragments from Jimi Hendrix's guitar and the 16th-century English warship *Mary Rose*, was launched as part of an art project to mark the 2012 London Olympics.

STAPLE ART▶ Artist Baptiste Debombourg created a huge, intricate mural in Prague, Czech Republic, using 450,000 metal staples.

ICE FESTIVAL▶ Twenty-two truckloads of ice—some 440 tons—were transformed by 29 international artists into 90 Disney characters, including Mickey Mouse, Simba, Aladdin and Buzz Lightyear, for the Bruges Snow and Ice Sculpture Festival in Belgium. To stop the characters melting while the festival was open between November 2011 and January 2012, the venue temperature was kept at 14°F (–10°C).

SPILLED MILK

▶ Christopher Boffoli, a photographer from Seattle, Washington, has captured popular food items in a bizarre new light. His miniature characters go kayaking in milk, mine for chocolate, and scuba-dive in cups of tea, among other daring activities. Christopher says that his humorous photos were inspired by the miniature scale toys of his childhood and America's food habits.

SEALED WITH A KISS

▶ *Japanese photographer Haruhiko Kawaguchi, like many artists, likes to capture couples in love. However, in his case he captures them in giant vacuum-sealed plastic bags! Although the concept may terrify some, all of his subjects, around 80 in total, volunteered for the* Flesh Love *project. Kawaguchi sucks all the air out of the large furniture bags with a vacuum cleaner and then has a matter of seconds in which to take his shots before the models start to panic. He says that while there have been no adverse effects, the men are genuinely more scared than the women, and he always keeps a supply of oxygen nearby for emergencies. Kawaguchi's methods are extremely dangerous and definitely never to be attempted at home!*

BLOOD ARTIST▶ New York City artist Nick Kushner has been painting with his own blood for 15 years. He says the pain he feels when drawing the "paint" from his body is cathartic.

LIVING ART▶ Belgian artist Ben Heine covers models in acrylic paint to create living works of art. He spent over three hours on each piece for his series called *Flesh and Acrylic.*

GALLERY BIRTH▶
Performance artist Mami Kotak from Norwood, Massachusetts, set up a birthing pool in a New York City art gallery and, as the culmination of her work, gave birth there in front of 20 people to a boy she named Ajax, on October 25, 2011. A video of the birth at the Microscope Gallery in Brooklyn was added to her exhibition *The Birth of Baby X.*

TALLEST TOWER▶ In May 2012, 4,000 children in South Korea worked together to build a 105-ft-high (32-m) LEGO® tower in front of Seoul's Olympic stadium—the world's tallest LEGO tower. It used over 500,000 LEGO bricks and took five days to construct.

CAR-HENGE ▶ To celebrate the 2012 summer solstice, artist Tommy Gun created a replica of the ancient English monument Stonehenge using 18 scrap cars stacked bumper-to-bumper in London. It took him three months to build the structure that stood 16 ft 5 in tall (5 m) and weighed nearly 40 tons. It was designed to withstand a Force 12 hurricane.

SECRET SMILE ▶ By turning Leonardo da Vinci's *Mona Lisa* on its side, New York City artist Ron Piccirillo claims to have spotted hidden, symbolic images in the 500-year-old painting, including the heads of a lion, an ape and a buffalo, which he says show that the painting is actually a representation of envy.

SINGLE LINE ▶ Singaporean artist Chan Hwee Chong has reproduced some of the world's most famous paintings—including Leonardo da Vinci's *Mona Lisa*, Johannes Vermeer's *Girl with a Pearl Earring* and Vincent van Gogh's self-portrait— with just a single spiral line. His work is so precise that if he makes even the smallest mistake he has to start all over again.

STICK MAN ▶ *Walking Man*, a 6-ft-tall (1.8-m) stick man sculpture by Swiss artist Alberto Giacometti, sold at an auction in London, England, in 2010 for more than $104 million.

DICE TRIBUTE ▶ New York City artist Frederick McSwain created a giant portrait from 13,138 dice. The portrait was of his friend, Canadian artist and designer Tobias Wong, who died in 2010 at 35 years of age or, to be precise, 13,138 days old.

MILLION BEADS ▶ In New Orleans, Louisiana, German-born artist Stephan Wanger used over a million recycled Mardi Gras beads to create the world's largest bead mosaic, measuring 8 x 30 ft (2.4 x 9.1 m). Titled *Sanctuary of Alegria*, the mosaic, which was completed in January 2012 after 14 months of work, depicted a view across the Mississippi toward downtown New Orleans.

ROYAL BEAN ▶ Micro sculptor Willard Wigan of Birmingham, England, sculpted a portrait of Queen Elizabeth II on a 0.08-in (2-mm) coffee bean to mark her Diamond Jubilee. It took him four weeks and he painted it with a hair plucked from the back of a housefly.

PANIC ROOM ▶ A bedroom at the Au Vieux Panier hotel in Marseille, France, is decorated half in white and half in bold graffiti. The hotel owner, Jessica Venediger, invited street graffiti artist Tilt to add bubble letters and tags on the walls, floor, furniture and even the bed linen to create the "Panic Room."

ART BARBIE ▶

▶ French artist Jocelyne Grivau has creatively combined the great paintings she admires with a childhood Barbie obsession to create these quirky and clever reworkings of famous masterpieces, starring the world's most famous doll. In this alternative art, Barbie takes the place of the mysterious *Mona Lisa*, by Leonardo da Vinci and Vermeer's *Girl with a Pearl Earring*. It can take Jocelyne days to prepare Barbie for a single photo. She says that the criticism of Barbie dolls inspires her to dress the doll up as iconic women in art.

MELON HEADS ▶ Clive Cooper from Vancouver, Canada, carves human and animal faces from brightly colored watermelons. Each artwork takes up to six hours to create but lasts only a day.

BASKETBALL PORTRAIT ▶ Malaysian artist Hong Yi used a basketball dipped in red paint to create an amazingly detailed portrait of Yao Ming, a basketball player who recently retired from the NBA team, the Houston Rockets.

TITANIC REPLICA ▶ In April 2012, to mark the centenary of the sinking of the *Titanic*, Stan Fraser unveiled a 100-ft-long (30-m) replica of the ship in the backyard of his home in Inverness, Scotland. He spent 12 years making the 1:10 scale model, using two old trailers to form the hull.

TOWERING TRANSFORMER ▶ Students at Hangzhou University, China, built a giant, 32-ft-tall (10-m) Transformer from discarded auto parts.

SLEEPING BEAUTY ▶

Ukrainian-Canadian artist Taras Polataiko staged an exhibition in Kiev where five young women took two-hourly turns to slumber on a bed at the gallery as the fairytale princess Sleeping Beauty. In keeping with the story, the Beauties promised to marry any visitor who woke them with a kiss, although the marriage pledges were not legally binding.

TONGUE PAINTER ▶

Ani K, a drawing teacher from Kerala, India, paints with his tongue. He was inspired to coat his tongue with paint and then lick the canvas after reading about an artist who painted with his foot. Ani first tried painting with his nose but found that his tongue offered greater control and he has even managed to grow immune to the paint fumes, which used to give him headaches and stomach cramps. He has completed more than 20 watercolors, including an 8-ft-wide (2.4-m) version of *The Last Supper*, which took him five months to paint.

KIT CAR ▶

To commemorate the Aston Martin DBR1 sports car that won the famous Le Mans 24-Hour Endurance Race in 1959, the Evanta Motor Company from Hertfordshire, England, handcrafted a life-size artwork of the car in the style of an Airfix construction kit toy. Measuring 21 ft (6.3 m) wide by 11 ft (3.3 m) tall, the artwork shows the car broken up into kit form with the individual pieces affixed to a gray frame and is valued at £25,000 ($40,000).

COFFEE PORTRAIT ▶

Artists in Hawaii created a 16 x 25 ft (4.9 x 7.6 m) portrait of Elvis Presley—an image from his 1961 movie *Blue Hawaii*—from 5,642 cups of coffee, incorporating ten different coffee shades.

ROADKILL POTTERY ▶

Marion Waldo McChesney presses the mummified corpses of dead animals into clay to create unique pottery designs. Her artistic roadkill collection began more than 15 years ago when she found a frog—which she subsequently nicknamed Dorset George— dead but uncrushed in a Vermont driveway. She still uses George for her pottery impressions, along with a dozen other dead frogs, seahorses, starfish, lizards and chopped-off bird's feet.

IMAGINATIVE ART ▶

Two New York City artists sold a piece of art that nobody can see for $10,000. Known collectively as *Praxis*, Delia and Brainard Carey founded the Museum of Non-Visible Art where, instead of purchasing a tangible picture, collectors buy an authentication letter and a small card bearing the artist's description of the work. Then they hang it on their wall and use their imagination to describe the piece of art to their friends.

HUMAN BODYWORK

▶ Here's a car with unique bodywork—made up of 17 naked men and women. The car was created by body-painter Emma Hack of Adelaide, Australia, who, working from a photo of a car that had been involved in a minor accident, covered her human models in shades of blue, white, black and silver, to include alloy wheels and a license plate, before arranging the models in the car shape. She took 18 hours to achieve the perfect finish.

CLEANER'S BLUNDER ▶

An overzealous cleaning woman at Ostwall Museum in Dortmund, Germany, ruined a modern sculpture worth $1.1 million after mistaking it for a mess and scrubbing all the paint off it.

WORKING MODEL ▶

Louis Chenot of Carl Junction, Missouri, spent an estimated 15,000 hours building a 1:6 model of a 1932 Duesenberg car from scratch. He completed the model in 2010 and it has more than 6,000 parts, including an operational engine.

FINGERLESS EMBROIDERY ▶

Despite losing all her fingers in a fire as a child, Peng Jiangya from Yinjiang Tujia, China, can create intricate cross-stitch designs at a speed faster than many able-bodied artists. She uses her arms to hold and thread the needle and through hours of practice has perfected a skill that draws tourists to her remote village to buy her beautifully embroidered landscapes.

New York artist Vincent Castiglia has been painting with his own blood for more than ten years. He makes a preliminary pen or graphite sketch before extracting just enough "paint" in the privacy of his own studio. He describes his macabre medium as "liquid flesh" and his larger works take up to three months to create, sometimes fetching over $25,000. Human blood contains iron oxide, a pigment found in many paints.

BLOOD ARTIST

LIVING DRAWINGS

▶ With just an ordinary pencil and a flat piece of white paper, Dutch illustrator Ramon Bruin creates 3-D illusion drawings that look as though they are jumping off the page. Using an airbrushing technique that he calls "anamorphosis," he draws incredible images of snakes, birds and insects, and when he puts his hand on the pictures, he really brings them to life.

PIN MONEY ▶ New York City artist Andre Woolery makes portraits of famous people—including rappers Jay-Z and Kanye West—from thousands of colored thumbtacks. He has also created a replica $100 bill from 23,850 green, silver and black thumbtacks, replacing the picture on the bill of Benjamin Franklin with one of Benjamin Banneker, the 18th-century African-American scientist and astronomer most famously known for being part of the team that surveyed the boundaries for the original Washington, D.C.

SOCCER STUD ▶ Using a powerful microscope, engraver Graham Short from Birmingham, England, painstakingly etched the full names of all 38 England World Cup goal-scorers onto a single tiny soccer boot stud. It took him six months to complete, as the slightest movement meant he had to start all over again. For that reason he wore a stethoscope so that he could engrave between heartbeats and worked only at night to avoid the vibration from any passing daytime trucks. He has previously engraved the Lord's Prayer on the top of a gold pinhead.

JELLY BEAN MURALS▶
Kristen Cumings of Martinez, California, re-creates famous artworks by the likes of Van Gogh and Vermeer using jelly beans. Each of her murals—some of which measure 4 x 6 ft (1.2 x 1.8 m)—uses around 12,000 jelly beans and can take her 50 hours to make. She starts by studying a reference photo of the artwork and then paints an acrylic version of it onto a blank canvas. Once that has dried, she begins applying the beans with spray adhesive, matching the colors to the original as best she can.

BEACH PATTERN▶
Instead of a brush and paints, Gunilla Klingberg used a modified tractor to create her patterned artwork *A Sign in Space* on a Spanish beach. A pattern made of truck tire treads was attached to a large metal cylinder and mounted on to the beach-cleaning tractor and when the vehicle was driven across Laga beach, it imprinted the star pattern in the sand. Whenever footprints destroyed the design, it was remade at the next low tide.

BANANA TATTOOS▶
Artist Phil Hansen from Minneapolis, Minnesota, has re-created famous artworks by Vincent van Gogh, Sandro Botticelli, Edgar Degas and Michelangelo, using only a push-pin and a banana. He effectively tattoos the banana by spending hours puncturing the peel repeatedly with the pin, after which the banana skin slowly rots and blackens to reveal his intricate designs.

COOL STATUES▶
To create their *Street Stone* series, French photographer Léo Caillard and art director Alexis Persani dressed ancient sculptures at Paris's Louvre Museum in modern clothes. Caillard photographed the statues and then got his friends to model in identical poses but wearing skinny jeans, checked shirts and Ray-Bans. Persani combined the two sets of pictures in Photoshop so that they merged seamlessly.

BLOOD ART▶
New York City artist Jordan Eagles uses animal blood collected from slaughterhouses as paint to make artworks as big as 32 ft (9.7 m) long. He uses fresh, decomposed and pulverized blood to vary the shades and textures.

HENNA HURRY▶
Pavan Ahluwalia became the world's fastest henna artist when she painted a staggering 511 armbands in one hour at a school in Essex, England, on February 27, 2012. Each design was unique and she beat her previous record by a massive 131 tattoos. Once the henna is applied, it needs to be left to dry for around 20 minutes, after which time the henna comes away to reveal the intricate designs underneath. The self-taught artist has been practicing henna design since she was just seven and has seen her colorful creations used on hats, scarves, shawls, shoes and even wallpaper and works of art.

▶TOY
SCULPTURES

▶*Australian artist Freya Jobbins has created more than 30 sculptures of famous and imaginary figures out of recycled plastic toys. By painstakingly positioning each toy, she has built models including "Kerri-Anne," the Roman goddess Juno built from dolls' heads and Barbie doll legs, and a head of Arnold Schwarzenegger with "hair" made of toy soldiers.*

BALL GAMES

▶ This mysterious giant "RedBall" has been appearing in bizarre urban locations all around the world. The man behind its appearance is New York artist Kurt Perschke, who has inflated the 15-ft-high (4.6-m), 250-lb (113-kg) ball in cities including Taipei, Toronto, London, Sydney, Abu Dhabi, Barcelona and Chicago since 2001. The ball inflates only briefly, often squeezed into an unusual spot, before disappearing and traveling to its next stop. Understandably, the "RedBall Project" gets attention wherever it goes, and Kurt is regularly approached by people who want the ball to appear in their own city.

PLAIN DOTTY▶ Nikki Douthwaite from Cheshire, England, turns the paper dots created by a stationery hole punch into celebrity portraits. For each picture, she uses tweezers and glue to stick up to 600,000 punched dots in a precise order.

CANDY MAGIC

▶ Los Angeles, California-based artist Jason Mecier has created this portrait of Harry Potter made entirely from black and red licorice! The sweet sorcerer forms part of Jason's *Licorice Flix* series, which also includes Willy Wonka, Freddy Krueger, Charlie Chaplin and E.T. Licorice Harry is now hanging in Ripley's Baltimore Odditorium.

COIN MOSAIC▶ A total of 412 employees from a bank in Tallin, Estonia, teamed up to create a 215-sq-ft (20-sq-m) coin mosaic from 53,757 coins. The mosaic comprised 46,241 ten-cent coins and 7,516 five-cent coins, giving it a total value of 4,999.90 euros ($6,190) and a weight of 482 lb (219 kg).

GLOWING CORPSES▶ Japan's Iori Tomita transforms the corpses of fish and other small animals into glowing, luminescent artworks. He acquires the discarded carcasses from butchers and fish markets and chemically strips them down to the toughest part of their remains before dying them with bright colors. He has made more than 5,000 pieces since 2005, the biggest of which took a year to complete.

BALLOON SPIDER▶ Even though he is scared of spiders, balloon-twisting artist Adam Lee used 2,975 balloons to create a giant spider measuring 45 ft (13.7 m) wide at Grand Mound, Washington State. Lee has also created balloon versions of famous people including Barack Obama, Queen Elizabeth II and The Simpsons.

STAIN PORTRAIT▶ Malaysian artist Hong Yi created an amazingly lifelike portrait of Taiwanese songwriter Jay Chou using nothing but coffee ring stains from the bottom of a coffee mug. She often uses unconventional media to create works of art, and has previously utilized sunflower seeds, chili paste and basketballs.

WALK-ON SCULPTURE▶ The *Tiger and Turtle* sculpture in Duisburg, Germany, is shaped like a roller-coaster track but is designed to be walked and climbed on. Made from 99 tons of galvanized steel and perched on top of a mining waste dump, Ulrich Genth's sculpture is 721 ft (220 m) long and has 249 steps on the walkway, the handrails of which are illuminated by LED lights at night.

CAVE ART▶ Rock analysis of sophisticated drawings of bears, rhinos and horses found on the walls of the Chauvet-Pont-D'Arc cave in the Ardèche region of France indicate that they are the oldest cave drawings in the world, dating back 30,000 years. The paintings depict some 13 different species of animal altogether.

TROUSER MOSAIC▶ Volunteers in Zhengzhou City, China, made a giant, 68,685-sq-ft (6,381-sq-m) mosaic from more than 23,000 pairs of trousers. It took over five hours to create and depicted an ancient Chinese cauldron and two Chinese characters that, translated, meant "fashion."

AUTO COWS▶ Miina Äkkijyrkkä, a Finnish sculptor, painter and designer, buys dozens of used cars and then creates giant, colorful sculptures of cows from the scrap auto parts. Her love of cows began when she attended a dairy farming school in the 1960s and she regularly uses them as a subject for her works of art.

GROWING PICTURES ▶

Zachary Copfer, a microbiologist-turned-photography student at the University of Cincinnati, has created ingenious portraits of Albert Einstein and Charles Darwin by growing bacteria in Petri dishes. He begins the process, which he calls bacteriography, by spreading the bacteria across the dish. He then places a photographic negative of his subject on top of the dish and exposes it to radiation, thereby controlling how and where the bacteria grows so that the image can be re-created in fine detail.

TOY DINOSAUR ▶ The U.S. Space and Rocket Center at Huntsville, Alabama, is home to a life-sized T-rex sculpture made from 160,000 pieces of K'NEX. The K'NEX dinosaur stands 12 ft 6 in (3.8 m) high and 33 ft 8 in (10.3 m) long, and weighs 10 lb (4.5 kg).

ATHLETIC BUS ▶ For the 2012 Olympics, Czech artist David Cerny turned one of London's famous red double-decker buses into a robotic sculpture that performs push-ups. The six-ton 1957 bus, which Cerny bought from an owner in the Netherlands, is powered by wiring and suspension gear to move up and down on bright red arms, with each push-up being accompanied by the sound of a prerecorded groan.

AMMO MODEL ▶ To comment on the role that religion has played in some of the major conflicts in history, California artist Al Farrow used gun parts and bullets to create a 6-ft-long (1.8-m) model cathedral.

BOTTLE-NOSED

▶ Constructed from thousands of discarded plastic bottles, these enormous fish appeared on Botafogo Beach, near Rio de Janeiro, Brazil, in June 2012 to highlight the problem of plastics polluting the world's oceans.

PAPER CITIES ▶ Dutch origami architect Ingrid Siliakus creates entire cities featuring New York-style skyscrapers by painstakingly cutting and folding pieces of paper. Spending up to two months on each cityscape, she uses no glue or adhesive, and calculates the spaces between the folded lines to 0.01-mm accuracy.

MIRACLE GLOW▶ Thousands of worshipers flocked to Saint Dimitrija Church in Skopje, Macedonia, in April 2012 after several frescoes of saints inexplicably brightened in color without being restored or cleaned. For years the murals had been blackened by the residue of candle smoke, but then suddenly—beginning with the picture of the Virgin Mary—the soot fell off them one by one in what churchgoers described as a "miracle."

POP (TART) ART▶ Tyler Kozar of Pittsburgh, Pennsylvania, won a million pop tarts in a contest and, after donating the food, used the packaging and wrappers to make works of art—including a 16-ft-tall (4.9-m) foil T-rex dinosaur that is now on display in Ripley's Baltimore Odditorium.

MODEL THEATER▶ Eighty-two-year-old Cyril Barbier from Birmingham, England, has built a working model of a local movie theater in his bedroom. Fully lit, the cinema has a moving curtain in front of the screen as well as an organ that can be powered to rise up out of the floor and drop back down again. Meanwhile, a hidden DVD player plays movies on the 15-in (38-cm) flat screen, which is in perfect proportion to the theater's original 1930s screen.

ARTISTIC VANDAL▶ Polish-born Wlodzimierz Umaniec was jailed for two years in December 2012 for defacing a multi-million dollar Mark Rothko painting, *Black on Maroon*, at the Tate Modern gallery in London, England, by scrawling his signature on it with a black marker pen—and then claiming that the vandalism itself was a work of art. Repairing the mural will take up to two years and cost about £200,000 ($300,000), as Rothko's complex layering style mixes eggs, glue and resin with traditional oil paint.

UNUSUAL SUSPECT▶ When the world's most famous work of art, Leonardo da Vinci's *Mona Lisa*, was stolen from the Louvre in Paris, France, in 1911, one of the suspects was Spanish artist Pablo Picasso. French police took him before a magistrate for questioning, but he was later released without charge. Ironically, he was in possession of a pair of Bronze Age Iberian statues, which had been snatched from the Louvre by a Belgian masquerading as a French baron, but the arresting officers never noticed the stolen artworks in Picasso's studio.

SHAMPOO PAINTER▶ Philadelphia artist Alex Da Corte makes paintings from dried shampoo. He often incorporates unusual materials into his artworks—past projects have featured soda bottles, Christmas trees and fingernails.

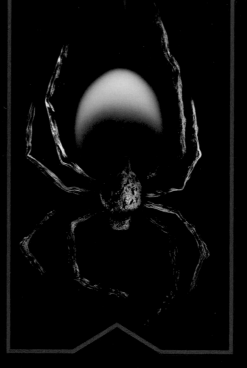

STRIKING IMAGES

▶ Fascinated by the incredible patterns that form in the blackened carbon of used wood after striking a match, Russian photographer Stanislav Aristov bends the spent matches into beautiful miniature sculptures of flowers, insects, fish, a lightbulb and even the Eiffel Tower.

SOOT PORTRAITS▶ Canadian artist Steven Spazuk uses the soot that rises from candles as a medium to create portraits. His technique involves holding a thick sheet of paper to a flame and then manipulating the soot left behind into an incredibly detailed monochromatic image.

FISHHOOKS▶ Cuban artist Yoan Capote created a 26-ft-wide (8-m) seascape mural from 500,000 fishhooks, intertwined and nailed onto plywood. Even with the help of 30 assistants working in rotation, it took him over six months to complete.

NICE PROFIT▶ German artist Gerhard Richter's *Abstraktes Bild*, a painting described by Sotheby's as a "masterpiece of calculated chaos," sold for $34 million at an auction in London, England, on October 12, 2012—the highest amount ever paid for a work by a living artist. The seller was rock guitarist Eric Clapton, who had bought the colorful abstract piece as part of a set of three for $3.4 million in 2001.

HANGING OFFENSE▶ In December 2011, Polish art student Andrzej Sobiepan snuck one of his paintings into the National Museum in Wrocław, where it hung for three days before being noticed. Far from being angry, the museum director praised Sobiepan's initiative as a "witty artistic happening" and kept the small picture of a green leaf on display, albeit in the museum's café.

PRETTY PRINTS▶ Connecticut-based artist Kevin Van Aelst has created a series of giant fingerprints using everyday objects, including mustard, yarn, cheetos and cassette tapes— and each artwork is a detailed re-creation of his own fingerprints.

ANIMAL LOVER▶ Leonardo da Vinci (1452– 1519) was a vegetarian and an animal rights activist who used to buy caged birds, which in Italy at that time were sold as food as well as pets, just to set them free.

MINIATURE MANHATTAN▶ Using nothing but hundreds of staples, Israeli artist Tofi Stoler built a miniature Manhattan, measuring just 4 x 14 x 20 in (10 x 35 x 50 cm) high. She has also made a model of her ukulele-playing boyfriend and re-created the scene from Francisco Goya's famous painting *The Third of May 1808*—all with metal staples.

COOKIE MOSAIC▶ The Bright School and Chattanooga Bakery of Chattanooga, Tennessee, together made a giant cookie mosaic from 16,390 Moon Pies, covering nearly 1,360 sq ft (126 sq m).

CHAIN DOGS

▶ *Israeli artist Nirit Levav Packer has created a series of life-size dog sculptures from discarded bicycle chains. Inspired after seeing chains, gears and pedals being thrown away at her son's bicycle store, she now scours garages and bike shops across Tel Aviv for suitable parts before soldering them into place. Her chain dog sculptures, which include greyhounds, poodles, a cocker spaniel, an Afghan hound and a Rottweiler, sell for up to $10,000 each.*

NIGHT SHIFT▶ French artist Anne-Louis Girodet (1767–1824) was at his most creative at night. In order to see in the dark, he would light as many as 40 candles on the brim of his hat. He determined his fee according to the number of candles burned while painting the picture.

TEA QUEEN▶ English artist Andy Brown created a portrait of Queen Elizabeth II by stitching together 1,000 used tea bags.

CARPET FLUFF▶ Brazilian artist Tonico Lemos Auad made his name by fashioning sculptures of squirrels, lions and cats out of pieces of carpet fluff.

CHAIN SMOKER▶ U.S. artist Jackson Pollock (1912–56) would often paint with a cigarette hanging from his lips. He used dropped cigarette ash in some of his greatest works to add texture.

NAILED IT!

▶ British artist Marcus Levine creates stunning pictures of the human body by hammering up to 50,000 metal nails into wooden boards. By varying the height and distance of the nails and rotating their heads, he can achieve different tones to give the overall effect of a pencil or charcoal drawing.

11

FOOD ▶

CREEPY CAKES

The world's most gruesome cake shop popped up in the Pathology Museum at St. Bart's Hospital, London, England. It featured such creepy confectionery as a bleeding heart perched on a wedding cake, a stitched-skin celebration cake, and cupcakes made using a range of toppings, including blood cells, maggots, severed body parts, lumps of flesh and even stool samples.

The brainchild of Emma Thomas (aka Miss Cakehead), the three-day "Eat Your Heart Out" event graphically represented diseases and body parts in edible form. Many of the foodstuffs were so lifelike they made visitors retch. And what better way to wash down a blood-cell cupcake than with a stool-sample cocktail—a creamy drink made by James Dance using cocoa, strawberry syrup and pieces of fudge?

WHO ATE BAMBI?▶ Andrea Canalito from Houston, Texas, designed a sculpture called *Twinkle Twinkle Baby* made from giant cupcakes with the heads of baby deer sticking out from the top. The nonedible cupcakes took three months to construct from foam, modeling material and paint.

FRUIT BAN▶ People in Indonesia are not allowed to eat durian fruit in many public places because of its foul smell—described as "pig droppings, turpentine and onions."

VEGETARIAN SHARK▶ Florence, a nurse shark at an aquarium in Birmingham, England, prefers to eat only vegetables, forcing handlers to sneak the fish that she needs to survive inside pieces of cucumber or celery. The 6-ft (1.8-m) shark used to eat meat but following a 2009 operation to remove a rusty hook from her jaw, she has used her razor-sharp teeth to rip through lettuce leaves instead of flesh.

FRUIT MOUNTAIN▶ Cooks at McGill University in Montreal, Canada, created an 11,197-lb (5,083-kg) fruit salad that featured 4,960 lb (2,250 kg) of watermelon, 2,230 lb (1,012 kg) of pineapple, 357 lb (162 kg) of strawberries and 220 lb (100 kg) of apples.

PUB TREK▶ Cathy Price from Preston, Lancashire, England, has visited more than 300 British pubs, all called the Red Lion. It has taken her two years and 10,000 mi (16,100 km) of travel. She plans eventually to visit all 724 Red Lions—the commonest pub name in Britain.

Brain

Nail

Maggot therapy

Eyeball

Stitches

Finger

SPONGE CAKE▶ Pastry chefs took three days to create a 2.8-ton sponge cake depicting the coat of arms of the town of Seiersberg, Austria. The cake—made from 3,000 eggs and 1,100 lb (500 kg) of fruit—was cut into 10,000 pieces and had to be made in a sports hall as no kitchen was large enough to accommodate it.

CHICKEN BAN▶ In an attempt to combat rising food prices, Iran's National Police Chief Esmail Ahmadi Moghadam has proposed a TV ban on images of people eating chicken.

HOT BUTTER▶ A new spicy peanut butter called Instant Regret registers an eye-watering 12 million on the Scoville scale that measures the heat of chili peppers. This make it six times hotter than law-enforcement pepper spray. It contains a mixture of peanuts, King Naga chilies and habanero chili extract, and each jar comes with ten safety warnings!

FUNNY TASTE▶ For two years workers at an air force base in Blekinge, Sweden, unwittingly drank coffee made with radiator water after a pipe from the coffee machine was mistakenly connected to the heating system. The brown radiator water was roughly the same color as coffee, and although it tasted strange, nobody noticed the error until the heating was shut down during maintenance work.

BACON FESTIVAL▶ The 2013 Blue Ribbon Bacon Festival in Des Moines, Iowa, featured more than 10,000 lb (4,540 kg) of bacon served in bizarre ways, including chocolate-dipped bacon and bacon-flavored cupcakes and gelato.

EXPENSIVE DRINK▶ Bartender Joel Heffernan made a cocktail that sold for $12,916 at a club in Melbourne, Australia. Taking 16 hours to prepare, the drink contained two nips of prized 1858 Croizet Cognac, which sells for $157,000 a bottle.

GINGERBREAD HOUSE▶ San Francisco cookie artist Curtis Jensen created an amazing scale model of Downton Abbey out of gingerbread. Curtis, whose past projects include a gingerbread model of Notre Dame, took more than a week to construct the elaborate Jacobean country house from the popular U.K. TV series using gingerbread, icing and colored candies.

GIANT CHOCOLATE BAR▶ Chicago, Illinois-based company, World's Finest Chocolate created an enormous chocolate bar weighing 12,290 lb (6 tons) and measuring 21 ft (6.4 m) long, 4 ft (1.2 m) wide and a chunky 3 ft (0.9 m) tall.

Tongue

Hook

Flesh turret

BRIDE'S POTATO ▶ A potato variety known as the Bride's Potato gets its name from an Inca practice of requiring a bride to peel potatoes to prove her skills as a good wife.

EXTRA LEGS ▶ A woman from Changsha, China, freaked out when she got home and realized that the frozen chicken she had bought from a supermarket had four legs!

MEATY MOUTHFUL ▶ For the 2012 launch of reality TV show *Man vs. Food Nation* on Food Network U.K., chef Tristan Welch created a sandwich filled with 40 different cuts of meat. Standing 14 in (35 cm) high and 24 in (60 cm) wide, the sandwich took four hours to make and weighed about 28 lb (12.7 kg). It contained 11 lb (5 kg) of meat, including salami, turkey, bacon, ham, sausage and chorizo.

COKE WAVE

▶ Phil Hansen boiled 12 two-liter bottles of Coca-Cola for seven hours to create a fizzy version of Japanese artist Katsushika Hokusai's painting *Great Wave Off Kanagawa*. The U.S. artist achieved the varying shades of brown on the 8 x 6 ft (2.4 x 1.8 m) canvas by boiling the syrupy mixture to different thicknesses—up to 0.4 in (1 cm) in the darkest spots.

PANCAKE STACK ▶ On February 21, 2012— Shrove Tuesday—chef Andy Wrobel built a 30-in-high (76-cm) stack of 60 pancakes in Melbourne, Australia. He flips over 100,000 pancakes every year at the restaurant where he has worked for more than 25 years.

BURGER PIZZA ▶ In 2012, Pizza Hut launched its Crown Crust Burger pizza in the Middle East—a pizza crust lined with a dozen cheeseburgers.

CAT CAFÉ ▶ In a bid to introduce Japanese culture to Vienna, Austria, Takako Ishimitsu has opened the Café Neko, a cat café where customers can play with five resident cats while enjoying their coffee. There are around 40 cat cafés in Tokyo, Japan, where they are very popular.

STILL EDIBLE ▶ Hans Feldmeier of Rostock, Germany, received a tin of lard in 1948 from a U.S. food-aid program and finally decided to eat the 64-year-old contents in 2012.

PAPER BOTTLE ▶ Martin Myerscough from Suffolk, England, has invented the world's first paper wine bottle. The bottle combines a paper outer casing with a thin plastic lining to keep the wine fresh.

LARGEST LASAGNA ▶ On June 20, 2012, chefs in Krakow, Poland, made the world's biggest lasagna, weighing more than an adult African elephant. Tipping the scales at 15,697 lb (7,120 kg), the lasagna took ten hours to bake before being sliced into 10,000 portions. It was made in support of the Italian soccer team who were based in the city for the Euro 2012 soccer championships.

STUCK ON YOU

▶ For nearly 20 years, people have been sticking pieces of chewing gum to a 50-ft-long (15-m) brick wall in Seattle, Washington, so that the sticky deposits are now several inches thick in places. At first, they used the gum to stick coins to the wall in Post Alley, but now it's just gum. Newlyweds have even chosen the gum wall as a backdrop for their wedding pictures, and it was also featured briefly in the 2009 Jennifer Aniston movie, *Love Happens*.

THAT'S QUACKERS!

▶ Wayne Algenio won a New York City speed-eating competition by having the stomach to devour 18 balut—boiled fertilized duck fetuses complete with beak, soft bones and moist feathers—in five minutes. A high-protein Filipino delicacy, balut is eaten in its shell and is usually dipped in salt and washed down with beer.

CREEPY RECIPES▶ A 2012 Dutch book, *The Insect Cookbook*, suggests dozens of ways of incorporating insects into everyday meals, such as adding worms to chocolate muffins and grasshoppers to a mushroom risotto.

CUPCAKE CROWN▶ On April 14, 2012, at the Isle Waterloo World Cupcake Eating Championship in Iowa, Patrick "Deep Dish" Bertoletti ate a world record 72 cupcakes in just six minutes.

VOLCANIC GRILL▶ The staff of the El Diablo restaurant, on the island of Lanzarote in the Canary Islands, Spain, cook food over the heat of an active volcano. A giant grill over the volcanic vent enables them to cook meat and fish dishes at temperatures of between 840°F (450°C) and 930°F (500°C).

LUCKY LEG▶ A bullfrog was saved from being made into soup in Zhuzhou, China, when a chef spotted that it had a fifth leg. Instead of being eaten, the freaky frog was sent to a zoo.

COOKIE TOWER▶ On March 16, 2012, students at Woodrush High School, Worcestershire, England, made a cookie tower more than 6 ft (1.8 m) high from 11,500 cookies.

FAVORITE DRINK▶ Claire Ayton from Warwickshire, England, drank 8.4 pt (4 l) of Diet Coke every day for ten years. In total, that's 30,855 pt (14,600 l) at a cost of nearly $20,000. She also gained 42 lb (19 kg) in weight.

CARNIVOROUS COCKTAIL▶ The Ruby Lo bar in London, England, used to serve "True" Bloody Marys—alcohol mixed with pasteurized blood.

CAKE CAR▶ Carey Iennaccaro and Mike Elder built a 95-percent cake car that reached a speed of 28 mph (45 km/h) in Kansas City, Missouri, on March 4, 2012—the world's fastest cake car. The 716-lb (325-kg) car was edible except for the tires, aluminum chassis and brakes. At the wheel, Iennaccaro wore a chocolate helmet and sat on a cake cushion watching a frosting speedometer!

GOAT DROPPINGS▶ Argan oil, a popular delicacy in Morocco, where it is used for dipping bread and to flavor couscous and salad dressings, is collected from the droppings of native Tamri goats. After the goats have feasted on the fruits of the argan tree, they leave behind the hard nuts in their droppings. The droppings are then collected by local women and sifted to remove the kernels, which are ground up to produce the valuable oil.

BEER SPILL▶ A truck crashed in Sachsen Anhalt, Germany, spilling 27 tons of beer crates and sending beer flowing for several hundred yards down the autobahn. Firemen, wearing breathing apparatus to protect them from the beer fumes, had to close the road for several hours.

MINE HOST▶ Muru, a restaurant near Helsinki, Finland, offers customers the chance to dine 262 ft (80 m) underground in the Tytyri Mine Museum. Diners wear safety helmets for the descent and during their meal can go down an additional 1,150 ft (350 m) via an elevator shaft.

WATER BUGS

▶ Food shoppers at Tung Kwian market in northern Thailand can buy a traditional local dish of water bugs. Their legs tied up with green string, the insects are sold alive so that they stay fresh before being fried.

DIRTY DISHES▶ Customers at a French restaurant in Tokyo, Japan, pay $110 to eat dirt. Toshio Tanabe, chef at Ne Quittez Pas, devised the dirt menu after winning a cooking contest with his earthy sauce. He uses a special black soil that has been tested for safety and then serves up such delights as potato starch and black dirt soup, followed by a vegetable salad with a black dirt dressing, sea bass with a dirt risotto, dirt ice cream, and finally dirt mint tea.

TALLEST CAKE▶ At Luoyang, China, in March 2012, a total of 20 chefs spent more than 24 hours perched on scaffolding to make a giant cake that weighed nearly 4,400 lb (2,000 kg) and stood a staggering 26 ft 2 in (8 m) tall. The eight-tiered cake, which was held in place by metal plates to prevent it from toppling over, required 1,100 lb (500 kg) of eggs, 572 lb (260 kg) of flour, 440 lb (200 kg) of cream, 220 lb (100 kg) of fruit and 176 lb (80 kg) of chocolate.

$900 BEER▶ A single bottle of Samuel Adams Utopias, a dark beer brewed by the Boston Beer Company of Massachusetts, was sold on eBay for a staggering $900 in 2013. Sold in a ceramic bottle, the beer has high alcohol content and is aged for up to 20 years in a variety of casks. Only a limited number of bottles are released each year.

BAT FLAKES▶ A German man was horrified when he poured out a bowl of cornflakes for breakfast—and found a mummified bat in the pack. Experts in Stuttgart believe the bat had flown into the packaging by mistake and had suffocated to death.

BONE IDOL

▶ U.K. butcher Tony Dunphy has turned his work into an art form by using meat in his paintings! He combines gloss paint with lamb and chicken bones to create 4-ft-high (1.2-m) artworks—such as this portrait of Amy Winehouse—which he says are inspired by pop art pioneer Andy Warhol.

MONSTER PIZZA▶ Big Mama's and Papa's Pizzeria of Los Angeles, California, offers the world's largest deliverable pizza—a monster pie measuring 54 x 54 in (1.35 x 1.35 m). It costs $200, feeds up to 70 people and is so big it has to be delivered in truck beds and maneuvered through doorways.

CUPCAKE MOSAIC▶ To celebrate Singapore's 47th birthday, 1,200 youth volunteers created a mosaic—in the shape of a pair of hands around the national flag—from 20,000 cupcakes. The mosaic measured 52 x 26 ft (15.8 x 7.9 m), and was made from 1,320 lb (600 kg) of cupcake mix, 770 lb (350 kg) of eggs and 660 lb (300 kg) of vegetable oil. It required 16 decks of ovens and more than 18 hours of baking.

BULLY BEER After announcing that it was making beer from bull testicles as an April Fool's Day joke, the Wynkoop Brewing Company of Denver, Colorado, received such a positive response to the idea that it decided to produce the beer for real. Taking the local name for fried bull's testicles— a delicacy in Colorado—Rocky Mountain Oyster Stout has a dark brown color with flavors of chocolate syrup and espresso.

WHISKY GALORE▶ Czech glassmakers blew by hand the world's biggest whisky bottle to meet an order from Glenturret, one of Scotland's oldest whisky distilleries, as part of its 107-year anniversary celebrations. Standing 5 ft 5 in (1.6 m) tall and weighing 110 lb (50 kg), the 482-pt (228-l) bottle took three hours to fill with Glenturret's whisky. It went on display in August 2012 at the Glenturret visitor center, which annually welcomes more than 200,000 whisky lovers.

MAKIN' BACON ▶ Farmer Huang Demin from Hunan Province, China, has built a 10-ft (3-m) wooden diving board for his pigs to jump off because he says it makes their meat taste better. Since his pigs have been diving headfirst into a pond each day, he has been able to charge three times the price of normal pork for their meat.

TORTA TREAT ▶ Over 50 cooks in Mexico City prepared a 173-ft-long (53-m), 1,540-lb (700-kg) torta sandwich made from 70 different ingredients, including thousands of pieces of bread, lettuce, onion and tomato and hundreds of pints of mayo, mustard and spicy sauces.

GOLD CUPCAKE ▶ Made from the finest chocolate and coated in edible 23-carat gold sheets, the Golden Phoenix cupcake went on sale in Dubai for a staggering $1,010, making it the world's most expensive cupcake.

POTATO PILE ▶ A hefty 92,500 lb (42,000 kg) of locally grown potatoes were arranged in nearly 10,000 bags at Sobeys store in Charlottetown, Prince Edward Island, Canada, on October 3, 2012, to form a gigantic potato display.

NAAN BREAD ▶ Using a 20-ft-wide (6-m) oven, volunteers in Xinjiang, China, took ten hours to bake a giant naan bread 9 ft (2.7 m) in diameter and stuffed with meat dumplings. It included 66 lb (30 kg) of mutton, 275 lb (125 kg) of flour and 35 lb (16 kg) of onion.

LICKABLE WALLPAPER

▶ *Wallpaper featuring 1,325 lickable chocolate and orange Jaffa cake-flavored stickers was pasted on to an elevator at a communications firm in London, England. Inspired by the movie* Willy Wonka & the Chocolate Factory, *the art installation, called* Spot of Jaffa, *was inspired by chef Heston Blumenthal and artist Damien Hirst. To prevent the spread of germs, each sticker could be licked only once before an attendant removed it and replaced it with a fresh one.*

HORSE SAUSAGE ▶ Chefs in Xinjiang, China, used meat from 38 horses to make a 700-ft-long (213-m) sausage weighing 2,769 lb (1,256 kg).

CRAB CAKE ▶ At the 2012 Maryland State Fair, cooks made a 300-lb (136-kg) crab cake from around 1,600 crabs. They used 200 lb (90 kg) of crabmeat, and eggs, breadcrumbs and seasoning.

OPPOSUM-SPIT COFFEE ▶ A coffee plantation in Pedra Azul, Brazil, is charging $450 for a kilo (2.2 lb) of exclusive coffee beans that have been chewed by a gray four-eyed opossum, or cuica. Plantation owner Rogério Lemke observed the marsupials eating the shell and sweet sticky substance that surrounds the coffee bean but spitting out most of the bean itself. Tests showed that the animals selected only the best fruit, so the beans they spat out were the cream of the crop.

DUCK HEADS

▶ *Tourists from all over the world flock to Donghuamen Night Market in Beijing, China, where dozens of stalls sell exotic street snacks including fried scorpions, sea horses, silkworm cocoons, centipedes, locusts, spiders, water beetles and snakes on a stick. As for these roast duck heads, put them on the bill.*

PUMPKIN ZOMBIES

▸ For Halloween 2012, a team of pumpkin sculptors led by Ray Villafane created a zombie pumpkin invasion at New York City's Botanical Garden. The Haunted Pumpkin Garden featured 500 spooky carvings of scarecrows, bats, bugs, spiders and snakes as well as zombies. The pumpkins were sprayed with water to keep the sculptures fresh, but they became even scarier when they eventually started to decompose.

CHOCOLATE RECORD

▶ FOUND, a band and art collective from Edinburgh, Scotland, released the world's first fully functional chocolate record. The limited-edition chocolate disk, made by baker Ben Milne using the same negative metal templates involved in producing vinyl versions, can be played on any record player—but only about ten times before it wears down. The sleeve and label for the band's single "Anti Climb Paint" are also edible, made from rice paper and icing sugar respectively.

CLEAN LIVING▶ Owing to a rare disorder called pica, which causes victims to eat objects that are not food, Kerry Trebilcock, a dental nurse from Cornwall, England, has eaten more than 4,000 washing-up sponges and 100 bars of soap. At one point she used to munch through five sponges a day, usually topped with BBQ sauce, ketchup, mustard or honey.

POTATO COOKIE▶ Chef Felice Tocchini of Worcester, England, has created a cookie that can be dipped in a cup of tea for two minutes without falling apart. Most cookies begin to crumble after ten seconds in a hot drink, but the new cookie's special ingredient, sweet potato, means it can stay whole for up to 12 times longer.

ONE-TON BURGER▶ The Black Bear Casino Resort near Carlton, Minnesota, cooked a bacon cheeseburger that measured 10 ft (3 m) in diameter and weighed a whopping 2,014 lb (914 kg). The burger included 60 lb (27 kg) of bacon, 50 lb (23 kg) of lettuce, 50 lb (23 kg) of sliced onions, 40 lb (18 kg) of pickles and 40 lb (18 kg) of cheese. It took four hours to cook the patty at 350°F (175°C) using an outdoor oven heated by propane torches, and more than seven hours to bake the bun. A crane was used to hoist and flip the giant burger as it cooked. Whereas a standard quarter-pound bacon double cheeseburger has 580 calories, this monster contained an unbelievable 4.1 million calories!

LUXURY DESSERT▶ Diamond merchant Carl Weininger treated guests at a party in London, England, to a £22,000 ($34,750) chocolate dessert laced with edible gold, champagne and caviar and topped with a two-carat diamond. Each mouthful cost around £800 ($1,250) and the whole dessert took just 15 minutes to eat.

CHERRY PIE▶ The giant cherry pie baked annually in George, Washington, for the 4th of July celebration weighs about half a ton, is prepared in an 64-sq-ft (6-sq-m) pan, and serves more than 1,500 people.

LOTTA LOLLY▶ To celebrate National Lollipop Day, See's Candies of Burlingame, California, created a 7,000-lb (3178-kg) chocolate lollipop—that's about twice the weight of an average car—that was nearly 6 ft (1.8 m) tall and 3 ft 6 in (1.06 m) wide. It came complete with an 11-ft-10-in (3.6-m) stick.

JESUS TOAST▶ Burnt Impressions, a firm from Danville, Vermont, created a toaster that produces an image of Jesus on every slice of toast. Creator Galen Diveley came up with the idea of the Jesus Toaster after reading reports of people seeing images of Jesus in various inanimate objects.

FROZEN BEER▶ When 52-year-old Clifton Vial was stranded in his truck for three days during a snowstorm in Nome, Alaska, he survived by eating and drinking nothing but frozen cans of beer.

CHICKEN GUTS

▶ Fried chicken innards—the heart, gizzard, liver and intestines—are a popular delicacy in the Philippines, where, instead of throwing out a dead chicken's internal organs, residents cook them.

HIGH TEA▶ A new restaurant has been named "3440" because it is located 11,286 ft (3,440 m) up a mountain in the Austrian Alps. The diner is perched on top of the Pitztal Glacier—the highest in the Tyrol—and is accessed via a ski lift up Wildspitze Mountain.

SYRUP HEIST▶ Millions of dollars' worth of maple syrup was stolen from a vast warehouse in St.-Louis-de-Blandford, Quebec, which holds the equivalent of nearly 50 percent of the annual maple syrup production of the entire U.S.A. Overall, Quebec produces a whopping 80 percent of the world's maple syrup.

COSTLY TIPPLE▶ On March 15, 2012, a bottle of 55-year-old Glenfiddich Janet Sheed Roberts Reserve whisky, one of only 11 bottles in the world, was bought at a New York City auction by Atlanta, Georgia, businessman Mahesh Patel for $94,000, making it the most expensive bottle of whisky ever sold.

CRACK COOK▶ Corey Peras, a cook from Ottawa, Ontario, cracked an incredible 3,031 eggs in an hour with one hand on June 22, 2012.

KING CABBAGE▶ At the 2012 Alaska State Fair, Robb Scott from Palmer, Alaska, exhibited a colossal cabbage weighing 138.2 lb (62.7 kg)— the heaviest in the world. An average cabbage weighs just 6 lb (2.7 kg).

BREATHALYZER JACKET▶ Matt Leggett from Wellington, New Zealand, has invented a special jacket that tells the wearer if they have drunk too much for it to be safe for them to drive. The wearer blows into a nozzle in the collar and a sensor in the pocket detects the amount of alcohol in the breath, displaying the results on a strip of lights stitched into the sleeve of the jacket. The more lights that glow, the more the person has had to drink.

ATE BRAIN ▶ Andy Millns of London, England, ate a replica of his own brain, made from chocolate. Experts at a technology company took an MRI scan of his head, fed a map of his brain into a computer and printed it out on a 3-D printer. A latex mold of the brain was then created and filled with liquid chocolate.

CHOCOLATE TEMPLE ▶ In May 2012, staff at Qzina Specialty Foods in Irvine, California, made the world's biggest chocolate sculpture—a replica model of an ancient Mayan temple weighing 18,239 lb (8,280 kg). It took 400 hours to build and the finished product stood 6 ft (1.8 m) tall with a 10 x 10 ft (3 x 3 m) base.

KILLER CURRIES ▶ A curry-eating competition in Edinburgh, Scotland, on October 1, 2011, featured curry so hot that contestants started vomiting, fainting and writhing on the floor in agony. One participant was so ill after sampling the "Kismot Killer" that she was rushed to a hospital twice in a matter of hours.

BREAKING THE MOLD

▶ *Estonian artist Heikki Leis takes close-up photographs of fruit and vegetables, which have been left to rot for months, to create images of weird sci-fi creatures and spectacular landscapes. Among his artworks are a moldy rutabaga (right) that resembles a hydrogen-bomb mushroom cloud and a rotten beet that looks like an alien monster (below).*

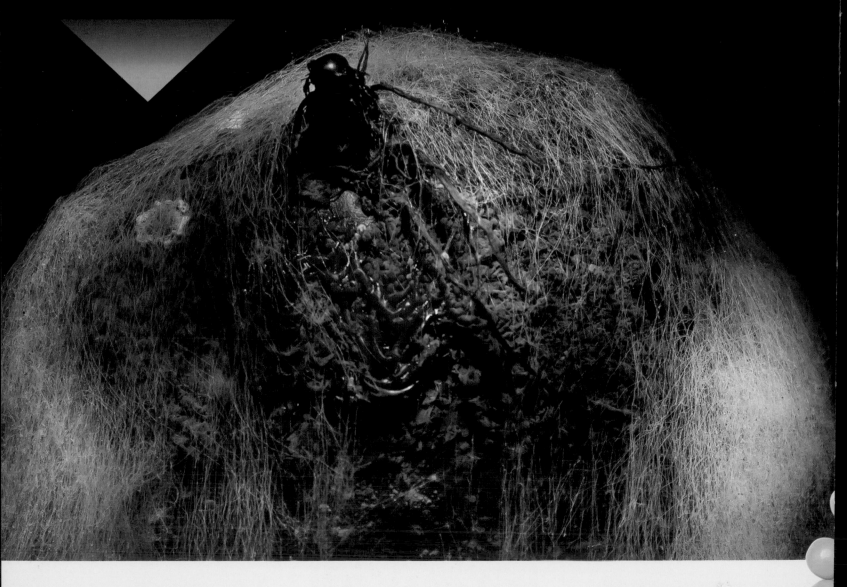

LONG LOG ▶ Eighty chefs at the Pudong Shangri-La Hotel in Shanghai, China, created a 3,503-ft-long (1,068-m), vanilla-flavored Yule log cake. Made using 904 eggs over a period of 24 hours, the giant cake was set out on 156 tables.

GRAVEYARD DINER ▶ The Lucky Hotel restaurant in Ahmedabad, India, was built in the 1960s over a graveyard—and today customers drink tea at tables next to 22 tombs set in the floor. Waiters jump over the green tombs to serve food, but these are not the restaurant's only unusual features—a large tree runs through the middle of the dining room and extends out through the roof.

PEDIGREE DOG ▶ On May 31, 2012, Mike Brown, the owner of Capitol Dawg in Sacramento, California, created the world's most expensive hot dog—a $145.49 luxury dog. It featured an 18-in (45 cm), 12 oz (340 g) all-beef frankfurter, expensive and rare moose cheese from Sweden, white truffle butter, whole grain mustard from France, and New Hampshire bacon marinated in maple syrup.

GREEN HONEY ▶ Bees at apiaries in Ribeauville, France, have been producing green and blue honey! The unusual coloring is thought to have been caused by the bees eating the sugary residue from containers of M&M's® candy that were being processed at a nearby biogas plant. Unfortunately, the pretty honey was not considered sellable.

BUG PIZZA

▶ Taiwanese water bugs, joro spiders, caterpillar moths and larvae were the interesting insect toppings served on a pizza at a bug-eating party in Tokyo, Japan. While insects are a good source of protein, eating them has traditionally been associated with people who couldn't afford to buy animal meat. However, bug eating is steadily growing in popularity as more and more people look to sustainable food sources in our over-populated world.

MAYO LOVER ▶ Philippa Garfield of London, England, loves mayo so much she eats it on sandwiches, on cookies, on fruit—and even puts it in her tea instead of using milk. Not content with that, she washes her hair with mayo and also uses it as face cream!

▶ FLAMINGO TONGUE AND ROAST PARROT WERE POPULAR DELICACIES AT ROMAN FEASTS. ◀

TITANIC FEAST ▶ A restaurant in Houston, Texas, commemorated the 100th anniversary of the *Titanic* sinking on April 14, 2012, by offering a recreation of the last meal served to the ship's first-class passengers for a price of $1,000 per person.

PRICEY PIZZA ▶ The Steveston Pizza Company in Vancouver, Canada, created a $450 pizza, made with lobster thermidor, Alaskan black cod and a side of Russian osetra caviar.

CHESTNUT CHAMP ▶ On March 17, 2012, at the TooJay's World Class Corned Beef Eating Championship in Palm Beach Gardens, Florida, Joey "Jaws" Chestnut from San Jose, California, won by devouring 20 corned-beef sandwiches—each weighing 8 oz (225 g)—in just ten minutes. Also in 2012, he consumed 390 shrimp wantons in eight minutes at the finale of the CP Biggest Eater Competition in Bangkok, Thailand.

MONSTER PIE ▶ In Moscow, Russia, chefs used hundreds of pounds of flour, berries and sugar plus 500 eggs to make a gigantic blueberry pie weighing 660 lb (300 kg) and measuring 230 ft (70 m) long.

PICNIC PARTY ▶ On July 15, 2012, in Kitchener, Ontario, some 5,000 people ate their lunches on more than 1,000 picnic tables, which stretched along the street for almost 1½ mi (2.3 km).

METEORITE WINE ▶ A vineyard in San Vicente, Chile, owned by British-born Ian Hutcheon, has launched 2010 Meteorito, a Cabernet Sauvignon wine infused with a 4.5-billion-year-old meteorite. The wine has been fermented for 12 months in a barrel containing the 3-in (7.5-cm) meteorite, which Hutcheon, a keen astronomer and winemaker, loaned from an American collector.

SAY CHEESE!

▶ Artist Jason Baalman created portraits of 2012 U.S. presidential candidates Barack Obama and Mitt Romney from more than 2,000 Cheetos. Jason from Colorado Springs, Colorado, spent over 100 hours carefully positioning and gluing the cheese-flavored snacks onto a black canvas to create an edible artwork measuring 3 x 4 ft (0.9 x 1.2 m). Jason, who has also used ketchup and barbecue sauce in his pictures, has previously made Cheetos portraits of talk-show host Conan O'Brien and singer Cee Lo Green.

LOOK-ALIKE NUGGET▶ Rebekah Speight of Dakota City, Nebraska, sold a three-year-old McDonald's Chicken McNugget that resembled the profile of George Washington for $8,100 on eBay.

SPAGHETTI STRUCTURE▶ Students in Iran used 100,000 ft (33,000 m) of spaghetti—that's over 20 mi (33 km)—to build a gridlike structure that measured 79 ft (24 m) long, 16 ft (5 m) tall and 18 ft (5.5 m) wide and weighed 226 lb (103 kg). It took them two months to make.

PARTY PIE▶ For a 2012 St. Patrick's Day party, chefs in Wildwood, New Jersey, created a 1,805-lb (819-kg) meat and potato pie, made up of 880 lb (400 kg) of minced beef, 775 lb (352 kg) of potatoes, 110 lb (50 kg) of carrots and 100 lb (45 kg) of onions.

ROYAL LANDLORD▶ In keeping with a 500-year-old tradition, the landlord of the Ship Inn on the half-mile-long Piel Island off the northwest coast of England is entitled to call himself the King of Piel.

OWL CURRY▶ For more than 30 years, the only meat that taxidermist Jonathan McGowan of Bournemouth, England, has eaten has been roadkill—including such dishes as owl curry, rat stir-fry, adder in butter, badger stew and squirrel pie. He first developed a taste for roadkill at age 14 after cooking a dead adder snake that he had discovered and deciding it tasted like bacon rind. He says squirrels ("like rabbit, but not as overpowering"), foxes ("lean and never any fat") and rats ("like pork but quite salty") are particularly delicious, but he is not as keen on mice ("very bitter"), hedgehogs ("all fatty meat") and moles ("horrible with a rancid taste").

PAPER SNACKS▶ Ann Curran of Dundee, Scotland, has developed a taste for eating her local newspaper. She says the Dundee *Evening Telegraph* is the "only newsprint with the proper flavor" and keeps shredded copies in her handbag for when she feels like a snack.

MARSHMALLOW ROAST▶ On March 24, 2012, 1,272 people gathered at Marion, Kansas, to roast marshmallows simultaneously around a giant bonfire that was 660 ft (201 m) long, 6 ft (1.8 m) wide and 3 ft (0.9 m) tall.

ROOF FLOCK▶ Wei Xingyu keeps a small flock of sheep on the roof of his four-story house in Changsha, China, so that his baby daughter has a regular supply of fresh milk. He has put down grass for his sheep to graze on, and if they get too hot on the roof, he walks them to his parents' house.

LIZARD FILLING

▶ Ian Lock from Derbyshire, England, was horrified to find this 6-in (15-cm) lizard crawling in a bag of supermarket wild arugula salad from Italy as he was about to make a sandwich.

EGGSTRAORDINARY!
▶ Ripley's were sent this picture by Josh Scott from Corbin, Kentucky, showing him holding an unbelievable 21 eggs in one hand!

KILLER COCKTAIL▶ Nick Nicora made a 10,500-gal (32,176-l) margarita cocktail at the 2012 California State Fair in Sacramento. The drink was poured into a 25-ft-tall (7.6-m), 20-horsepower blender.

BEER TRAIN▶ Instead of using waiters, the Vytopna Restaurant in Prague, Czech Republic, delivers drinks to its customers on a 1,300-ft-long (396-m) model railroad that runs through the restaurant building.

GASSY DISHES▶ As well as serving food as a solid or a liquid, the Juniper Kitchen and Wine Bar in Ottawa, Ontario, serves it as a calorie-free gas to be inhaled by the customer. Liquid-based foods such as soups are poured into a device called Le Whaf, a large glass cylinder with an ultrasound attached. The ultrasound agitates the mix, creating a vapor cloud that is filled with the flavor of the soup, but without any of the calories.

RECORD ROLL▶ A group of 285 chefs cooked a 1,525-ft-long (465-m) fried spring roll in Semarang, Indonesia—that's more than a quarter of a mile long! It needed an incredible 2,156 lb (980 kg) of bamboo shoots and 15,000 spring roll skins, as well as five frying pans, to create the whopper.

CAN OPENER▶ British merchant Peter Durand invented the tin can in 1810, but it was not until 1858 that Ezra Warner of Waterbury, Connecticut, invented the can opener! Before that, cans had to be hammered open.

POOP TEA▶ Businessman An Yanshi from Sichuan, China, purchased 11 tons of poop from a giant panda breeding center—and used it to make the world's most expensive tea, selling for over $200 a cup. He says his panda dung tea is special because the animals absorb only a fraction of the nutrients in their food—70 percent of the nutrients are passed in their feces.

DOUBLE EGG▶ Sean Wilson from Hampshire, England, was surprised when his hen Rosie laid a colossal egg that weighed 6.4 oz (181 g), and was even more amazed when he cracked the egg open and found another egg shell inside! The "rare egg inside an egg video" quickly became an online sensation with 500,000 views in a week.

ONE-TON PUMPKIN▶ Ron Wallace of Greene, Rhode Island, grew the world's first one-ton pumpkin, and his 2,009-lb (911-kg) giant, nicknamed "The Freak II" earned him more than $15,000 when he exhibited it at the 2012 Topsfield Fair in Massachusetts. His record-breaking pumpkin reached that weight in just one growing season, starting from a single tiny seed.

SPACE BURGER▶ Five students from Harvard University, Massachusetts, launched a burger nearly 100,000 ft (30,000 m) into space tied to a helium balloon. Using an attached camera, they filmed it soaring where no burger has ever gone before until the balloon burst and the burger fell back to Earth, landing in a tree outside Boston.

SUPER SAUSAGE▶ Ptacek's IGA grocery store of Prescott, Wisconsin, celebrated its centenary on October 6, 2012, by making a 52-ft-2-in-long (16-m) bratwurst. The super sausage, which slotted into a bun made from 40 lb (18 kg) of dough, was so big that it took a dozen people to turn it every few minutes while it was grilling.

EDIBLE QUEEN▶ Food artist Michelle Wibowo from Brighton, England, made a life-size sculpture weighing 55 lb (25 kg) of Queen Elizabeth II fashioned from sugar paste, accompanied by a royal corgi dog made from fruitcake.

BLOODFEAST

▶Fifty guests at the Livingston Restaurant in Atlanta, Georgia, paid $85 each to eat eight blood-inspired dishes. Masterminded by head chef Zeb Stevenson, the special Blood Dinner menu included currant bread mixed with bacon and pork blood and served with bone marrow butter, smoked eel in an eel blood broth, blood sausage and, for dessert, pomegranate and pork blood-enriched crème anglaise (pictured here) drizzled into liquid nitrogen.

SWEET SNAKE

▶ U.S. company Vat19 has created an edible gummi python that measures 8 ft (2.4 m) long and weighs 27 lb (12.2 kg). Selling for nearly $150, the monster snake boasts scary eyes, blended colors, ridged coils, thousands of individually carved scales and comes in blue raspberry flavour with either green apple or red cherry sections. The Party Python contains a whopping 36,000 calories—18 times an adult's recommended daily allowance.

STICKY FINGERS Scientists at England's University of Leicester say that criminals with a taste for fast food run a greater risk of being caught. The creators of a new forensic fingerprint say people who eat foods with a high salt content have "sticky fingers," which are more likely to leave a telltale mark at a crime scene.

BLIND FAITH▶ Vietnamese cook Christine Ha won the 2012 series of Fox's *MasterChef*—even though she is blind. Suffering from an autoimmune disorder that affects the optic nerves, she lost sight in one eye in 1999 and was completely blind by 2007, but uses her heightened sense of smell and taste to compensate for her lack of vision. She has spent years re-creating her mother's favorite recipes, purely by taste.

LOCAL GRUB

▶ Mopane worms are a traditional delicacy in southern Africa as, ounce for ounce, they contain more protein than roast chicken breast. The worms, which are really caterpillars, are usually fried with tomatoes, garlic and onions, but they don't taste much better than they look. People say they are very chewy, difficult to swallow and taste like a combination of earth, salt and dry wall!

LONGEST PARSNIP In 2012, Peter Glazebrook from Nottinghamshire, England, grew a record-breaking parsnip that was an incredible 18 ft 6 in (5.6 m) long—36 times the length of a normal parsnip. He has previously held the record for the longest beet at 21 ft (6.4 m), and the largest potato at 8 lb 4 oz (3.7 kg).

TOP DOG▶ At Little Rock, Arkansas, in May 2012, vendor "Hot Dog Mike" Juliano sold four hot dogs for charity, each costing a whopping $1,501. TheONEdog was made up of lobster tails, gold flakes, saffron and high-quality beef.

MOUSE BACON Wan Shen's butcher's shop in Guangdong Province, China, sells nothing but freshly caught, free-range mice, a dish considered so tasty by locals that pound for pound it is more expensive than chicken or pork. Among Wan Shen's specialties is cured mouse bacon, where the rodent is delicately carved into tiny slices.

CAKE PORTRAIT▶ To mark the Diamond Jubilee of Queen Elizabeth II in 2012, German-born baker Gerhard Jenne created a portrait of the Queen from 3,120 individually colored, iced cakes—one for every week of her reign. It contained around 1,000 eggs, 200 packets of butter, 150 bags of sugar and 79 lb (36 kg) of marzipan.

SUNDAE BEST On May 6, 2012, at Lake Forest, California, some 400 volunteers built the world's longest ice-cream sundae, measuring a whopping 222 ft 9¾ in (67.9 m).

SPACE LETTUCE▶ Mizuna lettuce was the first plant to grow in space successfully through two generations—aboard the *Mir* Space Station.

CHOCOLATE HEAVEN Germans are the world's most enthusiastic chocolate eaters, consuming an average of 25 lb (11.3 kg) of chocolate per person every year.

TEMPTING FATE▶ On February 11, 2012, a man suffered a heart attack while eating a 6,000-calorie Triple By-Pass Burger at the Heart Attack Grill in Las Vegas, Nevada.

DEER MENU South Korean international soccer player Park Ji-Sung was such a frail youngster that his parents boosted his strength by feeding him a dish of boiled frogs, antlers and deer blood. He says it smelled like intestines and tasted so vile that he would sometimes throw up after eating it, but the weird menu worked wonders and eventually earned him a place playing for Manchester United.

OVERSIZE OMELET▶ 150 chefs in Santarém, Portugal, teamed up to cook a giant omelet that weighed 14,225 lb (6,466 kg)—that's more than 7 tons. The omelet used 145,000 eggs—equal to the weekly yield from 9,000 chickens—880 lb (400 kg) of oil and 220 lb (100 kg) of butter. It took six hours to cook in a special pan that measured over 32 ft (10 m) in diameter.

MOO-TON CADET▶ In an attempt to produce the best beef in Europe, some farmers in southern France give their cows a daily feed of up to two bottles of fine wine, mixed in with barley and hay.

COFFEE BLAST▶ Over 1,000 baristas gathered in the main square at Zagreb, Croatia, to operate 22 coffee machines and, in just over three hours, fill a giant coffee cup with 4,252 pt (2,012 l) of cappuccino—the largest ever cappuccino coffee.

SLICE OF LUCK▶ When Liz Douglas of Stirling, Scotland, was involved in a serious car crash, her life was saved by a loaf of bread. The medium-sliced loaf fell from her shopping bag and cushioned her head when her car plowed into a telephone pole, allowing her to escape with only minor cuts and bruises.

KING KEBAB▶ In June 2012, cooks in Ankara, Turkey, created the world's biggest kebab—a 2,641-lb (1,198-kg) monster made from the meat of seven cows. The kebab stood over 8 ft (2.5 m) tall and needed a crane to haul it into place. The ten cooks had to work on scaffolding to prepare it.

DOG GONE▶ In 2012, Joey Chestnut won his sixth straight Nathan's 4th of July Hot Dog Eating Contest at Coney Island, New York. He devoured 68 dogs and buns in ten minutes, beating his closest rival by an impressive 16 dogs!

BURGER MUMMY

▶ *This 5-ft-2-in-tall (1.57-m) mummified skeleton was made by Texas artist Ben Campbell from $200 of ground-up burgers and French fries! After drying the food out, he ran it through a blender, mixed it with adhesive resin and then packed it into rubber molds before bonding together the cast pieces. He says: "As long as it is kept dry, it should last for thousands of years, like a real mummy."*

12

BEYOND BELIEF ▶

MUMMIFIED PETS

Dozens of pet owners have chosen to have their favorite pets mummified after death, preserving their corpses in animal-shaped caskets to keep them as fresh as the day they died. The bodies of beloved cats, dogs, rats, finches and even peacocks have been sent to the world's only pet mummification company to undergo the traditional burial routine of the Ancient Egyptians.

When a client's pet dies, the vet packs the body in ice and transports it to the Salt Lake City, Utah, headquarters of Summum, whose office building is, appropriately, pyramid-shaped. The pet's organs are removed and cleansed before being placed back inside the body. The corpse is then hydrated by submerging it in a water tank for at least 70 days. The Egyptians preferred to dehydrate bodies, but Summum finds that they are better preserved by doing the opposite. The dead pet is then smeared with lanolin and wax, wrapped in bandages and given a fiberglass finish.

▲ *A number of humans have also signed up to be mummified— one of the benefits of the process being the fact that it could soon be possible to remove a person's DNA for cloning after death by drilling into the casket. Ron Temu, a client counselor at Summum, says: "Being able to take out DNA at a later date has real appeal for people. They like the idea of being able to clone themselves."*

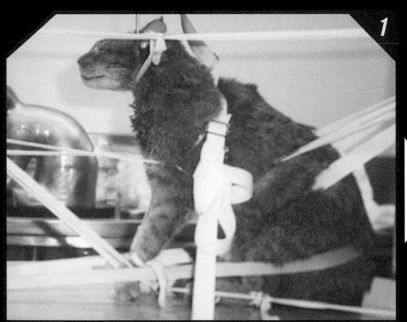

After its organs are removed, cleaned and put back inside the body, the hydrated dead cat is suspended in position ready to be wrapped in bandages.

The body is swathed in several layers of cotton gauze in keeping with Egyptian mummification tradition.

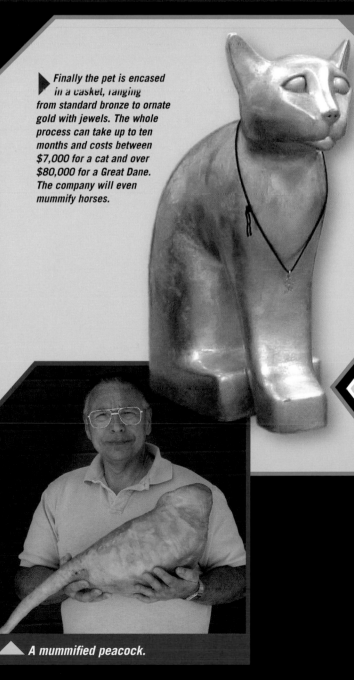

Finally the pet is encased in a casket, ranging from standard bronze to ornate gold with jewels. The whole process can take up to ten months and costs between $7,000 for a cat and over $80,000 for a Great Dane. The company will even mummify horses.

A mummified peacock.

A polyurethane membrane is then coated over the gauze to form a permanent seal before adding a layer of fiberglass and resin.

Pet caskets or mummiforms come in bronze, marble and, in this case, exotic gold leaf that is applied with a range of brushes.

SKATEBOARDING CAT ▶

MODERN CAVEMAN ▶ Daniel Suelo has lived without money since giving it up in 2000. He left his last $30 in a phone booth and walked off into the wilderness, where he has lived in caves, stayed in communes and camped outdoors. For several years he made his home in a vast cave on the edge of a cliff in the Arches National Park, Utah, where he carved a bed out of rock, foraged for food, drank from springs and bathed in a nearby stream. He pays no taxes and accepts no financial help from the government.

SHARED GRAVE ▶ Archeologists excavating a 5th-century cemetery in Cambridgeshire, England, discovered the grave of a woman who had been buried with a cow. Male Anglo-Saxon warriors were sometimes buried with horses, but finding a woman sharing a grave with a cow was described by experts as "genuinely bizarre."

DECOY RESCUE ▶ Answering distress calls from members of the public, a team of 25 firefighters performed a hazardous nighttime rescue to save a swan stuck in a frozen pond in Straubing, Germany, only to find that the bird was a plastic decoy put there by fishermen to scare away other birds.

HOT HEAD

▶ Alan Sailer, a photographer from California, has created twisted versions of popular Christmas gifts, dolls and toys by blowing them up and capturing the carnage with very high-speed photography. This head is filled with red gelatin, and the explosion is courtesy of a firecracker concealed within the toy and electronically controlled. Do not try it at home!

▶ *Romeo, a male purebred Bengal cat from Seattle, Washington, has learned to skateboard! He puts all four paws on the board to ride around the house. Romeo can also jump through hoops, leap over hurdles, give a high-five, walk backward on his hind legs and play a cat-sized piano.*

CAT MAYOR ▶ In 2012, Stubbs, a cat with no tail, celebrated his 15th year as mayor of Talkeetna, Alaska, making him one of the longest-serving mayors in the U.S.A. He has more than 1,000 friends on Facebook, which is 100 more than the town's entire population.

SLEEPING ZOMBIE ▶ On the morning of November 1, 2012, a passerby called police in Birmingham, Alabama, after seeing what looked like a woman shot dead in her car and slumped over the steering wheel—but when officers arrived, they actually found a drunken Halloween reveler who had passed out wearing a zombie costume splattered with fake blood.

SMUGGLED FRIEND ▶ A man convicted of smuggling in Sweden outsmarted his jailers by sneaking in a friend to serve most of his one-year sentence. The replacement convict arrived with a driving license in the smuggler's name but bearing his own photograph. The deception was discovered only when he was released on probation after serving two-thirds of his friend's sentence.

DEAD BEDMATE ▶ After his wife died in 2003, Le Van of Quang Nam, Vietnam, was so upset that he slept on top of her grave for 20 months. When the wind and rain finally became unbearable, he excavated a tunnel into the grave, dug her up, wrapped her bones in gypsum, dressed her, put a dummy mask on her face and has slept in bed next to her ever since.

RITUAL SURGERY ▶ In 2011, Simon Eroro, a journalist in Papua New Guinea, traveled into the jungle and, as part of a ritual cleansing ceremony, agreed to be circumcised with bamboo sticks just to get an interview with a group of rebels.

TIP OFF ▶ An armed robber fled with money from the cash register of a store in Albuquerque, New Mexico, but left behind a piece of his finger.

COFFIN CLASS ▶ Randy Schnobrich, a woodworker from Grand Marais, Minnesota, teaches a "Build Your Own Coffin" class for those who want to be buried in their own handiwork.

WHEELY CRAZY ▶ Drew Beaumier from Fountain Valley, California, has turned himself into a real-life Transformer. By designing a hinged robot costume with wheels on the arms and legs, he can fold into car form and "drive" along the street. Then when he stands up, the outfit opens into an Optimus Prime pose. He made the costume in eight weeks by dismantling a toy car, reassembling the parts with hinges and gluing it to a sports undergarment so that he can wear it like a suit.

LOUDEST PURR ▶ Smokey, a cat owned by Ruth Adams of Northampton, England, has the world's loudest purr, officially measured at 67.7 decibels, but she has also been known to purr at 92 decibels, equivalent to the noise of a lawn mower, a hair dryer, or a Boeing 737 coming in to land. Most cats purr at around 25 decibels, but Smokey's deafening sounds make it difficult for anyone to hear the TV or radio if she is in the room.

BUFORD
POP 1
ELEV 8000

TOWN SOLD

▶ In 2012, Buford, Wyoming, was sold for $900,000 to a buyer from Vietnam after the town's sole resident and owner since 1992, Don Sammons, decided to move to Colorado to be nearer his son. Buford was once home to 2,000 people, but in recent years Sammons was the only resident for miles around—although 1,000 visitors a day did descend on the place in summer, curious to see the town with a population of one.

FAT FIRE▶ The burning fat from an obese corpse caused a fire that almost destroyed a crematorium in Graz, Austria. The fire started when large amounts of burning fat from a 440-lb (200-kg) woman's body blocked an air filter, leading the system to overheat.

HANGING ON▶ Traffic policeman Second Lieutenant Nguyen Manh Phan clung for more than half a mile to the windshield wipers of a bus traveling at 30 mph (48 km/h) through the streets of Hanoi, Vietnam, after the bus driver sped off before he could be ticketed.

BACON COFFIN▶ A food company based in Seattle, Washington State, has created a $3,000 coffin painted in a bacon design.

BIG BANG▶ Instead of the planned 30 minutes' entertainment for a crowd of hundreds of people, a 2011 Community Fireworks Display in Oban, Scotland, lasted only one minute after a technical hitch resulted in all of the fireworks going off at once.

MOBY SICK

▶ While walking on a beach in Dorset, England, eight-year-old Charlie Naysmith discovered a 21-oz (600-g) piece of whale vomit that is worth up to $60,000. Sperm whale vomit that has solidified over time into a waxy substance is called ambergris or "floating gold" and is valuable because it is used in expensive perfumes to prolong the scent.

HAND GRENADE▶ Students were evacuated from a school in Newcastle, New South Wales, Australia, in 2012 when an 11-year-old brought a hand grenade to class for show-and-tell. The children were taken to a nearby park while police and bomb appraisal technicians examined the inactive World War II grenade.

TURTLE RECALL▶ In 1965, 13-year-old Jeff Cokeley carved his initials and the date into the shell of a box turtle he found on his family's farm in southwestern Pennsylvania—and 47 years later his father Holland was walking a dog on the farm when he stumbled across the same turtle with its markings still in place.

MOVING KISS▶ After their wedding in Yuxi, China, bride and groom Li Wen and Lu Ben exchanged the traditional kiss—while sitting in different moving cars. The newlyweds traveled in separate vehicles to the reception, and on the way the drivers inched close together so that the couple could wind down their windows and share a kiss on the highway.

CRAZY THIEF▶ While trying to break into an electrical substation, Michael Harper of Leicester, England, suffered serious burns and knocked out the power to 2,000 homes when he urinated on a transformer.

IN PIECES▶ A mentally ill woman in Sichuan, China, tore up 50,000 yuan (about $8,000) in bank notes. Her husband took the scraps to the bank where 12 members of staff worked for six hours trying to piece them back together, but in that time they managed to complete just one.

Odd Marriages

▶ Erika La Tour Eiffel from San Francisco, California, married the Eiffel Tower because she had fallen hopelessly in love with the French landmark.

▶ Chen Wei-yih from Taipei, Taiwan, married herself to demonstrate how happy she was in her own company.

▶ Korean Lee Jin-gyu married a pillow decorated with a picture of his favorite female animated character, Fate Testarossa.

▶ In Possendorf, Germany, Uwe Mitzscherlich married his cat Cecilia after being told that his pet did not have long to live.

▶ Two-year-old Sagula Munda was married to a dog at a ceremony in Jaipur, India, to protect the boy from further bad luck after he contracted a rotten tooth.

▶ Sharon Tendler married Cindy the dolphin at a special ceremony in Eilat, Israel. Cindy was rewarded with a kiss and a piece of herring.

DONKEY WEDDING

▶ At a festival in Zamora, Spain, to celebrate Saint Anthony, the patron saint of animals, groom Isidro Fernandez Rodriguez chose as his beautiful bride his donkey Matilde.

PARTY TIME▶ Over 140 political parties contested the 2010 U.K. general election, including the Fancy Dress Party, the Monster Raving Loony Party, the Nobody Party, the Pirate Party, and the Bus Pass Elvis Party.

ACCIDENTAL MAYOR▶ Fabio Borsatti became mayor of Cimolais, Italy, after running for office only to help his friend, Gino Bertolo, the one other candidate, who did not want to stand unopposed.

VAMPIRE SKELETONS▶ Bulgarian archeologists discovered two 800-year-old "vampire" skeletons during excavations near the Black Sea. The two men had been stabbed through the stomach and chest with iron rods as part of a ritual designed to prevent them turning into vampires after death.

GORILLA DUMPED▶ A 15-ft-high (4.5-m) metal gorilla statue was found mysteriously dumped on a path in Cambridgeshire, England, in March 2012. Enforcement officers described it as the most unusual case of illegal dumping they had known.

MASS WEDDING▶ In March 2012, 2,000 couples from 54 countries attended a mass wedding at a stadium in Gapyeong, South Korea.

TWICE LUCKY▶ Virginia Fike of Berryville, Virginia, won two Powerball lotteries on the same day—April 7, 2012—winning a total of $2 million.

BEST DOG▶ When Sue and Michael Hopkins got married in Swansea, Wales, their 11-year-old lurcher dog Snoopy was their best man. The dog kept the rings in a bag around his neck and barked to let guests know that the service had finished.

WRAP ARTISTS

▶*Wes Naman from Albuquerque, New Mexico, is a photographer who has created a series of distorted portraits by wrapping his friends' faces in sticky tape. He had the idea for his Scotch Tape Series after applying tape to himself to test a lighting rig set-up—and was so impressed by the weird, zombie-like results that he encouraged more than 30 of his friends to have their noses, lips, ears and eyebrows temporarily twisted.*

TALL PEOPLE

Only 17 people in history are known to have reached a height of 8 ft (2.4 m) or more—and measuring 8 ft 11.1 in (2.72 m) from head to toe, Robert Wadlow (1918–40) was the tallest man ever to have lived. Even today's contenders for the title of world's tallest person don't come anywhere near his great height. Known as the "Alton Giant," after his hometown of Alton, Illinois, Robert wore size 37 shoes that cost $100 a pair—equivalent to $1,500 today—and he traveled everywhere in a car that had the passenger seat removed so that he could sit in the back and stretch his long legs.

When he died from an infection, aged 22, Wadlow was buried in a specially made 10-ft-6-in-long (3.2-m) steel coffin that was interred in a vault of solid concrete because his family feared that his body might be stolen. Like most excessively tall people, he had suffered from an over-active pituitary gland, which resulted in an abnormally high level of human growth hormone.

▶ Weighing 356 lb (162 kg) and standing 7 ft 4 in (2.23 m) tall, New Jersey-born Aurelio "Al" Tomaini (1912–62) spent most of his adult life as a circus performer despite taking medication to curb his growth. While appearing in Cleveland in 1936, he met his future wife Jeanie—the "Half Girl"—who was born with no legs and stood just 2 ft 6 in (76 cm) tall. They toured for years as the "World's Strangest Married Couple," with Al usually propping Jeanie on his shoulder or carrying her at his side.

▲ Raised in Willow Bunch, Saskatchewan, Canada, and the oldest of 20 children, Edouard Beaupré (1881–1904) wanted to be a cowboy but was so tall that his legs were too long for him to ride even the tallest of horses comfortably. Instead, he toured with sideshows as the "Willow Bunch Giant," wrestling strongmen and performing incredible feats of strength. His most celebrated stunt was crouching beneath a 900-lb (408-kg) horse and lifting it up on his shoulders. When he died he was 8 ft 3 in (2.51 m) tall and his body was embalmed and displayed at a Montreal circus until the city's university acquired it for research into abnormal growth. In 1990, 86 years after his death, Beaupré was finally laid to rest and cremated.

▲ Although he was a normal-sized baby, Robert Wadlow grew so fast that even at elementary school they had to make a special desk for him. He was 6 ft (1.8 m) tall by age eight and when he joined the Boy Scouts at 13 he stood 7 ft 4 in (2.2 m) tall. It required 14 yd (13 m) of 3-ft-wide (1-m) material to make his uniform. When he died aged only 22, he was still growing, so he would almost certainly have become the only person ever to stand over 9 ft (2.74 m) tall.

John Rogan (1868–1905) from Sumner County, Tennessee, was the second tallest person in history, growing to a height of 8 ft 8 in (2.64 m). He underwent a rapid growth spurt at age 13, which eventually left him unable to stand or walk. So he got around by converting his bed into a cart, which was pulled by goats. Rogan, whose hands were 11 in (28 cm) long, earned a living by selling portraits and postcards of himself at a train station.

Born in Letcher County, Kentucky, Martin Van Buren Bates (1837–1919) became known as the "Kentucky Giant" after a sudden growth spurt sent his height rocketing to 7 ft 9 in (2.36 m). He was a captain in the Confederate Army during the Civil War, his size prompting Union soldiers to tell tales of a "Confederate giant who's as big as five men and fights like 50." After the war, he joined a circus where he met 7-ft-5-in-tall (2.27-m) Anna Haining Swan, and in 1871 the couple married in London, England, drawing a crowd of thousands to witness "the wedding of the giants."

Welshman George Auger (1881–1922) started out as a policeman but, because of his 7-ft-5-in (2.26-m) size, he created a disturbance wherever he went. It was said that there was enough cloth in one of his suits to fit out an entire family. At 5 ft 4 in (1.6 m), his wife Bertha often used a ladder to kiss him and was afraid to sit on his lap for fear of falling off. When the couple went to see the Barnum & Bailey Circus, Auger found that he stood a full head taller than the show's giant and was hired and given the name the "Cardiff Giant," going on to tour the U.S.A. as a circus performer. In 1922, Auger was asked by comedy star Harold Lloyd to appear in the silent movie Why Worry?, but unfortunately he died shortly after filming began.

Standing 7ft 6½ in (2.3 m) tall, singer and actor William Olding was hailed as the tallest man in England in the 1930s. When he appeared as an angel in a 1936 play, more than 19½ yd (18 m) of cloth were required to make his costume and the dressmaker had to climb a stepladder to reach his shoulders.

INVISIBLE MAN▶ In February 2012, paramedics and a deputy sheriff responded to a call from a 28-year-old man from Winder, Georgia, who had phoned 911 to report that he was invisible.

NAKED AMBITION▶ Eager to escape the rat race, Masafumi Nagasaki, 79, has been living naked as the sole inhabitant of the Japanese desert island of Sotobanari for more than 20 years. The only time he puts on clothes is when he makes his weekly trip to a nearby island to collect water and rice cakes.

HIDDEN SNAKES▶ A man was arrested on suspicion of stealing five exotic snakes from a pet store in Mesa, Arizona, by hiding them down his shorts for more than an hour.

LIZARD KING▶ Businessman Tyler Gold of York, Nebraska, legally changed his name to Tyrannosaurus Rex in 2012 because he thought it was cooler than his real name. His full legal name is Tyrannosaurus Rex Joseph Gold.

DISNEY WEDDING▶ Jason Webb-Flint and his wife Julie celebrated 20 years of marriage by renewing their wedding vows dressed as Mickey and Minnie Mouse. All the guests at the wedding in Kent, England, turned up as Disney characters, with the couple's teenage sons attending as Donald Duck and Goofy and no fewer than four people dressing up as Pocahontas. Disney songs including "Colonel Hathi's March" from *The Jungle Book* were played during the service.

Nice parking!

WHAT'S IN THE TRUNK?
▶ Passersby in Warwickshire, England, were startled to see a car 15 ft (4.6 m) up in the branches of a tree! The fiberglass shell of the Reliant Robin three-wheeler was hauled there with ropes by prankster Gregan Thompson and three friends.

CHICKEN STOLEN▶ A man was arrested after an 8-ft-tall (2.4-m) fiberglass chicken was stolen from a chicken farm in Ontario, Canada. The thief made off with the bird after severing it at the legs.

SECOND ARK▶ Dutch millionaire Johan Huibers built a replica of Noah's Ark—a full-size vessel measuring 450 ft (137 m) long by 70 ft (21 m) wide. Complete with life-size plastic animals, it was inspired by a dream he had in 1992 in which the Netherlands was flooded by the North Sea. The ark took Johan four years to build.

SARDINE SPILL▶ The highway near Kolobrzeg, Poland, was closed for hours after a truck driver forgot to shut his rear door properly and spilled 26 tons of sardines onto the road.

RODENT'S REVENGE▶ Dale Whitmell of Ontario, Canada, was lucky to escape with his life when he accidentally shot himself in the forehead while trying to kill a mouse with the butt of his rifle. He had not realized the gun was loaded.

POOPER HERO▶ In 2011, a mysterious superhero called SuperVaclav donned a helmet, mask and tights to patrol the parks of Prague, Czech Republic, and wage war on dog owners who failed to clear up their pets' poops.

LOST BET▶ A 21-year-old man was stuck for nine hours overnight in a park at Vallejo, California, after betting his friends $100 that he could fit into a children's playground swing. With the help of liquid laundry detergent, he managed to slide his legs into the swing, but then he became stuck and his friends vanished. Fire crews cut him free the next morning.

BEST FRIENDS
▶ Anzac the baby kangaroo and Peggy the baby wombat became best friends after the orphaned pair shared a pouch at an animal rescue center in Victoria, Australia. The youngsters constantly huddled together, taking comfort from each other's movement and heartbeat.

PENGUIN CANDIDATE▶ Campaigning while dressed as a penguin, Professor Pongoo (aka Mike Ferrigan) polled 444 votes in the Pentland Hills ward for the City of Edinburgh Council, Scotland, in 2012, thereby receiving more votes than both the Liberal Democrats and the Green Party. If elected, he had promised to attend council meetings in the penguin costume.

TREE TRIBUTE▶ As a tribute to his late wife Janet, who died in 1995, farmer Winston Howes of Gloucestershire, England, planted 6,000 oak trees in a 6-acre (2.4-hectare) field leaving a perfect heart shape in the middle—with the point facing in the direction of her childhood home.

TASTY TAPE▶ A 23-year-old woman from Marietta, Georgia, eats 6,000 ft (1,830 m)— that's more than a mile—of Scotch tape every month. She has been addicted to eating tape for over nine years and goes through three rolls a day, chewing each piece for about 30 seconds before swallowing.

ADDED INTEREST▶ A driver in Sicily was handed a whopping $44,500 fine for illegal parking after an Italian police officer mistakenly added on 1,800 years of interest because he calculated the fine back to the year AD 208 instead of 2008.

DOZY TOURIST▶ Italian security guards checking the baggage at Rome's Fiumicino Airport were alarmed when they spotted on an X-ray a Norwegian tourist curled up fast asleep among the suitcases on the moving belt. The man traveled for around 160 ft (50 m) on the belt before police caught up with him.

MEMORY MAN▶ Community police officer Andy Pope has such an incredible memory for faces that he successfully identified more than 130 wanted people in 12 months on the streets of Birmingham, England, having memorized their images just from CCTV stills. He even recognized a serial robber in the street a whole year after his image had appeared on TV.

BEARDED LADY▶
A woman robbed a bank in Cottondale, Alabama, dressed as a man, completing her disguise with a beard drawn on with a black marker.

SPACE CHICKEN

▶ *Wearing a knitted spacesuit and helmet, and with a modified lunchbox as a spacecraft, Camilla the rubber chicken floated to the edge of space in March 2012 to test levels of radiation during an intense solar storm. She was launched into space attached to a helium balloon by Bishop Union High School students in California and sent to an altitude of 120,000 ft (36,575 m). Carrying four cameras, a cryogenic thermometer and two GPS trackers, the chicken spent 90 minutes in the stratosphere before the balloon popped and she parachuted safely back to Earth.*

DRUNKEN BEASTS

■ **A black bear passed out on the lawn of a resort in Baker Lake, Washington, in 2004 after drinking 36 cans of beer.**

■ **A gang of drunken monkeys rampaged through an Indian village in 2005 after stealing potent liquor that had been carefully stored in pots for a religious festival.**

■ **A horse in Romania tested positive for alcohol in 2008 after the cart it was pulling hit an elderly man who was sitting on a bench. Ion Dragan had just bought the horse, which may have been given liquor by its previous owners to make it look strong and healthy before being sold.**

■ **Drunk on a fermented-rice-based liquor being prepared for a local festival, a herd of 70 elephants went on a four-day rampage in eastern India in 2010, killing three people and destroying 60 homes.**

■ **In 2011, a number of parrots in Palmerston, Australia, began behaving raucously and falling over after getting drunk as a result of eating alcoholic plants.**

■ **A herd of cows gate-crashed an outdoor party in Boxford, Massachusetts, in 2012 and began drinking the beer that the fleeing partygoers had left behind.**

RADDNINGSTJÄNSTEN STC

DRUNKEN MOOSE

▶ *Per Johansson of Särö, Sweden, arrived home from work to find a drunken moose stuck in his neighbor's tree. In autumn, moose eat fallen, fermented apples, which make them intoxicated. This animal tried to climb into the tree to reach an apple but it became stuck with one hoof on the ground and the other three up the tree. Eventually freed by firefighters, the moose stumbled away from the tree, collapsed on the ground and went to sleep. Having sobered up overnight, it got up and walked slowly off the next morning.*

CHAIR RAGE ▶ A male passenger in Torbay, Devon, England, was caught on camera causing £200 ($300) of damage to a bus seat by chewing it.

NUMBERED HEADS ▶ Tan Chaoyun of Shenzhen, China, the mother of six-year-old identical quadruplet boys, shaved the numbers 1, 2, 3 and 4 into her sons' heads so that people could tell them apart at school.

BIRTHDAY BLUES ▶ As a birthday treat, Xiao Li bought girlfriend Wang Xue a $750 necklace and hid it in a cake—but then could only watch in horror as she wolfed the cake down whole and swallowed the necklace. She subsequently underwent endoscopic surgery in Qingdao, China, where a probe was passed down her throat and into her stomach to retrieve the necklace.

BODY BLOW ▶ Owing to severe overcrowding, the dead must be removed after six years from Hong Kong's public cemeteries.

DEAD LOAD ▶ When a pickup truck overturned on the highway in Luozhou, China, 16 bodies tumbled out onto the tarmac. Police thought they were investigating a serial killer until it emerged that the driver was a professor from the city's medical school who had bought the corpses of unclaimed murder victims for his students to use in class.

FISH ALERT ▶ Emergency services rushed to a suburb of Stockholm, Sweden, to investigate a reported gas leak, but when they arrived they found the smell was nothing more dangerous than fermented herring, a traditional Swedish delicacy.

POLICEMAN STOLEN ▶ A life-size cardboard police officer that was being used to reduce crime was stolen from a supermarket in Barnsley, England. The 6-ft-tall (1.8-m) figure, named P.C. Bobb, had been placed in the store to deter shoplifters.

GATOR PARTIES ▶ Reptile expert Bob Barrett from Tampa Bay, Florida, provides live alligators for children's pool parties. For $175, he takes an alligator, with its mouth taped shut, to people's backyard pools so that children can swim with it.

KILLER MOOSE ▶ In 2009, Ingemar Westlund of Loftahammar, Sweden, was arrested as a murder suspect in the death of his wife—but police released him when it was discovered that she had been killed by a drunken moose.

SYNCHRONIZED FLUSHING ▶ To help clear toilet waste that had accumulated in the city's sewers during days of water outages in September 2012, all residents of Bulawayo, Zimbabwe, were urged to flush their toilets simultaneously at 7.30 p.m. twice a week on Mondays and Thursdays.

KING TRUCKER ▶ Some historians believe the rightful King of England died in 2012—at a modest house in Jerilderie in New South Wales, Australia. Researchers claimed that Australian forklift truck driver Michael Hastings's ancestors were cheated out of the English crown in the 15th century.

DOUBLE PUNISHMENT ▶ When trying to feed a fish to a 9-ft-long (2.7-m) alligator, Florida airboat captain Wallace Weatherholt had his hand bitten off and was subsequently charged with unlawfully feeding the reptile. His hand was found, but could not be reattached.

BIRD'S EYE VIEW ▶ Italian tourist Nathalie Rollandin got a bird's eye view of San Francisco Bay—thanks to a greedy seagull. She had been photographing the Golden Gate Bridge when the seagull mistook her camera for food and snatched it while it was still filming. The bird flew off, but soon dropped the camera nearby, leaving behind 30 seconds of unique views of the bay at sunset.

DOUBLE LIFE ▶ In the U.S.A., Isaac Osei owns a New York City taxi company—but in Ghana, he is royalty. He is the chief of five towns, wears a crown, sits on a throne and lives in a palace.

WEBBED WONDERS

▶ On January 10, 2013, dozens of patients at All Children's Hospital in St. Petersburg, Florida, were amazed to look out and see three Spider-Men cleaning their windows and waving to them. Workers from Clearwater's High Rise Window Cleaners dressed in Spider-Man costumes so that the children could meet a superhero in person.

OLDEST NEWLYWEDS ▶ After dating for 18 years, of which 15 had been spent living together, 95-year-old Lillian Hartley and 98-year-old Allan Marks finally married in 2012 near their home in Palm Springs, California, to become the world's oldest bride and groom with a combined age of 193 years.

WIPED OUT ▶ Since brown tree snakes mysteriously made their way to the Pacific island of Guam in the 1940s, their numbers have grown to two million and they have driven nearly all the island's native birds to the brink of extinction.

PRISON BREAK-IN ▶ Police in Sacramento, California, arrested parolee Marvin Lane Ussery for attempting to break into Folsom Prison—from where he had been released two years earlier.

LICKED BOTTOM

▶ *Zhang Bangsheng, a devoted keeper at Wuhan Zoo, China, saved the life of a rare three-month-old Francois' langur monkey by licking its bottom for an hour to encourage it to defecate. He had noticed that the monkey had eaten a peanut and was in pain through being unable to pass it. As the monkey was too young to be given laxatives, Zhang cleaned its bottom with warm water and started licking. He was soon rewarded when the constipated monkey successfully passed the peanut.*

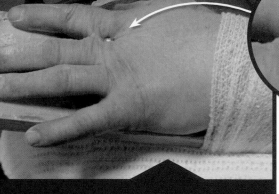

NAILED HAND▶ Alan Williams was trapped in his house in Shropshire, England, for nearly four hours after accidentally nailing himself to the floor. He was doing home improvements when he slipped at the top of the stairs and fired a high-powered 5-in (12.5-cm) bolt through his left hand. Pinned to the floor, he was unable to move or get help until his partner came home. He was then taken to hospital still attached to the floorboard, but luckily the nail missed vital tendons and veins, allowing him to regain full use of his hand.

LATE GUESTS▶ The Lastel Hotel in Tokyo, Japan, caters only to dead clients. Families check in their deceased relatives while waiting for an appointment at a crematorium.

SLOW DEATH▶ Lakeesha LaShawn Johnson of Seattle, Washington State, died on November 4, 2011. Her death was ruled a homicide owing to a gunshot wound she had received 13 years before.

ASH AMMO▶ Instead of having their ashes scattered in the traditional way when they die, hunters can have them turned into ammunition. Alabama company Holy Smoke puts cremated ash into live shells or cartridges—1 lb (2.2 kg) of ash is enough for 250 shells—which can then be loaded into shotguns and fired into the sky at birds or clay targets.

GOLD COINS▶ In February 2012, workers on a building renovation in Les Riceys, France, found a hidden stash of U.S. minted gold coins dating back to the 1850s and worth nearly $1 million.

SHORT CUT▶ Runner Rob Sloan from Sunderland, England, was stripped of his third-place bronze medal in the 2011 Kielder Marathon after he was found to have traveled part of the last 6 mi (9.6 km) of the race by bus.

STILL ALIVE▶ An 87-year-old Swedish woman discovered she had been declared dead by the Swedish Tax Agency after a doctor accidentally wrote her birth details into a death certificate. Although she called the authorities to say she was still very much alive, she was refused her prescription at the local pharmacy as their records stated that she was in fact a "non-existing person."

DENTIST DASH▶ Kurt Wagner from Mödling, Austria, drove 40 mi (64 km) the wrong way down the country's busiest highway, causing at least one accident and a major police operation—because he had a toothache and desperately needed to see a dentist. When arrested, he said he could remember nothing about the drive because he had taken a cocktail of strong medication and alcohol to numb the pain.

VANISHING ACTS

▶*For his book* Vanishing Act, *American photographer Art Wolfe captured a series of amazing shots of wildlife creatures perfectly camouflaged in their natural habitat. Can you spot a wolf peering out from behind a tree in a Montana forest (far right)? Or the giraffe in South Africa that blends in vertically with the shape and color of its surrounding vegetation (right)? And how about the great gray owl in the picture below, taken in Oregon?*

COFFIN THERAPY ▶ Coffin-maker Stepan Piryanyk, from Truskavets, Ukraine, helps people prepare themselves for the afterlife by allowing them to lie in a casket for 15 minutes in what he calls "coffin therapy." Clients relax to a soothing soundtrack of birdsong and falling water. Putting the lid on is optional.

GARDEN TRENCH ▶ To re-create the conditions faced by soldiers during World War I, historian Andrew Robertshaw excavated a 65-ft-long (20-m) trench in the back garden of his home in Surrey, England. It took volunteers about a month to remove the 220 tons of earth needed to make way for an authentic kitchen, infantry bedroom and officer's dugout.

BACK TO HER ROOTS ▶ Since 2008, Val Theroux has made an annual 9,000-mi (14,500-km) round trip from Canada to England—just to see a tree. The retired nurse from Kamloops, British Columbia, fell in love with the oak tree in Hampshire's New Forest while visiting her daughter and became so infatuated with it that she even tracked it down on Google Earth so she could see it from Canada. On her visits, she gets up early in the morning to be alone with the tree, then hugs it and admires it for a few hours. She says: "Some trees will not give you the time of day, while others are very welcoming. I get a lot of healing from this tree and go away feeling like I've seen an old friend."

EXPLODING AQUARIUM ▶ Shoppers fled in terror after a shark-filled aquarium suddenly burst open in a busy Dongfang, China, shopping mall, flooding the floor and showering people with flying glass and fish. Fifteen people were injured and three lemon sharks and dozens of smaller fish and turtles perished when the 10-in-thick (25-cm) protective glass of the huge 37-ton tank shattered without warning.

CLEAN EATING ▶ The larva of the emerald cockroach wasp disinfects its food before eating. The parasitic larva, which lives inside a cockroach, creates a clear liquid disinfectant solution in its mouth and then spits it out, covering the insides of its host. The disinfectant removes a common cockroach bacterium that is especially deadly to the wasp.

HUMAN TAIL ▶ Japanese inventor Shota Ishiwatari has invented a tail for humans, which wags when the wearer is excited. The "Tailly" is attached to a belt that monitors the wearer's pulse. The faster the pulse, the faster the wagging.

LOBSTER BOY

▶ Grady Stiles from Pittsburgh, Pennsylvania, was born in 1937 with two clawlike fingers on each hand and deformed legs. He was the sixth member of his family to be born with the congenital condition ectrodactyly, where the fingers and toes fuse together. In the 1940s he began appearing in circus sideshows with his family, and became known as the "Lobster Boy," a role he performed for almost 50 years.

HOPPING MAD ▶ A burglar who broke into a house in Plymouth, England, was caught out after coming face-to-face with the family's giant pet rabbit. Weighing 10 lb (4.5 kg), and measuring 2 ft (60 cm) long, Toby stomped so loudly on the floor of his cage that the intruder panicked and fled.

LENNON CRIMEWAVE ▶ Police in Belo Horizonte, Brazil, arrested three John Lennons in January 2013, while a fourth ended up in the city morgue, after allegedly being murdered. The Beatles were hugely popular in Brazil and hundreds of parents named their sons after John Lennon.

BRIDE AND GROOM▶ Retired schoolteacher Liu Fu from Zhengzhou, China, finally posed for her wedding pictures 30 years after her husband died. She played both the bride and groom in the glamorous photos, staged with the help of wardrobe experts, hairdressers and makeup artists. When she and husband Feng had married, they were short of money, but she had always wanted a proper wedding album.

NEIGHBORHOOD NINJA▶ Ken Andre, a volunteer Neighborhood Watch member, patrols the streets of Yeovil in Somerset, England, dressed as a ninja. The martial arts expert and father-of-two, also known as "Shadow," dons black Japanese robes to combat crime and has foiled dozens of street attacks.

CLOWN DOCTORS▶ Proving that laughter is the best medicine, Professor Thomas Petschner and Rita Noetzel founded Clown Doctors of New Zealand to promote the medical use of clowns in hospitals across the country. The Clown Doctors also donned their red noses and costumes to perform when a massive earthquake struck Christchurch. They spent weeks bringing light relief to the rescue teams.

SNOT NICE!▶ Yuk! This silicone, novelty nose-shaped dispenser squirts green shower gel through the nostrils to re-create the essence of fresh mucus from a really heavy cold.

ZOMBIE STORE▶ The Zombie Apocalypse store in Las Vegas, Nevada, sells a range of items for dealing with the undead, including 3-D bleeding ex-girlfriend zombie targets and Tasers disguised as cell phones.

DEAD CANDIDATES▶ At the 2012 U.S. elections, voters elected two dead politicians to represent them. Earl K. Wood, a Democrat standing in Orlando, Florida, and Alabama Republican Charles Beasley both recorded convincing victories despite having died weeks before polling took place.

DRESSED CRAB

▶ *Crabs with shells decorated with paintings of characters from popular TV shows are displayed on a market stall in Balikpapan, Indonesia. They are collected from the ocean and painted by a local man, Yanto, and then offered for sale at around $1 each.*

UNINVITED CLEANER▶ A woman broke into a house in Westlake, Ohio, took out the garbage, vacuumed the carpet, washed some dishes and tidied up the living room, then left the home owners a bill for $75 written on a napkin.

EVA'S TRAVELS▶ In 1955, three years after her death, the embalmed corpse of Argentina's First Lady Eva Peron was snatched—and it then went on a global trek for two decades. In turn it was kept in a van, behind a cinema screen in Buenos Aires and then inside the city's waterworks. After being secretly transported to Italy and buried under a false name, it was disinterred and taken to Spain before finally returning to Buenos Aires, where it now lies 16.4 ft (5 m) underground in La Recoleta Cemetery in a heavily fortified crypt.

▶▶ ABOUT 1.8 MILLION SHOPPING CARTS ARE STOLEN OR LOST EVERY YEAR IN THE U.S.A. ◀◀

CHEESE GAS▶ A road tunnel in northern Norway was closed for three weeks after a truck's cargo of 27 tons of carameliz ed brown goat cheese caught fire. Trapped in the tunnel, the cheese continued to burn for days, releasing potentially lethal gases.

TUTAN-ALAN▶ Following his death in 2011, Alan Billis from Devon, England, was mummified in the style of the Ancient Egyptians. After he had responded to a newspaper advert looking for someone to become a mummy, scientists at the University of York devised techniques to embalm his body using Ancient Egyptian methods. He could now remain preserved in his mummified state for 3,000 years!

MAZE MISERY▶ A family became so scared and disoriented while wandering around a cornfield maze in Danvers, Massachusetts, that they called emergency services for a rescue. They entered the spooky 7-acre (2.8-ha) maze, which was cut in the shape of a headless horseman, by daylight but panicked when night fell.

SUPER NAMES▶ Two men from Nottingham, England, officially changed their names to consist of 15 superhero or super-villain names each. Daniel Knox-Hewson became Emperor Spiderman Gandalf Wolverine Skywalker Optimus Prime Goku Sonic Xavier Ryu Cloud Superman Heman Batman Thrash, while Kelvin Borbridge opted for Baron Venom Balrog Sabretooth Vader Megatron Vegeta Robotnik Magneto Bison Sephiroth Lex Luthor Skeletor Joker Grind.

Ripley's Believe It or Not!®
www.ripleybooks.com

HANGING AROUND

▶ Suspension artist Deana Brown spent eight hours hanging like a piece of meat from the ceiling of a room in Baltimore, Maryland, by huge metal hooks inserted into the skin of her shoulders.

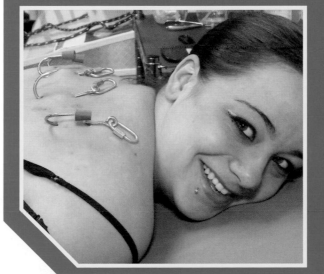

" When I'm suspended from hooks it feels like an enlightenment— when I do it I feel as if I'm free. It's also a great back stretcher and it's amazing to feel free even though you're hooked up like a piece of meat. "

HEADBANGER

▶ Swooping to catch prey, this unlucky owl collided head-on with a pickup truck and found itself wedged in the vehicle's grill. The trucker drove 8 mi (13 km), with the owl's head still trapped in the grill, before he was able to call the Vermont Fish and Wildlife Department to rescue the bird which, incredibly, was later released unharmed.

Ouch!

SINGING MICE▶ A breed of mouse that lives in the mountains of Costa Rica uses song to communicate. The mice "sing" to each other their mating calls, the sounds reaching over long distances in the form of up to 20 high-pitched chirps per second.

WAITING GAME▶ A man suspected of swallowing a diamond that he had stolen from a jewelry store in Windsor, Ontario, Canada, was held in custody until it finally passed through his system—nine days later. Richard Matthews was fed fiber-rich foods to speed up the process after an X-ray also revealed the presence of a pair of artificial diamonds in his intestines.

CORPSE'S COMPANION ▶
Two years after her husband died, grieving widow Adriana Villareal of Buenos Aires, Argentina, had moved into his tomb and set up a bed, a chair, a radio, a computer with Internet access and even a small stove next to his coffin. She visits the cemetery three times a year, spending three or four nights at a time sleeping next to her husband's embalmed corpse.

FELINE FELON▶ A cat was caught trying to smuggle a cell phone into a Brazilian prison. Officers who spotted the cat going through the main entrance of the Judge Luiz de Oliveira Souza prison found the phone, charger, batteries, drill bits and memory cards strapped to its body. The cat is believed to have been secretly raised by inmates and then given to visitors.

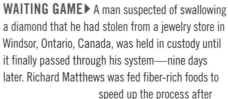

HUMAN VISE
▶ Ripley's were sent this submission by professional strongman Pat Povilaitis ("The Human Vise") from Oak Ridge, New Jersey, who can stick his hand into an authentic wolf or mountain-lion trap, then lift a 275-lb (125-kg) Ford 460 engine block with the hand in the trap!

EGGLESS CHICK▶ A hen in Welimada, Sri Lanka, gave birth to a chick without laying an egg. Instead of passing out of the hen's body and being incubated outside, the fertilized egg was incubated within the hen's reproductive system until it hatched inside her body. The chick survived but the hen died of internal wounds.

AGORAPHOBIC OWL▶ Gandalf, a Great Gray Owl at Knowsley Safari Park near Liverpool, England, was afraid of flying outside in the open, so his owners built a special aviary for him inside a brick shed.

GIRAFFE JOCKEY▶ Having hand-raised Mara, a three-month-old, 6½-ft-tall (2-m), giraffe, at the Lion Park conservation area near Johannesburg, South Africa, Shandor Larenty trained her to carry him on her back. Larenty's English great uncle, Terry, worked for the famous Chipperfield's Circus in the 1950s and was the only person at the time known to be able to ride a giraffe.

MIRACLE ESCAPE▶ Carlos Montalvo, a federal agent with the Tampa, Florida, Division of the ATF, lived to enjoy his retirement thanks to a "one-in-20-million shot" in 1987 when a drug suspect fired at him from close range, but instead of entering Montalvo's body, the bullet entered the barrel of his gun. Montalvo had moved in to make an arrest when the suspect fired from just 4 ft (1.2 m) away, but luckily both men were carrying the same kind of gun and the bullet entered the barrel of Montalvo's 9-mm Sig Sauer, where it smashed the bullet inside but spared the agent.

ROCK TV▶ Jason Antone, who suffers from the rare genetic disorder Friedreich's ataxia, broadcasts JROCK TV, a public access television show, from his home in West Bloomfield, Michigan, and in three years has received no less than 246 calls from celebrity guests endorsing the show, including actors Chevy Chase and Josh Gad, and talk-show host Regis Philbin.

GLAMOROUS GOLDFISH ▶ The world's first beauty contest for goldfish was staged in Fuzhou, China, in 2012. More than 3,000 fish from 14 different countries were lined up on rows of tables in giant bowls. There were 12 categories, including the longest and heaviest goldfish, and the fish were judged on five criteria: breed, body shape, swimming motion, color, and overall impression.

PULLED TRAIN ▶ With a harness strapped around his waist, Syrian strongman Adnan Ismail al-Awad used all his muscle power to pull a 65-ft-long (20-m) train that was full of passengers up an incline—a total weight of around 100 tons. Normally, it would take the strength of 100 horses to get the train and carriages to move.

CUCKOO CRAZY ▶ Jim and Jane Klingensmith have more than 300 cuckoo clocks in their Lake Placid, Florida, home. They began collecting the clocks in 1992 and their oldest clock dates back to the late 19th century.

▶ **IN 1975, WERNER ERHARD OF SAN FRANCISCO SENT 62,824 CHRISTMAS CARDS.** ◀

DUCK CALL ▶ Since 1974, the city of Stuttgart, Arkansas, has awarded a $2,000 scholarship annually to the high school senior who can make the best duck call. The scholarship honors the memories of Stuttgart's champion duck callers and duck-call makers, Chick and Sophie Major.

WRONG NOTE ▶ Two robbers hit the wrong note when they stole a jukebox from a restaurant in San Diego, California, after mistaking it for a cash machine. The dopy duo tried to back a pick-up truck through the glass door of the restaurant, only to find that the opening was too narrow—and then they compounded their error by towing away the jukebox instead of the ATM.

REPLICA SUPERCAR ▶ Wang Jian, a mechanic and farmer from Jiangsu Province, China, built his own replica of a $1.5 million Lamborghini Reventon supercar for just $9,000. Using scrap metal, he took over 15 months to build his dream car, but because he cannot get a license to drive it on the road, he uses it instead for transporting fertilizer!

ZIP IT!

▶ *These brilliant zipper lips were created by would-be makeup artists from New College, Worcestershire, England, as part of a challenge by international fashion and beauty photographer Alistair Cowin to create weird and wonderful lip designs. The students also made up lips in the design of a crab, a cat, a candy cane, a human skull and the Stars and Stripes, and used accessories, such as pearls, black caviar and baked beans.*

DEAD MAN WALKING▶ Terrified relatives fled a funeral in Alagoinhas, Brazil, when the deceased suddenly turned up—alive. A body at the morgue had been identified as car washer Gilberto Araujo by his brother, but the first Gilberto knew about it was when he bumped into a friend in the street who told him that he was supposed to be dead and that his funeral was taking place soon. "He told me there was a coffin and that I was inside it. So I said, 'But I'm alive. Pinch me!'"

VAMPIRE HUNT▶ When villagers near Dharmapuri, Tamil Nadu, India, thought vampires were killing their cattle in early 2012, officials offered a $2,000 cash reward to anyone who could prove conclusively that a vampire existed.

GRAVESIDE VIGIL▶ A faithful dog has refused to leave his dead master's grave for more than six years—even though the dog was never shown the location of either the cemetery or the tomb. German shepherd Capitan ran away from home after Miguel Guzman died in 2006, but a week later the family went to the cemetery in Villa Carlos Paz, Argentina, to pay their respects and were startled to find the dog howling by the grave. Capitan sometimes goes off for a walk during the day, but at 6 p.m. sharp he lies on the grave and stays there all night.

YELLOW SUBMARINE▶ Molly the West Highland terrier travels around the coastline of Cornwall, England, in owner Chris Garner's yellow, two-seater underwater vessel MSV Explorer to study marine life. The adventurous dog also joins him on motorcycle and quad-bike rides.

WALKING BACKWARD▶ Hu Xianwei of Handan, China, has trained his Pekingese Zhu Zhu to walk backward on his hind legs for more than 1 mi (1.6 km) every day. The dog even glances back over his shoulder to look out for obstacles.

STOREROOM SURVIVOR▶ Manuela the tortoise was found alive in a house in Rio de Janeiro, Brazil, despite having spent more than 30 years locked in a storeroom. She had vanished in 1982, but it was not until Leonel Almieda died in 2013 and his children began clearing out a locked second-floor junk room that they found the long-lost family pet—among a pile of broken electrical items. Animal experts believe the lucky tortoise survived all those years by nibbling termites from the wooden floor for food and licking condensation off smooth surfaces in order not to become dehydrated.

DAZZLING CEILING▶ Each Christmas, Sylvia Pope of Swansea, Wales, decks out the ceiling of her living room with an astonishing 1,750 Christmas baubles from all over the world.

FAKE CARS▶ Police in Wuxi City, China, have placed cardboard cutouts of squad cars by the sides of roads in a bid to slow down speeding drivers. The boards even have solar panels, which power flashing lights so that the fake cop cars look realistic at night.

LION DOG

▶ Panic spread through Norfolk, Virginia, in January 2013 after dog-owner Daniel Painter shaved the hair of his Labradoodle, Charles the Monarch, so that it looked like a lion. Worried residents called 911 to report that a big cat was roaming the streets and police officers checked with Virginia Zoo to make sure that none of its lions had escaped. Painter, who shaved his dog to look like the lion mascot of nearby Old Dominion University, said: "I tell people he's a Lab-a-lion, and half of them believe that!"

SMOOCHING POOCHES▶

A "love hotel" for dogs, complete with its own fitness center, opened in 2012 in Belo Horizonte, Brazil. Dog owners pay $50 a day for their pampered pooches to have a room that comes with a heart-shaped mirror on the ceiling, red cushions on the floor and dimmed lighting.

DRIVE-THROUGH FUNERALS▶

The Robert L. Adams funeral parlor in Los Angeles, California, offers drive-through funerals, allowing mourners to pay their last respects without having to leave the comfort of their car. The deceased is viewed through a long window made from bulletproof glass. The idea is intended to help people who have difficulty walking, as well as those with busy schedules.

HIDDEN LIGHT▶

A neon light that had been left on accidentally over 75 years ago was found behind a wall in the women's restroom during the 2012 renovation of the historic Clifton's Cafeteria in Los Angeles, California. The longest-lit neon light in the world, it had run up an estimated electric bill of $17,000 since the 1930s.

BEAR INVASION▶

Meteorologist Kurt Aaron's regular 11 p.m. weather forecast for WNEP-TV in Scranton, Pennsylvania, which is usually filmed in a landscaped outdoor area, was hastily relocated on April 23, 2012, after a mother bear and three of her cubs appeared unexpectedly on the set. Seeing the adult black bear just 10 ft (3 m) away, Aaron ran inside and did his report indoors from the studio instead.

FINGER FIGHT▶

When a suspect pointed a .38-caliber revolver at NYPD Sgt. Michael Miller, the officer managed to jam the gun by wedging his finger between the hammer and the cylinder. Although the man pulled the trigger several times, the gun would not fire and he was overpowered, leaving Sgt. Miller with nothing worse than a crushed bone in his finger tip.

DOGGIE WEDDING▶

On July 12, 2012, Baby Hope Diamond, a white Coton de Tulear rescue dog, married Chilly Pasternak, a poodle, in a wedding that cost $158,187—nearly six times the cost of the average human wedding. The doggie bride's wedding dress cost $6,000, and tickets were sold for the event to raise money for an animal charity.

MATH GENIUS▶

Using only mental calculation, India's Amit Garg solved ten math problems—each requiring him to divide ten digits by five digits—in just 5 minutes 45 seconds at Annapolis, Maryland, on March 15, 2012.

GOAT PEDICURE▶

Two people stole a tame goat from a petting zoo in San Diego, California, and returned him the next day after giving him a pedicure with pink toenails.

TATTOO RIDE

▶ Trying to keep a steady hand, Burnaby Q. Orbax tattooed his brother, Sweet Pepper Klopek, while the pair were riding on Canada's oldest and bumpiest wooden roller-coaster—at PNE Playland in Vancouver. Orbax, who had never tattooed anyone before, held the tattoo machine while the ink cap was duct-taped to Klopek's hands. The result inked on Klopck's upper right knee was a smiley face tattoo with a very long tongue.

Actually having his leg tattooed!

▶ The brothers also perform with the freak show Monsters of Schlock—Orbax has pulled a 4½-ton truck for more than 110 yd (100 m) using ropes attached to two hooks in his back, while Klopek has released 40 mousetraps on his tongue in one minute!

ACKNOWLEDGMENTS

COVER © darren whittingham - Fotolia.com, © Don Bayley - istockphoto.com; PAGE 4 (t/l) Annabel de Vetten, (t/r) Dale Porter/KillerImage.com, (b/l) Desre Pickers, (b/r) Vat19.com; 5 (t/l) M & Y Agency Ltd/Rex Features, (t/r) Shareef Sarhan, (c/r) Nirit Levav, (b/l) Gillian Bell, Deadbright.com/Miss Cakehead, (b/r) Steven Larimer & Cindy Rio; 6 (t/l) © kromkrathog - Fotolia.com; 9 (t) Cassandra Mardi; 12–13 (bg) © Juri Samsonov - Fotolia.com; 13 (t/l) © Tommy Schultz - Fotolia.com, (t/r) © ftlaudgirl - Fotolia.com, (c/l) © Ludovic LAN - Fotolia.com, (c/r) Imagebroker/Andrey Nekrasov/Flpa, (b/l) © Martin Wilkinson - Fotolia.com, (b/r) © Gino Santa Maria - Fotolia.com; 15 Dominic Deville; 16–17 Caters News; 18 (t/l) David Begiashvili, (b) Getty Images; 19 Startraks Photo/Rex Features; 20 Circus World Museum, Baraboo, Wisconsin; 21 (t) Hernandez Silva arquitectura/Rex Features, (b) Steve Rosenow/Loowit Imaging; 22 (t) Lisa Lin/Rex Features, (b) Reuters/China Daily; 23 Maskull Lasserre; 24 (t) © PA/Police Grossburgwedel, (b) Nikkie Curtis/Max Galuppo; 25 www.corsozundert.nl/Rex Features; 26 Caters News; 27 (t) Bournemouth News/Rex Features, (b) Dominic Deville; 28 Cover Asia Press; 29 (t) Caters News, (b) Yoshikazu Tsuno/AFP/Getty Images; 30 Reuters/Daniel Munoz; 31 (t) © Guido Vrola - Fotolia.com, (c) Erik Astrom/Scanpix/Press Association Images, (c/r) Rolf Hojer/Scanpix/Press Association Images; 32 (t) Annabel de Vetten, 33 (t) Sell Your Photo, (b) Dr Morley Read/Science Photo Library; 35 Paul Koudounaris, 36 (l, t/r, c) Reuters/Yusuf Ahmad, (b) Elang Herdian/AP/Press Association Images; 37 Reuters/Yusuf Ahmad; 38 Time & Life Pictures/Getty Images; 39 (t) Stephen Alvarez/National Geographic Stock, (b) Imagine China; 40–41 (t) Reuters/Vincent West/Files, (b) Sandra Church/Rimrock Humane Society; 41 Arturo M. Nikolai; 42 Imaginechina/Rex Features; 43 Redux/Eyevine; 44 (t/r) Roya Naini, (t/r) Jim Simandl, (b) Dick Larson; 45 Paul Koudounaris; 46–47 Chris Tangey - Alice Springs Film and Television; 48 Angel Vega; 49 (t, c) Caters News, (b) Dave Lee King; 50 Caters News; 51 (t) Caters News, (b) Ivan Dementievskiy; 52 Reuters/China Daily; 53 (t) Newsline Scotland, (b) Quirky China News/Rex Features; 54–55 Caters News; 56 (t) Caters News, (b) Courtesy Humboldt State University Library; 57 Caters News; 59 Liberty Mountain Resort; 60 (t) Reuters/Cris Toala Olivares, (b) Matt Roper; 61 (t) Matt Roper, (b) Reuters/Fred Thornhill; 62 (t) © Pete Oxford/NaturePL.com, (b) Charles Lam/Rex Features; 63 (t) Caters News, (b) Reuters/Chaiwat Subprasom; 64 (b/l) ZSSD/Minden Pictures/FLPA, (b/r) Michael Patricia Fogden/Minden Pictures/National Geographic Stock; 65 University of California at Davis Veterinary School; 66 (t) Europics, (b) Caters News; 67 Caters News; 68 (t) Imagine China, (b) Martin Amm; 69 Kyndra Batla; 70 Caters News; 71 (t) Caters News, (b) Photo by Bill Bouton; 72 NBCU Photo Bank via Getty Images; 73 (t) Caters News, (b) Albanpix Ltd/Rex Features; 74 Caters News; 75 (t) Draft FCB New Zealand/SPCA, (b) © Bruce Coleman/Photoshot; 76 (b) Dale Porter/KillerImage.com; 77 (t) Imagine China, (b) Europics; 78 (t) © NHPA/Photoshot, (b) © Eric Gevaert - Fotolia.com; 79 © David Shale/NaturePL.com; 80 (r) Leah Garcia, (b) © Sipa USA/Rex Features; 81 Caters News; 82 (l) Becky Stanford, (r) Robert Brooks; 83 Liberty Mountain Resort; 85 London News Pictures/Rex Features; 86 (l) Caters News, (r) Scott Markewitz; 87 (b/l) Grant Gunderson, (l) Caters News, (r) Alaska Stock Images/National Geographic Stock; 88 (t/l, t/r) Wenn.com, (b) Getty Images; 89 Caters News; 90 Caters News; 91 (t) AP/Press Association Images, (b) London News Pictures/Rex Features; 92 Desre Pickers; 93 (t, r) NTI Media Ltd/Rex Features, (b) © Ian Marlow/Demotix/Corbis; 94 KeystoneUSA-Zuma/Rex Features; 95 (t/l) Gregg Valentino, (b/r) Getty Images; 96 (t/l, r) Getty Images, (b) L.L.Bean/Rex Features; 97 Getty Images; 100–101 (dp) © Robert van der Hilst/Corbis; 101 (t/r) © Robert van der Hilst/Corbis; 102 (t) Reuters/Umit Bektas, (b) ChinaFotoPress via Getty Images; 104 © Bettmann/Corbis; 105 (r) Isaac Burrier, (l) Steve Duggan; 106–107 Cover Asia Press; 108 Imagine China; 109 (t/l, t/r) Phoenix Day Photography, (b) Chayne Hultgren (AKA: The Space Cowboy); 110 Helma van de Weide/Rex Features; 111 (t/r) Reuters/Ricardo Moraes, (l, b/r) SWNS; 112 (b/l) Body Art The Extreme Ink-ite 114 © Europics, (b) © Winston Link - Fotolia.com; 116 (b, b/r) Imagine China, (t/r) Wenn.com; 117 (t) Wenn.com, (b) Fantich & Young; 120 (bg) © marianna38 - Fotolia.com, (b) Getty Images; 122 (t) Ashley Savage, (b) Imagine China; 123 (sp, b/r) Imagine China, (t) Kathy Vick; 125 Kobi Levi; 126–127 Jeremy Telford; 128 Barcroft Media via Getty Images; 129–136 (bg) © Alexandr Zinchevici - Fotolia.com, marinamik - Fotolia.com, © marianna38 - Fotolia.com, © poplasen - Fotolia.com; 129 (sp) Jennifer Dawson (curator) and Vent Haven Museum KY; (t) Tom Ladshaw courtesy of Vent Haven Museum KY; 130 Jennifer Dawson (curator) and Vent Haven Museum KY; 131 (t) Getty Images, (c/l, b) Jennifer Dawson (curator) and Vent Haven Museum KY; 132–133 (dp) Jennifer Dawson (curator) and Vent Haven Museum KY; 132 Jennifer Dawson (curator) and Vent Haven Museum KY; 133 Jennifer Dawson (curator) and Vent Haven Museum KY; 134 (t/l) Bryan Simon/Jennifer Dawson (curator) Vent Haven Museum KY, (t/r, c, b) Jennifer Dawson (curator) and Vent Haven Museum KY; 135 (t/l, t/r, b/l) Jennifer Dawson (curator) and Vent Haven Museum KY, (b/r) James Kriegsmann/Michael Ochs Archives/Getty Images; 136 (sp) Jennifer Dawson (curator) and Vent Haven Museum KY, (b) Tom Ladshaw courtesy of Vent Haven Museum KY; 137 (t) Wenn.com, (b) TheSkillsShow.com/Wenn; 138 Kobi Levi; 139 (t/r) Faye Halliday, (c) Bewley Shaylor, (b/r) Ray Scott; 140–141 © Bettmann/Corbis; 142 M&Y Agency Ltd/Rex Features; 143 (t) Vat19.com, (b/l, b/c, b/r) Reuters/Sheng Li; 145 M&Y Agency Ltd/Rex Features; 148 (t) Caters News, (b) Western Times; 149 (t) AA/ABACA/Press Association Images; 150 M&Y Agency Ltd/Rex Features; 151 (t) Rex Features, (b) Europics; 152 Quirky China News/Rex Features; 153 (t) AAP/Press Association Images; 154 Quirky China News/Rex Features; 155 (t) Tim Hahn/AP/Press Association Images, (c) Ross Parry Agency, (b) Network Rail/Rex Features; 158–159 Caters News; 160 (t) Caters News, (b) Shareef Sarhan; 161 Quirky China News/Rex Features; 162 Jay Nemeth/Red Bull Content Pool; 163 (b/r) balazsgardi.com/Red Bull Content Pool, (t/r) Joerg Mitter/Red Bull Content Pool, (b/l) Red Bull Stratos/Red Bull Content Pool; 164 Imaginechina/Rex Features; 165 Reuters/Vincent Kessler; 166 (t) Top Photo Corporation/Rex Features, (t/r) Canadian Press/Rex Features, (b) Reuters/Vladimir Nikolsky; 167 Canadian Press/Rex Features; 168–169 Alexander Remnev/Solent News/Rex Features; 170 (t/l, t/c) Joe Salter, Flora Bama-Lounge Triathlon, (t/r) Jeff Nelson Studios, (c) Gennaro Serra; 171 (t/l, c) Jeff Nelson Studios, (t/r) Joe Salter, Flora Bama-Lounge Triathlon, (b) Reuters/Yves Herman; 174 (t) Vincent Thian/AP/Press Association Images, (b) Getty Images; 175 Reuters/Laszlo Balogh; 176 (t) HAP/Quirky China News/Rex Features, (b) Quirky China News/Rex Features; 177 AFP/Getty Images; 179 SWNS; 180–181 www.idrinkleadpaint/twitter @idrinkleadpaint; 182 (l) Pintofeed, (t) Gianluca Regnicoli; 183 (t) SWNS, (b) Caters News; 184 (t) Charlotte Howell, (b) Benoit Aquin/Polaris/eyevine; 185 (t) KPA/Zuma/Rex Features, (b) Caters News; 186–187 Cecelia Webber, www.ceceliawebber.com; 188 (t, c) Caters News, (b) SWNS.com; 189 Rayfish.com; 191 Freya Jobbins/Rex Features; 192–193 Chooo-San/Rex Features; 194 (t, b) Nikita Nomerz/Rex Features, (t/r) Reuters/Paul Hanna; 195 Getty Images; 196 Splash News; 197 (t/l, t/r) Cassander Eeftinck Schattenkerk, (b) Christopher Boffoli; 198 Photographer Hal; 199 (t/l) joce-barbiemamuse.com, (t/r) KeystoneUSA-Zuma/Rex Features, (b/r) © joce-barbiemamuse.com, (b/r) © Corbis, (bkg) © JackF - Fotolia.com; 200 Solent News; 201 Reuters/Andrew Burton; 202 (t/l, t/r) Ramon Bruin, (b) Freya Jobbins/Rex Features; 203 Getty Images; 204 (t/l, t/r) ©Kurt Perschke/www.redballproject.com, (b/r) © Bert Folsom - Fotolia.com; 205 (c, t/l, t/r) ©Kurt Perschke/www.redballproject.com, (b) Felipe Dana/AP/Press Association Images, (b/r) Marcos de paula/DPA/Press Association Images; 206 (t, b) Sell Your Photo; 207 (t, c) Nirit Levav, (b/l, b/r) Marcus Levine; 209 Melinda Chan; 210 (t/l, t/r, c, b/r) Gillian Bell, Deadbright.com/Miss Cakehead, (b/l) Sarah Hardy Cakes sarahhardycakes.co.uk/Miss Cakehead; 211 Gillian Bell, Deadbright.com/Miss Cakehead; 212 (t/l, t/c, t/r) HotSpot Media, (b) © Michele Westmorland/Corbis; 213 Reuters/Keith Bedford; 214 (t) © Rungroj Yongrit/epa/Corbis, (b) Caters News; 215 (t) Jaffa Cakes/Rex Features, (b) Melinda Chan; 216 Seth Wenig/AP/Press Association Images; 217 Ben Milne, (t) © Rolex de la Pena/epa/Corbis; 218 (t) Caters News, (b) Richard Jones/Sinopix/Rex Features; 219 (t/l, t/r) Caters News, (b) Reuters/Vincent Kessler, (b/l) © Liaurinko - Fotolia.com; 220 (t) Jack Dempsey/Invision for Cheetos/AP Images, (b) KNS News; 221 (t) Joshua Scott, (b) Caters News; 222 (t) Vat19.com/Rex Features, (b) Logan Cooper; 223 Wenn.com; 225 Rob Leeson/Newspix/Rex Features; 226–227 Worldwide Features; 228 (t,l, t/c, t/r) Steven Larimer & Cindy Rio, (b) Alan Sailer/Rex Features; 229 (t) Steven Larimer & Cindy Rio, (b/l, b/r) Donald L. Sammons; 230 (t) BNPS, (b) © Mariam A. Montesinos/epa/Corbis; 231 Wes Naman/Rex Features; 232 (t/r) Circus World Museum, Baraboo, Wisconsin, (b) Saskatchewan Archives Board R-A3465; 233 (t/l, b/r) Circus World Museum, Baraboo, Wisconsin; 234 (t) Hotspot Media, (b) Rob Leeson/Newspix/Rex Features; 235 Earth to Sky Calculus/NASA; 236 Jan Wiriden/GT/Scanpix/Press Association Images; 237 (t) © Cherie Diez/Tampa Bay Times/Zumapress.com/eyevine; 238 (b) Quirky China News/Rex Features; 238 Caters News; 239 Circus World Museum, Baraboo, Wisconsin; 240 (r) Getty Images, (l) www.50fifty-gifts.com; 242 (t/l, t/r) Vermont Fish & Wildlife Department, (c/l) Luke Kelly, (c/r, b) Ryan Ganley; 243 Alistair Cowin/Rex Features; 244 (t) Ross D. Franklin/AP/Press Association Images, (b) Stephen M. Katz/AP/Press Association Images; 245 Syx Langemann

Key: t = top, b = bottom, c = center, l = left, r = right, sp = single page, dp = double page, bg = background

All other photos are from Ripley Entertainment Inc. Every attempt has been made to acknowledge correctly and contact copyright holders and we apologize in advance for any unintentional errors or omissions, which will be corrected in future editions.

Ripley's ODDITORIUMS

There are 32 Ripley's Believe It or Not! Odditoriums spread across the globe for you to visit, each packed full with weird and wonderful exhibits from the Ripley collection.

Atlantic City
NEW JERSEY

Baltimore
MARYLAND

Bangalore
INDIA

Blackpool
ENGLAND

Branson
MISSOURI

Cavendish
CANADA

Copenhagen
DENMARK

Gatlinburg
TENNESSEE

Genting Highlands
MALAYSIA

Grand Prairie
TEXAS

Guadalajara
MEXICO

Hollywood
CALIFORNIA

Jackson Hole
WYOMING

Jeju Island
SOUTH KOREA

Key West
FLORIDA

London
ENGLAND

Mexico City
MEXICO

Veracruz
MEXICO

Myrtle Beach
SOUTH CAROLINA

New York City
NEW YORK

Newport
OREGON

Niagara Falls
CANADA

Ocean City
MARYLAND

Orlando
FLORIDA

Panama City Beach
FLORIDA

Pattaya
THAILAND

San Antonio
TEXAS

San Francisco
CALIFORNIA

St. Augustine
FLORIDA

Surfers Paradise
AUSTRALIA

Williamsburg
VIRGINIA

Wisconsin Dells
WISCONSIN

ORLANDO

ANNUALS

With ALL-NEW stories and pictures in every edition of this bestselling series, our books entertain, shock and amaze!

Amazing stories and images!

To see all of our books go to www.ripleybooks.com

ROBERT RIPLEY BIOGRAPHY

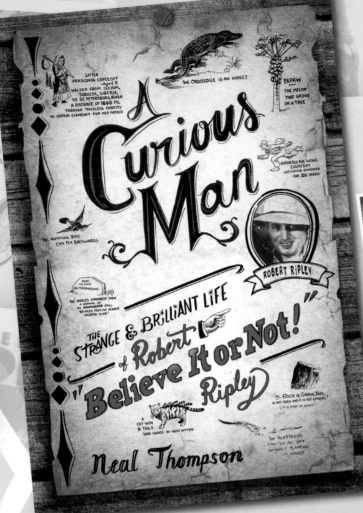

The definitive biography of Robert Ripley, A CURIOUS MAN, written by acclaimed biographer Neal Thompson, tells of the strange and brilliant life of this extraordinary person. The stuff of a classic American fairy tale, Ripley traveled the globe bringing the bizarre and unusual to the masses—and his legacy lives on today.

TWISTS

The award-winning TWISTS have all you ever wanted to know about these exciting subjects plus a bunch of jaw-dropping stories and unbelievable pictures from the crazy world of Ripley's Believe It or Not! Fascinating facts and heaps of fun—don't miss them!

SHARKS AND OTHER SCARY SEA CREATURES
fun, facts and sharks...it's sea creatures with a Ripley twist!

BRUTAL BEASTS Believe It or Not!
fun, facts and frights...it's brutal beasts... with a Ripley twist!

FUN FACTS & SILLY STORIES

FUN FACTS Ripley's Believe It or Not! KIDS SILLY STORIES

Book 2 out now!

Following hot on the heels of our successful FUN FACTS & SILLY STORIES comes a second volume in this fantastic series for younger Ripley fans. Incredible pictures and crazy facts will entertain kids for hours. Meet a four-eared cat and an elephant artist, and find out why the "happy face" spider got its name!